Darko Anicic

Event Processing and Stream Reasoning with ETALIS

Darko Anicic

Event Processing and Stream Reasoning with ETALIS

From Concept to Implementation

Südwestdeutscher Verlag für Hochschulschriften

Impressum/Imprint (nur für Deutschland/only for Germany)
Bibliografische Information der Deutschen Nationalbibliothek: Die Deutsche Nationalbibliothek verzeichnet diese Publikation in der Deutschen Nationalbibliografie; detaillierte bibliografische Daten sind im Internet über http://dnb.d-nb.de abrufbar.
Alle in diesem Buch genannten Marken und Produktnamen unterliegen warenzeichen-, marken- oder patentrechtlichem Schutz bzw. sind Warenzeichen oder eingetragene Warenzeichen der jeweiligen Inhaber. Die Wiedergabe von Marken, Produktnamen, Gebrauchsnamen, Handelsnamen, Warenbezeichnungen u.s.w. in diesem Werk berechtigt auch ohne besondere Kennzeichnung nicht zu der Annahme, dass solche Namen im Sinne der Warenzeichen- und Markenschutzgesetzgebung als frei zu betrachten wären und daher von jedermann benutzt werden dürften.

Coverbild: www.ingimage.com

Verlag: Südwestdeutscher Verlag für Hochschulschriften GmbH & Co. KG
Heinrich-Böcking-Str. 6-8, 66121 Saarbrücken, Deutschland
Telefon +49 681 37 20 271-1, Telefax +49 681 37 20 271-0
Email: info@svh-verlag.de

Approved by: Karlsruhe, KIT, PhD Thesis, 2011

Herstellung in Deutschland:
Schaltungsdienst Lange o.H.G., Berlin
Books on Demand GmbH, Norderstedt
Reha GmbH, Saarbrücken
Amazon Distribution GmbH, Leipzig
ISBN: 978-3-8381-3173-3

Imprint (only for USA, GB)
Bibliographic information published by the Deutsche Nationalbibliothek: The Deutsche Nationalbibliothek lists this publication in the Deutsche Nationalbibliografie; detailed bibliographic data are available in the Internet at http://dnb.d-nb.de.
Any brand names and product names mentioned in this book are subject to trademark, brand or patent protection and are trademarks or registered trademarks of their respective holders. The use of brand names, product names, common names, trade names, product descriptions etc. even without a particular marking in this works is in no way to be construed to mean that such names may be regarded as unrestricted in respect of trademark and brand protection legislation and could thus be used by anyone.

Cover image: www.ingimage.com

Publisher: Südwestdeutscher Verlag für Hochschulschriften GmbH & Co. KG
Heinrich-Böcking-Str. 6-8, 66121 Saarbrücken, Germany
Phone +49 681 37 20 271-1, Fax +49 681 37 20 271-0
Email: info@svh-verlag.de

Printed in the U.S.A.
Printed in the U.K. by (see last page)
ISBN: 978-3-8381-3173-3

Copyright © 2012 by the author and Südwestdeutscher Verlag für Hochschulschriften GmbH & Co. KG and licensors
All rights reserved. Saarbrücken 2012

Abstract

Event Processing (EP) is concerned with detection of situations under *time* constraints that are of a particular business interest. We face today a paradigm shift toward the real time information processing, and EP has therefore spawned significant attention in science and technology. Due to omnipresence of events, EP is becoming a central aspect of new distributed systems such as cloud computing and grid systems, mobile and sensor-based systems, as well as a number of application areas including financial services, business intelligence, social and collaborative networking, click stream analysis and many others.

However, there are a number of issues to be considered in order to enable effective event-based computation. A language for describing event patterns needs to feature a well-defined semantics. It also needs to be rich enough to express important classes of event patterns. Pattern matching should be supported in both, query-driven and event-driven modes. A number of other event operations, such as event aggregation, filtering, translation, enrichment and splitting, should be supported too. Since EP is a real time processing task, an EP language needs to feature an efficient execution model. Finally, processing only events is not sufficient in many applications. To detect complex situations of interest, EP needs to be enhanced by background *knowledge*. This knowledge captures the *domain* of interest. Its purpose is to be evaluated during detection of events in order to on the fly enrich events with relevant background information; to detect more complex situations; to *reason* about events and propose certain intelligent recommendations; or to accomplish event classification, clustering, filtering and so forth.

The ETALIS Language for Events (ELE) is a declarative rule-based language for EP. It supports the above mentioned features, and goes beyond the state of the art by providing stream reasoning capabilities. In this thesis, we first review related literature and extract requirements for modern EP systems. Then we present ELE as a novel expressive formalism that fulfils these requirements. Further on, we show how deductive stream reasoning capabilities of ELE, together with its EP capabilities, have the potential to provide powerful real time intelligence. We give a few extensions of the core ELE. A number of examples and use case scenarios are developed to show the power of the proposed EP framework. We provide a prototype implementation of the language, and present evaluation results for implemented scenarios. Finally, we summarise the results of this thesis and outline our view of the emerging future work.

Acknowledgements

On my journey to complete this thesis many people have contributed. Foremost, I would like to sincerely thank to my supervisor, Prof. Dr. Rudi Studer, who gave me the opportunity to work in his research group and continuously supported my work. Prof. Dr. Rudi Studer has created a unique research environment that made my research both possible and enjoyable.

I am grateful to Dr. Opher Etzion who was willing to serve as a second reviewer of this work. I wish to sincerely thank him also for inviting me to participate in many initiatives and collaborations within the event processing community – most notably the joint work on The Event Processing Manifesto, and participation in the implementation of Fast Flower Delivery use case in ETALIS.

I am indebted to my supervisor, Dr. Nenad Stojanovic, for his unmeasurable enthusiasm and inspiration throughout my PhD studies. Ha gave me the necessary freedom to pursue my ideas, and has continuously encouraged me to always further my work.

The work presented in this thesis would not be possible without my colleagues Dr. Sebastian Rudolph, Dr. Paul Fodor, Jia Ding, Ahmed Khalil Hafsi and Vesko Georgiev. Without Sebastian this thesis would not have the same level of technical profoundness. Since the time I started the work on ETALIS, Paul has been providing immeasurable help in implementation of ETALIS. Jia Ding, Ahmed Khalil Hafsi and Vesko Georgiev have also greatly contributed to successful development and testing of ETALIS.

I would like to thank all the (former and present) colleagues in the Rudiverse for providing such a friendly working atmosphere. I specially need to thank my colleagues from the iCEP group: Sinan Sen, Roland Stühmer, Jun Ma, Yongchun Xu and Dominik Riemer. Roland Stühmer has also generously helped with the early work on ETALIS.

My parents and sister receive my sincerest gratitude and love for giving me continuous support and encouragement in my work.

I thank my wife for giving me inspiration and energy throughout the time it has taken to complete this thesis.

Darko Aničić
Karlsruhe, June 2011

Contents

List of Figures   xi

List of Tables   xiii

List of Algorithms   xv

I   Introduction   1

1   Thesis Overview   **3**
- 1.1   Introduction 3
- 1.2   Shifting Event Processing Toward More Intelligent Event Processing . . . 5
- 1.3   Shifting Reasoning Toward Stream Reasoning 7
- 1.4   Aims and Objectives 11
- 1.5   Thesis Organization 14
- 1.6   Relation to Previous Publications 15

2   Introduction to Event Processing   **17**
- 2.1   What is an Event? 17
- 2.2   Event Programming Principles 18
  - 2.2.1   Events as a Means to Declare Changes 19
  - 2.2.2   Information Push Versus Information Pull 19
- 2.3   Event Processing Architecture 20

3   Introduction to Logic Programming   **25**
- 3.1   Background of Logic Programming 25
- 3.2   The Logic in Logic Programs 26
  - 3.2.1   Syntax of Definite Programs 26
  - 3.2.2   Semantics of Definite Programs 30
- 3.3   The Control in Logic Programs 33
  - 3.3.1   Immediate Consequence Operator 34
  - 3.3.2   SLD Resolution 35

4   State of the Art   **39**

4.1	Active Databases	39
4.2	Event Processing Systems	42
4.3	Approaches for Retraction in Event Processing	46
4.4	Approaches for Out-of-Order Event Processing	49
4.5	Logic-Based Approaches in Event Processing	50
4.6	Semantic-Based Approaches	52
	4.6.1 Temporal RDF	53
	4.6.2 Stream Reasoning Approaches	53

II ETALIS Language for Events   55

5 Logic-Based Event Processing: Design Principles and Requirements   57
- 5.1 Formal Declarative Semantics 57
- 5.2 Point-Based Versus Interval-Based Temporal Semantics 59
- 5.3 Seamless Integration of Events with Queries and Domain Knowledge 60
  - 5.3.1 Query Processing 60
  - 5.3.2 Knowledge Processing 60
- 5.4 Event-Driven Incremental Reasoning 61
- 5.5 Expressivity 61
- 5.6 Set at a Time Versus Event at a Time Processing 62
- 5.7 Simplicity and Ease-of-Use 63
- 5.8 Extensibility 65

6 ETALIS: A Rule-Based Language for Event Processing and Reasoning   67
- 6.1 Introduction 67
- 6.2 Syntax of the Language 69
- 6.3 Declarative Semantics of the Language 73
  - 6.3.1 Complexity Properties 75
- 6.4 Examples 75
  - 6.4.1 An Example Application 77

7 Operational Semantics of the Language   79
- 7.1 Overview 79
- 7.2 Execution Model for ETALIS 80
  - 7.2.1 Sequence 80
  - 7.2.2 Conjunction 84
  - 7.2.3 Concurrency 87
  - 7.2.4 Disjunction 87
  - 7.2.5 Negation 88
  - 7.2.6 Interval-Based Operations 88
    - 7.2.6.1 Duration 88
    - 7.2.6.2 Start 89
    - 7.2.6.3 Equal 89

		7.2.6.4	Finish 89
		7.2.6.5	Meet 90
	7.3	Iterative and Aggregative Patterns 90
		7.3.1	From Event Rules to Event Iterative Rules 90
			7.3.1.1 An Example Application with Iterative Rules 91
		7.3.2	Implementation of Aggregative Patterns 92
	7.4	Consumption Policies 96
		7.4.1	Consumption Policies Defined on Time Points 97
		7.4.2	Consumption Policies Defined on Time Intervals 98

8 The Event Processing Network in ETALIS — 101
- 8.1 Filtering 102
  - 8.1.1 Event Type Filter 102
  - 8.1.2 Event Content Filter 102
- 8.2 Pattern Detection 103
- 8.3 Transformation 103
  - 8.3.1 Projection 103
  - 8.3.2 Translation 104
  - 8.3.3 Enrichment 104
  - 8.3.4 Splitting 105
  - 8.3.5 Aggregation 106
  - 8.3.6 Composition 106
- 8.4 Knowledge-Based Event Processing Agents 107
  - 8.4.1 Event Processing with Transitive Closure Rules 107
  - 8.4.2 Rule-Based Event Classification 108
  - 8.4.3 Event Processing with Reasoning About Subclass Relationships . 110

III ETALIS Extensions — 113

9 Retraction in Event Processing — 115
- 9.1 Problem Statement for Event Retraction 115
  - 9.1.1 A Motivating Example: Processing Events with Transactions ... 116
    - 9.1.1.1 Event Retraction with External Complex Events 117
    - 9.1.1.2 Event Retraction and Compensations 117
    - 9.1.1.3 Summary of the Problem 118
- 9.2 ETALIS Formalism for Event Retraction 118
  - 9.2.1 Event Retraction Example 119
- 9.3 Operational Semantics for Retractable Event Processing 121
  - 9.3.1 Sequence 121
  - 9.3.2 Conjunction 123
  - 9.3.3 Time-Life Window for Event Retractions 126

10 Processing Out-of-Order Events — 127
- 10.1 Overview of Out-of-Order Event Processing 127

       10.1.1 Motivating Example 128
              10.1.1.1 Missed Complex Events due to Out-of-Order Events . . 130
              10.1.1.2 False Positive Complex Events due to Out-of-Order Events 130
              10.1.1.3 Summary of the Problem with Out-of-Order Events . . 131
  10.2 Out-of-Order Event Processing 131
  10.3 Memory Management 133
       10.3.1 Pushed Constraints 134
       10.3.2 General and Pattern-Based Garbage Collection 135

11 EP-SPARQL: Extending ETALIS for the Semantic Web   137
  11.1 Introduction 137
  11.2 The Semantic Web with Event Processing 139
  11.3 Syntax of EP-SPARQL 140
  11.4 Semantics of EP-SPARQL 143
  11.5 An Example of EP-SPARQL Application 146
  11.6 Operational Semantics of EP-SPARQL 147
       11.6.1 Sequence 148
       11.6.2 Filter Expression 150
       11.6.3 Background Knowledge 151
       11.6.4 Equals 151
  11.7 Memory Management and Time Windows in EP-SPARQL 152

IV Practical Considerations   153

12 Implementation   155
  12.1 ETALIS Architecture 155
  12.2 EP-SPARQL Implementation 158
  12.3 Interacting with ETALIS 159

13 Evaluation   161
  13.1 Performance Evaluation 161
       13.1.1 Data Sets 162
       13.1.2 Run-Time Tests for Common Event Patterns 163
       13.1.3 Performance Evaluation for Knowledge-Based Event Processing . 166
       13.1.4 Performance Evaluation for Event Processing with Retractions . . 167
       13.1.5 Performance Evaluation of Out-of-Order Event Processing 171
              13.1.5.1 Knowledge-Based Event Processing with Out-of-Order events 172
              13.1.5.2 Test with Real Dataset and Out-of-Order Events 174
       13.1.6 Performance Evaluation for Iterative Patterns 174
              13.1.6.1 Test 1: Sum with Sequance 175
              13.1.6.2 Test 2: Average with Sequence 175
              13.1.6.3 Test 3: Maximum with Disjunction 176

                    13.1.6.4   Test 4: Count with Negation 177
                    13.1.6.5   Application 1: Supply Chain 178
                    13.1.6.6   Application 2: Stock Trade 179
          13.1.7   Experimental Results for EP-SPARQL 181
                    13.1.7.1   Test 1: Stream Reasoning 181
                    13.1.7.2   Test 2: Example Applications 182
    13.2 Use Case: On The Live Measurements of Environmental Phenomena . . . 184
          13.2.1   Additional Use Cases 191

V Conclusions and Outlook   193

14 Summary and Conclusion   195
   14.1 Summary of the Results 195
   14.2 Future Work 198
          14.2.1   Event-Driven Business Processes 199
                    14.2.1.1   A Unifying Framework for Event-Driven Ad-Hoc Processes 199
   14.3 Conclusions 200

A Appendix   203
   A.1 Linked Sensor Data for Weather Stations 203
   A.2 Distance Calculation 204

Bibliography   205

Index   219

List of Figures

2.1	An event processing network	21
3.1	Example definite program	29
3.2	Example definite rules with built-in predicates	30
3.3	Example Herbrand interpretations of the program P	33
3.4	Iterative generation of immediate consequences	34
3.5	Example construction of the minimal Herbrand model	35
3.6	An SLD tree for our example definite program	37
6.1	ETALIS Conceptual Architecture	68
6.2	Language for Event Processing - Composition Operators	71
6.3	Definition of extensional interpretation of event patterns. We use $P(x)$ for patterns, $q_{(x)}$ for rational numbers, $t_{(x)}$ for terms and PR for event predicates. . . .	74
7.1	Example program	85
9.1	Conceptual interaction of events and transactions	117
10.1	Received vs. real order of events	130
12.1	System Diagram: ETALIS	156
12.2	System Diagram: EP-SPARQL	158
12.3	ETALIS interfaced with event producers and event consumers	159
13.1	Experiments for sequence operator - (a) Throughput (b) Throughput vs. Predicate Selectivity	163
13.2	(a) Sequence - Throughput vs. Workload Change (b) Negation - Throughput vs. Selectivity	164
13.3	(a) Negation - Throughput vs. Workload Change (b) Conjunction - Throughput	164

13.4 (a) Experiments for Disjunction Operator - Throughput (b) Evaluation of Transitive Closure - Workload Change 165

13.5 Experiment for Testing Computation Sharing for Sequence Operator . . . 166

13.6 EP combined with Stream Reasoning 167

13.7 (a) Throughput comparison (b) Negation and revision 167

13.8 (a) Sequence - 1st event retracted (b) 2nd event retracted 168

13.9 (a) Parallel - 1st event retracted (b) Conjunction - 1st event retracted . . . 169

13.10 (a) Disjunction - 1st event retracted (b) Event latency 169

13.11 (a) Revision time-based windows (b) Stock price change on a real data set 170

13.12 (a) Throughput comparison (b) Memory consumption 172

13.13 Throughput change as the size of companies' relations varies from 100 to 1000 173

13.14 Memory consumption in the knowledge-based EP test 173

13.15 Stock price change on a real data set: (a) throughput (b) memory consumption 174

13.16 SUM-SEQ: throughput vs. window size 175

13.17 AVG-SEQ: throughput vs. window size 176

13.18 MAX-OR: throughput vs. window size 177

13.19 COUNT-NOT: throughput vs. window size 177

13.20 (a) Throughput comparison (b) Memory consumption 178

13.21 Average and maximum stock prices 180

13.22 Delay caused by stream reasoning 181

13.23 Goods Delivery System: (a) Delay caused by processing (b) Memory consumption 182

13.24 Tsunami detection histogram 184

13.25 Sensor Location Map 185

13.26 Sensor location map with marked wind areas 189

13.27 (a) Complex event throughput (b) Memory consumption 190

14.1 Conceptual architecture of event-driven ad-hoc processes. 200

List of Tables

8.1 Namespace abbreviations. 110

13.1 Complex Events from Live Sensor Data. 187

13.2 Computation for pattern (13.23) from live sensor data. 188

13.3 GeoNames locations nearby KSFO weather station (SFO Airport). 190

List of Algorithms

1	Sequence.	82
2	Conjunction.	84
3	Concurrency.	87
4	Negation.	88
5	Sequence with retraction.	121
6	Conjunction with retraction.	124
7	Sequence with out-of-order events.	132
8	Sequence with constraint checks.	134

Part I

Introduction

1

Thesis Overview

1.1 Introduction

The concept of Event Processing (EP) is not new. Sensing for particular observations and acting upon their detection have been a part of human nature ever since. For example, our organism reacts when the body feels warm. The same happens in our society – we sense for opportunities and threats, and act accordingly to avoid troubles or take advantages of a particular situation. As we move more to the era of Information and Communication Technology, we also see a dramatic increase in the number of *observable events*. A received phone call, a confirmation that a transaction has completed, a sensor reading, and so forth – are few examples of observable events. Coping with observable events assumes *detection* of events that are important, and a *response* to them in a timely fashion. Since the amount of available event data is rapidly expanding and detection needs to be performed with low latency, this task has turned to be rather challenging [ChEA11]. Hence we need novel concepts, techniques, and systems to automatically process events, and optimise them algorithmically to do that in a timely fashion. Due to these new requirements, EP has emerged as a substantial new field of computer science over the last decade.

Most businesses today collect large volumes of data continuously, and it is absolutely essential for them to process this data in real time, so that they can take time-critical actions [Luck02]. There are many reasons why today's information society abounds in large volume of continuous information (events). Few of them are to be mentioned here.

The amount of information that is available to users at nearly the moment it is produced is upraising on the Web. Electronic businesses and Internet explosion cause massive increase in event-driven interactions (instead of request-response interactions, that have been dominant so far). A new generation of computing, such as cloud computing, emerges with a need for an effective real time monitoring and management. In order to enable key characteristics of cloud computing, such as elasticity, multi-tenancy, reliability, scalability and metering – cloud computing requires autonomic computing that is to be extended with EP. Modern business processes management demands automation and changes according to business events. How to detect business events and trigger changes is a yet another topic related to EP. Efforts to make energy consumption more efficient have recently led to the creation of smart energy grids. By using an event-driven communication between involved parties (energy suppliers, consumers, marketplace players and so forth), smart energy grids aim to optimise energy consumption, and hence reduce the associated costs. Further on, a real time control in manufacturing processes increasingly interact with the underlying production machinery. The production machinery can be seen as a source of events, since it emits condition information about production equipment asynchronously. Asynchronous interactions are supported by an EP architecture, and this is a yet another reason to exploit EP in manufacturing processes. Finally let us mention the financial sector, that has dramatically changed due to new electronic business processes and a high competition. Financial institutions have started to use EP for feeding data into algorithmic trading systems as well as for finding dealing opportunities across available assets. Fraud detection and surveillance are also growth areas for EP, as well as risk monitoring that uses EP for managing market and liquidity risks in real time.

EP is fast becoming a foundation of today's computer and information systems. The reason for this lays in the fact that events are everywhere (above we have mentioned only few areas) and we need a way to make sense of them. EP is a set of techniques and tools to help us understand and control event-driven information systems [Luck02]. We will discuss concepts and techniques of EP in Chapter 2, however at this point it is worth to abstract what EP is about.

An event represents something that occurs, happens or changes the current state of affairs. For example, an event may signify a problem or an impending problem, a threshold, an opportunity, an information becoming available, a deviation and so forth. These events are directly related to specific, measurable changes of conditions. In many application it is however important to infer more abstract situations. It is the task of EP to effectively derive these situations based on occurrence (or non occurrence) of several single, ordinary events. EP therefore deals with a problem of identifying abstract situations that cannot be detected from looking only at single events. Instead, an abstract situation (a derived event) is usually a combination of ordinary (and possibly other derived) events that satisfy certain *temporal* and *semantic* conditions. Events together with temporal and semantic conditions, that are of interest to a particular application, are called *event patterns*, and are commonly specified in a special purpose languages, called *Event Processing languages*.

In the remaining parts of this work we investigate characteristics of EP languages and event-driven systems, in general. As a result, we spot possibilities for further advancements in EP, and propose (in Chapter 6) a new language called the ETALIS Language for Events (ELE). The language comes with a clean rule-based syntax and a declarative semantics. The language is expressive enough to capture all aspects important to EP. Moreover, we present features and extensions of ELE that go beyond the state of the art languages [ADGI08, BGAH07, ArBW06, KrSe09, CCDF$^+$03]. An outstanding feature of the ELE is a capability to do *logic reasoning*. This capability together with other ELE features is built into the language's operation semantics, thereby providing a unified framework for EP and logic reasoning. Moreover we provide the language's extensions to enable retractable EP (dealing with the circumstance that certain events may be *revoked*, in Chapter 9), out-of-order EP (dealing with *late* events, in Chapter 10), and most importantly, we provide an extension for EP and logic reasoning suitable in the realm of the Semantic Web (in Chapter 11).

1.2 Shifting Event Processing Toward More Intelligent Event Processing

Recently, there has been a significant paradigm shift toward *real time* information processing in research as well as in industry. As mentioned in the previous section, most businesses today collect large volumes of data continuously and it is absolutely essential for them to process this data in real time so that they can react quickly. Real time computing has raised significant interest due to its wide applicability in areas such as sensor networks (for on the fly interpretation of sensor data), financial services (for dynamic tracking of stock fluctuations as well as surveillance for frauds and money laundering), ad-hoc Business Process Management (to detect situations that demand process changes in a timely fashion), network traffic monitoring (to detect and predict potential traffic problems), location based services (for real time tracking and service operation), Web click analysis (for real time analysis of users interaction with a Web site and adaptive content delivery) and so forth.

Classical database systems and data warehouses are concerned with what happened in the past. In contrast thereto, EP is about processing *events* upon their occurrence, with the goal to detect what has just happened or what is about to happen. For example, an event may represent a sensor reading, a stock price change, a complied transaction, a new piece of information, a content update made available by a Web service and so forth. In all these situations, it is reasonable to compose simple (atomic) events into *derived* (complex) events, in order to structure the course of affairs and describe more complex dynamic matters. EP deals with *real time recognition* of such derived events, i.e., it processes continuously arriving events with the aim of identifying occurrences of meaningful derived events (according to predefined event patterns or event operations).

Derived events are detected for various reasons, e.g., to trigger a time-critical action, to be displayed on a dashboard (presenting information in real time), or to trigger another event and continue an event-driven computation. In existing approaches to EP, a derived event is represented either as a single event (that is filtered, projected, enriched and so forth), or as a composition of other events satisfying certain temporal or spatial relationships.

Digitalisation of information in markets, factories, and communication over Internet has caused large volumes of data that is continuously generated. EP offers concepts and techniques to process this data in real time. Consequentially, this means that EP needs to effectively fulfil two requirements – *high throughput* and *timeliness*. Facing the large volumes of generated events and the necessity of processing them in real time, EP creates indeed a challenge in its own right. Yet, the question remains whether sole functionality of today's EP is enough to meet sophisticated requirements of modern event-driven information systems. EP deals with operations that include reading, creating, transforming, and deleting events [EtNi10]. Some of these operations are computationally intensive, but not *intelligent*. Coming back to the vision from [Luck02], it is arguable whether EP supported by today's event-driven systems, are *expressive* enough to capture events in all their aspects. How likely is that critical decisions are taken merely on event patterns of the type, e.g., "event a is followed by event b in the last 10 seconds"? For some applications such patterns are expressive enough; however for *knowledge-rich* applications, they are certainly not. In many applications, real time actions need to be triggered not only by events, but also upon evaluation of additional *background knowledge*. This knowledge captures the *domain of interest*, or *context* related to critical actions and decisions. Its purpose is to be evaluated during detection of events in order to on the fly *enrich* events with relevant background information; to detect more complex *situations*; to *reason* about events and propose certain *intelligent recommendations*; or to accomplish event *classification, clustering, filtering* and so forth.

In this work, we advocate a *knowledge-rich* EP, which apart from events, also processes *contextual* knowledge (e.g., to additionally prove *semantic* relations among matched events or to describe the domain in which events are interpreted). Our approach employs formal *reasoning* methods to generate non trivial conclusions from the contextual knowledge. These non trivial conclusions are known as *implicit* knowledge, as opposed to knowledge that is *explicitly* stated (e.g., information from a database). Hence, in our approach complex events are derived not only from other events, but from implicit knowledge too. To give a reader some feeling what we mean by semantic relations and implicit knowledge, let us consider the following example.

Consider a traffic management system which detects roads with slow traffic, and automatically modifies a speed limit on these roads. For example, the traffic on a road is slow if two events, suggesting a slow traffic, have been reported within the last half an hour. So how can we identify events that *suggest* slow traffic? Traffic can be slowed down due to various reasons (e.g., an accident occurred, a ghost driver identified, or due to bad weather and so forth). Further on, there may be a number of classifications for each of these reasons. For instance, a traffic accident is classified as a head-on collision, side collision, rollover; and further, bad weather driving conditions can be caused by rain, snow, ice and so forth. There exist different types of observations which may influence the traffic, and for each of them there may be a different suggested speed limit.

All this, and similar information can be formally represented as a background knowledge (since they are fairly static). The system can evaluate the knowledge when certain events occur in order to better asses the situation. For instance, an event may report rain in a particular region, and a head-on collision may have happened on a road section in the same region. A similar situation, that requires the speed limit change, could be detected due to snowfall and a ghost driver. In all cases the system will *infer* that occurred events are *semantically* relevant with respect to the traffic monitoring, and will automatically modify the speed limit on that road section (given that those events additionally satisfy temporal constraints, i.e., they have occurred within a half an hour, as well as spatial constraints, i.e., events originate from the same region). Therefore, such a system enables us to specify a more *abstract, high-level* situations, while specific cases related to those situations may be *inferred* from the background knowledge. Moreover a situation can be assessed based on *implicit knowledge* (i.e., not only explicitly stated information). We believe that such a capability in today's EP systems would push them toward a more intelligent EP.

Formal knowledge representation enables machine processable knowledge, as well as derivation of *implicitly* stated knowledge. We want to utilise this capability to enable detection of *indirect* observations that may still make influence on the overall traffic situation, e.g., to detect intelligent recommendations, to better asses the context in which events are processed, and so forth. This powerful feature is beyond the state of the art of existing EP systems [ADGI08, BGAH07, ArBW06, KrSe09, CCDF$^+$03], and is required for an intelligent real time processing.

In this work we will further purse the topic of knowledge-based EP which may help in shifting today's EP toward a more intelligent EP. Yet to succeed in this, we need to adapt current knowledge processing and reasoning procedures to work over *streaming* events.

1.3 Shifting Reasoning Toward Stream Reasoning

Reasoning is ability to generate non-trivial conclusions from premises or assumptions. There exist different types of reasoning. Logical reasoning methods were mainly divided between *deductive*, *inductive* and *abductive* reasoning.

Deductive reasoning is reasoning that attempts to show that a *conclusion* necessarily follows from a set of *premises* or *hypotheses*. The conclusion is true when premises are true too. Logic *rules* define which conclusions may be drawn from which premises. By validating logic rules, deductive reasoning proves premises and effectively attempt to gain new knowledge. This knowledge (conclusions) is commonly called *implicit* knowledge.

Inductive reasoning is reasoning that starts from a specific case or cases and attempts to induce a general rule. That is, it begins with specific observations, and detects patterns and regularities in order to induce a much larger set of conclusions or theories.

Abductive reasoning is reasoning that starts from an observed phenomenon, and attempts to abduce a single explanation (or a few explanations) thereof (although, in general, there may be infinitely many of them). Deduction and abduction thus differ in the direction in which reasoning is performed. Deduction start from a set of hypotheses and deduces a conclusion, while abduction begins with a conclusion and abduces hypotheses.

While the all three methods of reasoning have their strengths in different cases, deductive reasoning starts with the assertion of a general inference rule and proceeds from there to a guaranteed specific conclusion. In terms of EP, a general inference rule corresponds to an event pattern, and a specific conclusion corresponds to an instance of a complex event. This analogy was the motivation for us to use deductive reasoning in EP. Hence in the remaining parts of this work, when saying reasoning, we refer to deductive reasoning (unless otherwise stated).

When we talk about knowledge representation and deductive reasoning, logic programming (LP) is a relevant field of computer science. The field began in the early 1970's[1] as a direct outgrowth of earlier work in automatic theorem proving and artificial intelligence (AI) [Lloy87]. The fundamental idea behind LP is to use *logic* as a programming language. This idea has proved to be useful in many areas including expert systems, problem-solving strategies, planning, game playing, and others – which in turn have been applied in the fields of accounting, medicine, process control, financial service, production, and human resources among others. But can concepts and techniques from LP be used for processing events?

In LP an inference procedure is applied to logic *rules* of the form: *If* $b_1, ..., b_n$ *Then* h, proving a conclusion h if it can prove premises $b_1, ..., b_n$. Rules, including premises and other artefacts that may be used for proving them, are kept in a knowledgebase (KB). This mechanism is close to EP if a derived event is treated as a conclusion (h), and is detected from more simple events ($b_1, ..., b_n$). Moreover, the condition part ($b_1, ..., b_n$) does not necessarily need to consist of events. Instead, it my contain other objects from a KB. It is convenient to use a KB, for example, to specify *relationships* between events, knowledge about the *domain of discourse*, and different *contexts* in which events are interpreted. More importantly, EP based on LP would enable *reasoning* over events, their relationships, entire states, and possible contextual knowledge available for a particular domain.

In deductive reasoning the argument's conclusion and premises are represented by logic (*deductive*) rules, and LP provides strategies for computing these rules. It has been already shown [APPS10, KoSe86, MiSh99, LaLM98, AlBB06, BrEc07a, Hale87, PaKB10] that EP approaches based on logic rules have various advantages. First, they are *expressive* enough and convenient to represent diverse event patterns and come with a clear *formal declarative semantics*; as such, they are free of operational side-effects. Second, integration of *query processing* with EP is easy and natural (including, e.g., the processing of *recursive* queries). Third, our experience with the deployment of logic rules is very positive and encouraging in terms of implementation effort for the main constructs in EP, as well as in providing extensibility of an EP system (e.g., the number of code lines is significantly smaller than in procedural programming). Ultimately, a logic-based event

---

[1] or even earlier, 1958, when John McCarthy published his paper "Programs with Common Sense".

1.3. Shifting Reasoning Toward Stream Reasoning

model allows for *reasoning* over events, their relationships, entire states, and possible background knowledge available for a particular domain.

To clarify what we mean by *reasoning* over events and and background knowledge, let us consider the following scenario. Suppose we use a navigation system to drive from a city A to a city B. Our goal is to find an optimal route between the two cities, with respect to the length of the route and the current driving conditions. Driving conditions are monitored in real time with a similar system as described in an example traffic management scenario from Section 1.2.

Further on, suppose that navigation system has the capability to perform deductive reasoning. For instance, all roads and road sections are represented as facts in its KB, and the system contains rules that explain how to find a path between two points. The KB also contains properties about roads (e.g., which routes are motorways, and which are single carriageway roads, toll roads, and so forth). Depending on constraints, the system deploys deductive reasoning to find an optimal route. This task can be done by the system, since the KB is static and we have a fixed goal to be solved. However if we want the system to navigate us with respect to the current driving conditions, it needs to reason *on-the-fly*. The initial optimal path may be altered due to the current driving conditions on a particular route section (during the drive). Therefore the system needs to reason about the current driving conditions (events) and the domain knowledge (existing routes, their properties and constraints). We refer to this type of (on-the-fly) reasoning as Stream Reasoning (SR).

Definition 1.1 *Stream Reasoning is the task of conjunctively reasoning over streaming events, and static or slowly evolving knowledge. It is, therefore, reasoning that takes streaming events as an input, and by consulting static or slowly evolving knowledge, it continuously derives a streaming output under time constraints.* ◇

Static or evolving knowledge represent background knowledge. This knowledge captures event patterns, as well as the *domain*, or *context* in which events are interpreted.

stream reasoning (SR) is a capability beyond many of the state of the art approaches in EP [ADGI08, MeMa09, BGAH07, ArBW06, KrSe09, CCDF$^+$03], despite the fact that there exists already a lot of (static or slowly evolving) knowledge on line available (which could be used in conjunction with EP). For example, the Linked Open Data (LOD) initiative[2] has made available on the Web hundreds of datasets and ontologies such as live-linked open sensor data[3], UK governmental data[4], the New York Times dataset[5], financial ontologies[6], encyclopedic data (e.g., DBpedia), linked geo-data[7]. This knowledge is commonly represented as *structured data* (using RDF Schema [BrGM04]). Structured data

---
[2] see http://linkeddata.org/
[3] Live linked open sensor data: http://sensormasher.deri.org/
[4] OpenPSI project: http://www.openpsi.org/
[5] Linked Open Data from the New York Times: http://data.nytimes.com/
[6] Financial ontology: http://www.fadyart.com/
[7] LinkedGeoData: http://linkedgeodata.org

allows us to define meanings, structures and semantics of information that is understandable for humans and intelligently processable by machines. Moreover, structured data enables *reasoning* over explicit knowledge in order to infer new (implicit) information. Current EP systems [ADGI08, MeMa09, BGAH07, ArBW06, KrSe09, CCDF+03] however cannot utilize this structured knowledge and cannot reason about it. In this work, we address this issue, and provide a framework for *event recognition* and *Stream Reasoning* over events and domain knowledge.

However, LP reasoning is not commonly used for highly dynamic KBs. Although LP deals with knowledge updates, reasoning algorithms in LP are not algorithmically optimised for reasoning over *streaming* events, i.e., for SR.

Apart from this, a significant difference between LP and EP systems is the underlying computation mechanism. Computation in LP is based on, so called, *request-response* interaction model while EP systems additionally support *event-driven* interactions (see Subsection 2.2.2).

For given a *request*, an LP system will evaluate available knowledge (i.e. rules and facts) and *respond* with an answer. This means that an LP system, used for EP, would need to check if an event pattern can be deduced or not. The check is performed at the time when such a request is posed. If satisfied by the time when the request is processed, a complex (derived) event will be reported. If not, the pattern is not detected until the next time the same request is processed (though it can become satisfied in-between the two checks). Contrary to this, EP demands *data-driven* or *event-driven* computation model (as handled by various approaches such as non-deterministic finite automata (NFA) [ADGI08], Petri Nets [GaDi92], the RETE algorithm [Forg82] and so forth). Unfortunately approaches grounded on NFA and Petri Nets do not feature reasoning capabilities; and RETE may be integrated with deductive rules as it is done in production rule systems [Alve09]. However, production rule systems in some aspects differ from event-driven systems. For example, in a RETE-based system many rules may be scheduled for firing when a certain event occurs. The execution order of these rules is defined by a conflict resolution strategy. For example, Drools system[8] (a RETE-based system) implements two conflict resolution strategies: salience and LIFO (last in, first out). In case of salience, a user can specify that a certain rule has a higher execution priority than other rules (by assigning a higher number to it). In that case, the rule with a higher salience will be preferred. LIFO priorities are based on recency, i.e., if two rules have the same priority, the rule that matches the most recent object will be fired first. While the latter is close to the recent event consumption policy [ChMi94], the former is not practically useful in EP systems as it is not feasible to assign a priority number for each event pattern rule. Having an event as a first class citizen would give us fine grain possibilities to select an event instance out of many possible. We will address this topic further in Section 7.4, and show that our approach can implement various consumption policies as defined in [ChMi94]. Moreover, having an event as a first class citizen will also enable our approach to easier implement various other aspects in EP (e.g., sliding windows, aggregates, retraction

---

[8]Drools: http://www.jboss.org/drools

in EP, and out-of-order EP). For further details between the RETE algorithm and our approach see Section 4.5.

How to effectively realise LP-based EP, thereby pushing EP toward more *intelligent EP*, and by pushing reasoning toward *SR* is a central topic of this work.

1.4 Aims and Objectives

The discussion, so far, emphasised the fact that events are everywhere, and we need to find a means to makes sense of them. EP has emerged in computer science as a new discipline which deals with events. Moreover by providing concepts, techniques and tools for events, today's EP offers a starting position for detection of complex situations in real time. Further on, we tried to stress importance of machine processable knowledge and reasoning in the context of EP, thereby shifting it toward a more intelligent EP. One approach to achieve this is to apply deductive reasoning and logic programming to EP.

This simple conclusion, however, disregards the fact that LP has not been used so far as a common computing paradigm in EP. Some underlying concepts of EP – most notably the event-driven interaction model (discussed in Subsection 2.2.2) – differ from the way LP has been used so far.

Faster detections of events leave more time to respond to them, but detections based on more accurate and complete information require more time for evaluation and less time for response [ChSc10]. It is a trade-off between faster detections of events, and detections based on a more accurate and complete information. An approach based on LP may help in enabling EP with more accurate and complete information. But a question, how feasible such an approach would be with respect to timeliness, remains open.

The principal objective of this work is therefore to advance the development in EP with a knowledge representation formalism that is grounded in LP. We summarise the following questions from the above discussion as the main research questions addressed in this work:

- Can we utilise knowledge representation (KR) techniques to formally express both, complex event patterns and background knowledge, in a uniform formalism for EP?

- How to effectively use logic inferencing to derive complex events in a timely fashion?

- By realising EP with concepts from LP, can we detect more real time situations that are otherwise undetectable with sole EP?

- Could an LP approach for EP be efficiently implemented with an event-driven computation model (instead of commonly used request-response interactions)?

- Would an LP approach for EP be extensible enough for other specific requirements in EP (e.g., event retraction and out-of-order EP)?

- How much do we need to compromise on faster detections of events, to get in return detections based on more accurate and complete information (complex event patterns with background knowledge)?

This is by no means an exhaustive list of research questions (related to knowledge-based EP). For example, how to utilise background knowledge for an automated creation of event patterns (pattern mining), and further, pattern maintenance and validation are relevant topics, see e.g., [SeSt10]. These and similar topics could be well investigated in the realm of an LP-based approach for EP too. However in this particular work they are out of scope, and might be a subject of our future work.

The main contributions of this thesis are as follows:

- **A uniform formalism for Event Processing and Stream Reasoning.** We define an expressive complex event description language, called *ETALIS Language for Events* with a rule-based syntax and a formal declarative semantics. The language features event and static rules. While event rules are used to capture patterns of complex events, the static rules account for (static or evolving) background knowledge about the considered domain. The proposed formalism is expressive enough to capture the set of all possible thirteen temporal relations on time intervals, defined in Allen's interval algebra [Alle83]. We further extended the language to express complex iterative patterns over unbound event streams, and apply certain aggregation functions over sliding windows. Since the language with its extensions is based on declarative semantics, it is suitable for *deductive reasoning* over event streams and the domain knowledge. The language is also general enough to support extensions with respect to other operators and features required in EP (e.g., event consumption policies).

- **Efficient execution model.** We develop an efficient, execution model to enable Event Processing and Stream Reasoning in *ETALIS Language for Events* (ELE).

We propose a novel operational semantics for ELE in which complex (derived) events are *deduced* or derived from simpler ones. Complex events are defined as *deductive rules*, and events are represented as *facts*. Every time an atomic event (relevant with respect to the set of monitored complex events) occurs, the system updates the knowledgebase, i.e., it adds a respective fact to the internal state of complex events. Essentially, this internal state encodes what atomic events have already happened and what are still missing for the completion of a certain complex event. Complex events are detected as soon as the last event required for their detection has occurred. Descriptions telling which occurrence of an event furthers the detection of complex events (including the relationships between complex events, events they consist of, or additional domain knowledge) are given by deductive

1.4. Aims and Objectives

rules and facts. Consequently, detection of complex events then amounts to an *inferencing* problem.

- **Event retraction model.** Events are often assumed to be immutable and therefore always correct. Retraction (revision) in EP deals with the circumstance that certain events may be revoked. This necessitates to reconsider complex events which might have been computed based on the original, flawy history as soon as part of that history is corrected. In this work we address the problem of *revision* in EP, and provide it as an extension of ELE.

- **Out-of-order Event Processing.** In most cases events, in an event stream, are assumed to be *totally ordered*: the order in which events are received by an EP system is the same as their timestamp order. This assumption is called *total order assumption* [LLDR+07]. In reality events may arrive *out-of-order*, for example, due to network latencies or even machine failures. In this work we describe the processing of complex events over event streams that may also contain *out-of-order* data. By handling *out-of-order* events an EP system needs to keep certain events longer than they are normally needed (in order to handle *late* events). Therefore, the problem of processing out-of-order events is strongly connected to another important issue – garbage collection (an effective removal of overdue events). This work provides a framework for processing events, including out-of-order events too.

- **Processing events in the context of the Semantic Web.** While existing semantic technologies and reasoning engines are constantly being improved in dealing with *time invariant* domain knowledge, they lack in support for processing *real time* streaming data (events). Real time Web data is valuable only if it is captured, processed, and delivered instantly.

  As already mentioned, there exists already a lot of (static or slowly evolving) knowledge available in the realm of the Semantic Web. However this knowledge has not yet been fully exploited in event-driven applications. To bridge the gap between the Semantic Web and EP we propose Event Processing SPARQL (EP-SPARQL) that extends the SPARQL language [PrSe08] with its EP and Stream Reasoning capabilities. As such, it is a language that can be used in processing real time data in the context of the Semantic Web applications too.

- **Implementation and evaluation.** We implement *ETALIS Language for Events* with its extensions in a Prolog-based prototype. The implementation is open source[9]. We describe the conceptual architecture of our implementation, and develop a set of experiments to evaluate its run time performance. When possible, we compare our evaluation results with results from a non logic programming EP system. We also conduct an evaluation case study. The study is related to a sensor network, dedicated to measurements of environmental phenomena (e.g., weather observations such as wind, temperature, humidity, precipitation, visibility and so forth). Finally, we present the study and show its implementation in ELE.

---
[9] ETALIS source code: http://code.google.com/p/etalis/

1.5 Thesis Organization

This work is organized in five parts, each containing several chapters.

The first part – Introduction – includes this chapter which gives an overview of the thesis, and provides background information for remaining parts of it. We introduce EP in Chapter 2 and LP in Chapter 3 as the two main building blocks of this work. The same chapters also provide terminology which is commonly used in the remaining parts of this thesis. Chapter 4 ends the first part by surveying the related work and comparing it to ours.

The second part – ETALIS Language for Events – develops the main work about a new formalism for EP and SR. We start this part by providing requirements and language design principles in Chapter 5. We introduce the language with its rule-based syntax and the declarative semantics in Chapter 6. The chapter also provides a number of examples which give the reader a better understanding about the language constructs and its use in practise. Chapter 7 describes in details an execution model of our language. It provides the operational semantics of the language, and explains how complex events are incrementally computed under time constraints. Chapter 8 shows how event operations, as commonly defined in an event processing network (EPN), are implemented in the proposed language.

The third part – ETALIS Extensions – provides few additional developments of ELE, thereby proving the extensibility of the language. We start this part by introducing the problem of event retraction, and give an execution model that handles revised events in Chapter 9. Revision in EP may cause certain events to be revoked (although they have already been detected). In contrast to this, out-of-order EP may cause additional detections of complex events (in presence of late events). Chapter 10 introduces problems in EP when out-of-order events are present, and provides an extension to our formalism to solve these problems. Chapter 11 motivates the need for EP in the context of Web, in particular, in the context of the Semantic Web. We provide EP-SPARQL which is a new language to address dynamic aspects in Semantic Web applications. It is as an extension of the commonly used SPARQL language [PrSe08]. We provide syntax and formal semantics of the language and devise an effective execution model for the proposed formalism.

The forth part – Practical Considerations – gives an overview of the Event-driven Transaction Logic Inference System (ETALIS). It is a prototypical system that implements all concepts developed in this work. In Chapter 12 we discuss an architecture of ETALIS, and give details related to practical use of the system. In Chapter 13 we present results from a number of tests that we have conducted with ETALIS. Results are divided into two categories. The first category reports on the performance results (i.e., run time characteristics of the system). The second category discusses a use case study, thereby demonstrating and emphasising functional capabilities of the system.

The fifth part – Conclusions and Outlook – summarises the presented work and gives an outlook for the future work. In Chapter 14 we give the summary of the achieved results, and provide more details about event-driven Business Process Management as a promising future direction in the context of our work. Finally, the same chapter also concludes this thesis.

1.6 Relation to Previous Publications

Most of the content in this thesis has been already published. The outline of the thesis was previously published in a short form in [AFRS[+]11b] and [ARFS12a]. Motivation to combine EP with logic reasoning has its roots in our previous work [ApSA09, AnSt09, AnSt08b, AFSS09]. The core of the second part – ELE with a rule-based syntax and the declarative semantics presented in Chapter 6 – was published in [AFRS[+]10]. An execution model – that is described in Chapter 7 – was introduced in [AFSS09, AFRS[+]10]. The work related to iterative and aggregative patterns – presented in Chapter 7 and Chapter 8 – was published in [ARFS11a]. In the part three, the work on event retractions (see Chapter 9) was published in [ARFS11b]. Out-of-order EP in ETALIS was presented in [FoAR11]. EP extended with Semantic Web technologies was motivated in [SASM[+]09]. Further on, we proposed a language called EP-SPARQL in [AFRS11a] (see Chapter 11). In the part four, Chapter 12 discusses an architecture of ETALIS which was published in [ARFS12b]. Chapter 13 gathers evaluation results from publications [AFRS[+]10, ARFS11a, ARFS11b, FoAR11, AFRS11a]. In the part five, Chapter 14 gives prospective areas where ETALIS can be effectively used, and provides the outlook for our unfinished and future work. In particular, the use of ETALIS for real time situational awareness in sensor networks was investigated in [XSSA[+]11, SMXS[+]11]. We proposed to apply ETALIS to process events and linked data in the context of the smart grids in [WASS[+]10]. Finally, basic concepts underlying event-driven business processes were initially proposed in [AnSt08a].

2

Introduction to Event Processing

Event Processing (EP) is a computer science discipline that has developed a set of techniques and tools to enable real time computing. EP techniques are grounded on principles of event programming. An EP architecture is an important concept in EP that helps us to better understand and control computing in EP applications. In this chapter we give an introduction to EP, including the underlying principles and an EP architecture.

2.1 What is an Event?

To understand what EP is about, let us start by explaining what is meant by an event.

In [EtNi10] an *event* is defined as an occurrence within a particular system or domain; it is something that has happened, or is contemplated as having happened in that domain. The word event is also used to mean a programming entity that represents such an occurrence in a computing system.

From this definition we see that events are considered within a particular domain. In many cases the domain endows events with a context in which they are interpreted.

In the first part of the definition, an event denotes something that happened in the real, physical world. The second part however treats an event as a programming entity in a computing system. Indeed, an event is a general term, and in most of the applications we start observing the physical world, and need a means to represent and process these observations in a computing system.

An event may also denote something that "is contemplated as having happened". In general, a computing system generates an event when something happens, however this does not necessarily correspond to actual occurrence. For example, a financial computing system triggers events whenever it suspects a fraud has been committed. These events however may be false positives, and do not need to correspond to real fraud happenings. Other examples, when an event denotes something that is contemplated as happened, occur in systems with failures (e.g., an event is reported either due to failure of a sensor, or failure of an event transmission system).

Later on, in Chapter 6 we will formally define an event as an entity denoted by an event name (type), the payload carried by the event, and a timestamp.

In practise, an event represents something that occurs, happens or changes the current state of affairs. For example, an event may signify a problem or an impending problem, a threshold, an opportunity, an information becoming available, a deviation and so forth. These events are directly related to specific, measurable changes of conditions. In many application it is however important to infer more abstract situations. It is the task of EP to effectively derive these situations based on (many) single, ordinary events.

In the remaining part of this chapter we describe basic principles which underlay EP and enable processing of events under time constraints.

2.2 Event Programming Principles

In this section we look at basic characteristics of event programming. To understand them, we start by looking at how applications typically interact when they are not using events.

Request-response or request-reply is one of the basic methods that computers (applications) use to interact. In such an interaction, one involved entity (e.g., computer) typically sends a *request*, and another entity replies by a *response*. We are used to such an interaction as this pattern, so far, has been widely used in computer systems (e.g., a user interaction with a web browser, or a user answering a telephone call, are typical examples of request-response interactions). The client-server model of computing implements request-response interactions, where the client represents a requester and the server is a responder.

Request-response interactions are typically implemented in a *synchronous* fashion. Such an interaction holds a connection open and waits until the response is delivered (or the timeout period expires). Therefore, in synchronous interaction a requester is expected to respond fairly promptly. Request-response interactions may also mix synchronous and asynchronous communications (referred to as "sync over async"). This happens when, for example, it is more efficient to close a connection due to a long-running intensive computation or awaiting a human response. However, in its essence, a request-response interaction is synchronous.

2.2. Event Programming Principles

In contrast, event programming is *asynchronous*. Requester and responder are replaced by an event producer and consumer, and there is no open connection in between them. Moreover, an event consumer does not wait for any respond. If (and when) there is one, it will be delivered by the event producer.

Based on this difference, between request-response and event-driven paradigms, we outline few characteristics of event-driven programming.

2.2.1 Events as a Means to Declare Changes

In declarative programming, we declare facts about things, stating that some of them are true and others are false[1]. Based on these facts, an inference procedure may be employed to possibly derive truth about other things (whose truth is not *explicitly* stated). However what is important is that we do not specify *who* may use a fact that something is true (or false), and we do not specify *when* one fact can be used to infer another one.

Similarly in event-driven programming, an event indicates that something has happened. That is, an event producer declares that something has occurred or there is a change in the current state of affairs. However, who may use this *fact* is not specified. Furthermore, when this fact may be used – to possibly infer another fact – is not predefined neither. Finally, the number of facts that may be derived from that fact is also not predetermined. The notion of *independence* between declaration of an event and possible consequences it may produce (e.g., to be used in derivation of unspecified number of other events, or to be used for any other purpose that has no influence whatsoever on the cause of that event) is in EP referred to as the *principle of decoupling* [EtNi10].

From this perspective, event-driven programming is close to the principles of declarative programming, whereas for example, programming based on request-response interactions is analogue to imperative programming. There, a requester asks for a certain processing to be done when the request is posed (similarly as an imperative program executes a sequences of commands when the sequence is called). The order – in which requests are processed – is important in event-driven programming, as well as in imperative programming though.

2.2.2 Information Push Versus Information Pull

One significant difference between event-driven and request-response interactions is the way how information is passed between a producer and a consumer of information. Event-driven interactions are based on information *push*, while in request-response interactions information is *pulled*. In the traditional client-server model, based on request-response interactions, the client asynchronously pulls information from a server. On the other

---
[1] For simplicity reasons, a two-valued logic (with *true* and *false*) is assumed. In general, there exist three-, four-, or many-valued logics too.

hand, in an event-based interaction model, information (event) is emitted through the asynchronous push mode.

This characteristic of event-driven programming is one of the main drivers for adoption of EP in modern ICT systems. The shift towards more asynchronous push interactions is a model of choice in many application areas like production monitoring and control systems, location-based services, algorithmic stock trading or logistics control. In all these applications, consumers of real time information do not know a priori when the information will be available. Hence to get the real time information, a consumer needs to constantly poll a producer. However a consumer does not necessarily know producers which it wants information to be pulled from. Moreover information producers typically interact with an a priori anonymous set of consumers. In all these interaction patterns, the push model eases the real time information exchange between a producer and a consumer.

Many Internet applications are based on the push model too, and in general, we see a trend of shifting many Web applications towards *Real Time Web* applications. The Real Time Web is a set of technologies and practices which enable users to receive information nearly as soon as it is published by its authors, rather than requiring periodic updates. Therefore there is no need to *pull* information, it will be delivered to users nearly at the moment it is published. Web applications, designed on the principles of service-oriented architecture (SOA), are now extended with principles of event-driven programming. For instance, no more waiting for web services to communicate from one polling instance to another. We notice a paradigm shift from information *pull* to information *push*; or from *request-response* based web services to *event-driven*, push-based, web services.

2.3 Event Processing Architecture

In the previous section we have described basic principles underlying EP. In this section we finally come to a definition of EP, and further present an architecture designed for event programming.

According to [EtNi10], *Event Processing* is computing that performs operations on events. Common event processing operations include reading, creating, transforming, and deleting of events.

Event Processing Technical Society (EPTS) has defined Event Processing similarly (see EPTS Glossary [LuSc11]). Note that in scientific literature and elsewhere, the term Complex Event Processing (CEP) is used to denote the same operations as EP, but performed on *complex* events [LuSc11]. Very often both terms are used interchangeably. All operations on *events*, that we discuss in the scope of this thesis, can be with no restriction applied to *complex* events too.

In this section, we will go from this rather general definition to a more detailed explanation what EP is about. However we will keep discussion close to topics relevant to this thesis. Moreover, some concepts presented here may be specific to the subject of the

2.3. Event Processing Architecture

thesis. For a more broad presentation of EP and an EP architecture, the interested reader is referred to [EtNi10, Luck02, ChSc10].

Event processing architecture is a software architecture pattern promoting the reading, creating, transforming, and deleting events. So what is an architectural pattern that may be applied by the design and implementation of EP applications? Applications differ in their domains (they are applied to) and requirements (they need to fulfil), however all EP applications consists of a set of common entities organised in an event processing network (EPN). Entities that an EPN consists of are: event producers, event consumers, and EP as an intermediate processing in between. Figure 2.1 presents the three main building blocks of an EPN. In the following we briefly describe each of these three entities. For a more detailed discussion on this topic, the interested reader is referred to [EtNi10].

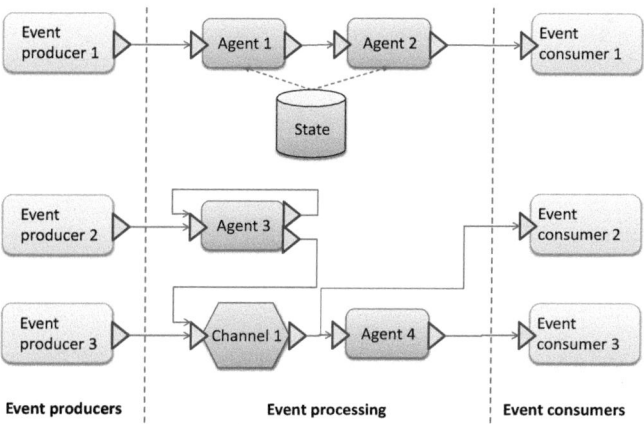

Figure 2.1: An event processing network

An *event producer* is an entity that introduces events into a system which implements an EP architecture. An event producer is also known as an event source. An event producer "listens" to an environment that is attached to, and provides events from that environment to an attached event processing agent (EPA) (see Figure 2.1). For example, an event producer can be attached to a physical sensor, so that when the sensor detects a change, the producer creates an object that represents the change and emits it as an event. In other cases, an event producer may simply be a proxy that relays events from somewhere else.

An *event consumer* is an entity that receives events from a system which implements an EPA. An event consumer "consumes" events, for instance, by reading events and using them for business analytics, or further computation, visualisation and so forth. In other cases, it may consume events by writing them into a log or triggering actions by them (e.g., calling a service or generating other events).

Processing, that take place between the producers and consumers, is actual EP (see Figure 2.1). As said, this processing may involve operations on events such as reading, creating, transforming, and deleting events. In general case, this processing is not monolithic – it consists of a set of agents, each performing certain operation on events.

An *EPA* is a software module that processes events [LuSc11, EtNi10]. An EPA takes events as input and, by applying an EP operation, it outputs *derived* (or *complex*) events. Authors in [EtNi10] give the following classification of EPAs.

- *Filter agent* – filters out irrelevant events with respect to a filtering condition. For instance, an agent may filter out stock price events whose price is below 10$. The goal of a filter agent is to increase performance of an EP application by discarding uninteresting events.

- *Pattern detection agent* – detects an event pattern based on certain conditions (e.g., temporal, spatial, and various other semantic relations that can be established among events). For instance, an agent may detect the stock price increase when a certain number of stock events happen, denoting the price increase of X % within a particular time (as defined by an event pattern).

- *Transformation agent* – transforms input events according to a transformation operations.

Transformation agents may further be classified upon transformation operations. The following operations have been recognised.

- *Split agent* – takes a single event as input and emits two or more copies of the input event.

- *Aggregate agent* – takes multiple events as input and produces a single derived event by applying an aggregation function over input events.

- *Compose agent* – joins two event streams similarly as two relations are joined in relational algebra.

- *Translate agent* – translates an input event into an output event according to a translation operation.

A translation operation may take one of the following two forms.

- *Enrich agent* – augments an input event with additional information (taken from an external information source, e.g., a database or an ontology).

- *Project agent* – deletes certain information carried by an input event (similarly as a relation from relational algebra is projected based on certain attributes).

2.3. Event Processing Architecture

EPAs are connected to event producers and consumers, as well as to themselves through event channels (denoted by directed edges in Figure 2.1).

An *event channel* is a processing element that receives events from one or more source processing elements, makes routing decisions, and sends the input events unchanged to one or more target processing elements in accordance with these routing decisions [EtNi10].

There are two reasons to use the concept of an EPN. The first reason is about *usability* when designing an EP application. Namely, an architect may have better understanding of the application when the internal intermediate EP is represented as an EPN [EtNi10]. The second reason is *efficiency*. Careful design of an EPN can reduce event flow within the network, and therefore increase the overall application's performance. An EPN may also enable implementation of EPAs on a distributed architecture, which can additionally increase performance and scalability of an application [EtNi10].

An *event processing language* enables a high-level specification of an EPN. In some EP languages, a user directly creates event flows that are mapped into an EPN. In others, a user writes language statements which are then compiled into an EPN.

In this thesis we provide a general language for EP [AFRS$^+$10, AFRS$^+$11b]. The language is found on event programming principles (see Section 2.2). It enables specification of an EPN, but the focus of the thesis is on the language itself, its underlying principles, and EPAs that can be realised with the language (rather than on the whole EP architecture, which additionally involves event producers, consumers, and event channels).

EP is a field of computer science that has a great potential for further research. Basic underlying concepts of EP and their further development toward a new Logic Programming approach for EP, are major topics of this work. In response to that, in the following chapter we introduce basic concepts of Logic Programming that are important to remaining parts of this work.

3

Introduction to Logic Programming

One of the main motivations of this thesis is to use *logic* to compute events. Our intention is to exploit the fundamental idea behind logic programming (LP) – to use logic as a programming language. In the remaining parts of this work, we will devise a logic-based formalism for expressing permitted operations on events. As preliminaries to that goal, in this chapter we introduce basic concepts underlying LP.

3.1 Background of Logic Programming

LP began in the early 1970's as a direct outgrowth of earlier work in automatic theorem proving and artificial intelligence (AI) [Lloy87]. The idea to use *logic* as a programming language has proved to be useful in many areas including bio-informatics, medicine, social network analysis, natural language processing, fraud detection, the Semantic Web, virtual worlds, process control, financial service, intelligent tutoring systems, and so forth.

There has been recently renewed interest in using LP in many areas outside the traditional ones. Examples include work on cloud computing [ACCE[+]09], declarative networking systems [CCHM08], natural language processing [EiGS05], robotics [ARDRSP[+]07] and so forth.

Historically looking, LP has significantly evolved around Kowalski's idea [Kowa79b]. According to that idea, an algorithm can be regarded as consisting of a *logic* component, which specifies the knowledge to be used in solving problems, and a *control* component, which determines the problem-solving strategies by means of which that knowledge is used. The logic component determines the meaning of the algorithm whereas the control component only affects its efficiency [Kowa79a].

In the nutshell, the logic explains *what* the problem an algorithm solves, while the control states *how* the problem is solved. Kowalski has argued that such a conceptual separation would enable computer programs to be more correct, and more easily improved and modified. Moreover, a programmer could focus on specifying the logic component of an algorithm while leaving the control to be handled solely by the logic programming system itself. While this goal would require purely declarative programming (which has not been fully achieved by Prolog-like logic programming systems), the separation of an algorithm to its logic and control part had a strong influence on LP in general [Lloy87].

Later on in this work, we will devise a formalism for EP that is based on logic. Our formalism comprises the logic and the control part, hence in this chapter we will go into fundamentals of each of these two components. Moreover the main goal of this chapter is to provide a concise terminology that is used later in this work. Our attention will however not cover general LP. Instead, it will focus to *definite programs*, as they are an important part of LP which are also in the scope of this work. Readers without prior knowledge to LP are referred to a more extended text on the subject [Lloy87, Apt90, vEKo76, NiMa95, Ullm88].

3.2 The Logic in Logic Programs

This section explains what is commonly understood under the term *logic* in logic programs. As already said, the notion of logic is considered here in the scope of definite programs, and in this section we explain what they are.

3.2.1 Syntax of Definite Programs

The *syntax* of a programming language is the set of rules used for constructing sentences from symbols and words of that language. Therefore, the syntax of a program is concerned with correct structures of that program with respect to the program's language. The meaning of a program – written in a programming language – is defined by the language *semantics*. In this subsection we talk about the syntax of logic programs, while in Subsection 3.2.2 we will introduce the semantics thereof.

Logic programs are built from *atomic formulas* of type: $p(t_1,t_2,...,t_n)$, where p is a *predicate symbol* and $t_1,t_2,...,t_n$ are *terms*. An atomic formula (or more simply, an *atom*) is a formula that cannot be divided into strict sub-formulas. Hence, it is the simplest well-formed formula which is used, together with logic connectives, to build compound formulas. The following examples are atomic formulas.

3.2. The Logic in Logic Programs

$$\text{age}(john, 30)$$
$$\text{marriedTo}(john, X)$$

The first formula defines an atom with a predicate name age, and two terms – *john* and 30. Intuitively, in a logic program we would use such an atom to denote that *john*'s age is 30. The second formula defines an atom, marriedTo, which is a relation between *john* and someone denoted by X. A term can therefore be a constant (e.g., *john*) or a variable (e.g., X). Constants and predicate names commonly start with lower case letters, while variables begin with upper case letters.

We also construct *compound terms* to implement functions. A function is an expression of type $f(t_1, t_2, ..., t_n)$ where f is a function symbol of arity n and $t_1, t_2, ..., t_n$ are terms. 0-ary function symbols denote individual constants, and are thus terms.

For instance, functions can implement arithmetic operations such as addition +, subtraction -, less than < and so forth. These atomic formulas have predicates with predefined meaning, often referred to as *built-in* predicates. Built-in predicates are used in practise to implement commonly used functions. For instance, apart from the mentioned arithmetic operations, Prolog provides various built-in predicates to perform routine activities like to determine the length of a list, to realise input and output operations, to communicate with the operating system, and so forth.

An interpretation of a function does not necessarily produce a finite set of results. For example, the less than operation ($X < Y$) may produce infinitely many results when X and Y range over an infinite domain. Variables in a function can be limited in range by other atomic formulas, thereby limiting the function itself. For example, a variable can be limited by appearing in a ground atom. In such a case, an interpretation of a function can be determined as a *fixed interpretation* (e.g., by selecting or joining certain constants from a set of ground atoms). In Chapter 6 we will propose a formalism which deals with functions that have a fixed interpretation.

Since the atom age(*john*, 30) contains only constants, it is also termed as a *ground* atom. A *literal* is either an atomic formula or a negated atomic formula. If $p(t_1, t_2, ..., t_n)$ is an atom, $p(t_1, t_2, ..., t_n)$ is said to be a *positive* literal, and $\neg p(t_1, t_2, ..., t_n)$ is said to be a *negative* literal. A disjunction of (negative or positive) literals is called a *clause*. A clause with the most one positive literal is called a *definite* clause or *Horn* clause. A definite (Horn) clause is written as:

$$p_0(t_1, t_2, ..., t_i) \vee \neg p_1(t_1, t_2, ..., t_j) \vee ... \vee \neg p_n(t_1, t_2, ..., t_k) \quad (3.1)$$

Based on these notions, we can now give a formal definition of definite programs (Horn logic).

Definition 3.1 *A signature* $\langle \mathbf{C}, \mathbf{F}, \mathbf{P}, \mathbf{V} \rangle$ *for a definite program consists of a finite set of individual names (or constants)* $\mathbf{C}$, *a finite set of* function symbols $\mathbf{F}$, *a finite set of* predicate symbols *(or* predicates*)* **P**, *and a finite set of* variable names **V**, *all of which are mutually disjoint. The function* ar : $\mathbf{F} \cup \mathbf{P} \to \mathbb{N}$ *associates a natural number* $\text{ar}(p)$ *with each predicate* $p \in \mathbf{F} \cup \mathbf{P}$ *that defines the (unique) arity of p.*

Based on a signature for Horn logic $\langle \mathbf{C}, \mathbf{F}, \mathbf{P}, \mathbf{V} \rangle$*, we define the following notions:*

- *A* term *is defined such that*
    - *if* $t \in \mathbf{C} \cup \mathbf{V}$*, i.e., t is an individual or variable name, then t is a term, or*
    - *if* $f \in \mathbf{F}$ *with* $\text{ar}(f) = n$*, and if* $t_1, \ldots, t_n$ *are terms, then* $f(t_1, \ldots, t_n)$ *is also a term.*

    Terms without variables are called ground terms.

- *An* atom *is a formula of the form* $p(t_1, t_2, \ldots, t_n)$ *given that* $t_1, \ldots, t_n$ *are terms, and* $p \in \mathbf{P}$ *is a predicate name of arity n, i.e.* $\text{ar}(p) = n$*. Atoms that contain only ground terms are called ground atoms.*

- *A* literal *is either an atomic formula* $p(t_1, t_2, \ldots, t_n)$*, or a negated atomic formula* $\neg p(t_1, t_2, \ldots, t_n)$*.*

- *A* definite (Horn) clause *is a formula of the form:*
  $p_0(t_1, t_2, \ldots, t_i) \vee \neg\, p_1(t_1, t_2, \ldots, t_j) \vee \ldots \vee \neg\, p_n(t_1, t_2, \ldots, t_k)$
  where $p_0, \ldots, p_n$ *are atoms, and every* t_i *that occurs within these atoms is a term.*

- *A* fact *is a Horn clause that contains a single positive literal, e.g.,* $p_0(t_1, t_2, \ldots, t_i)$*.*

- *A* definite goal *is a Horn clause that contains one or more negative literals, e.g.,* $\neg\, p_1(t_1, t_2, \ldots, t_j) \vee \ldots \vee \neg\, p_n(t_1, t_2, \ldots, t_k)$*. A definite goal can be also written in the form of an implication:*
  $\leftarrow p_1(t_1, t_2, \ldots, t_j) \wedge \ldots \wedge p_n(t_1, t_2, \ldots, t_k)$

A set of definite (Horn) clauses is called a Horn program *or a* definite program. ◇

In the remaining part of this work we will often use the term *Horn rule*, which is a Horn clause that contains one positive literal and one or more negative literals. For notational convenience, a Horn rule is written in the form of an implication:

$$p_0(t_1, t_2, \ldots, t_i) \leftarrow p_1(t_1, t_2, \ldots, t_j) \wedge \ldots \wedge p_n(t_1, t_2, \ldots, t_k). \qquad (3.2)$$

The premise of a Horn rule is called the rule *body* while the conclusion is called the rule *head*.

Notation in (3.2) is a common way to represent a Horn rule as it is a natural expression of an inference. The rule states that one way to prove a conclusion $p_0(t_1, t_2, \ldots, t_i)$ is to prove premises $p_1(t_1, t_2, \ldots, t_j) \wedge \ldots \wedge p_n(t_1, t_2, \ldots, t_k)$. In the remaining parts of this work, we

3.2. The Logic in Logic Programs

(1)   shipment(s_1,s_2).
(2)   shipment(s_2,s_3).
(3)   dlvPath(X,Y) :− shipment(X,Y).
(4)   dlvPath(X,Y) :− shipment(X,Z),dlvPath(Z,Y).

Figure 3.1: Example definite program

shell use Prolog style for expressing definite (Horn) rules. The following rule is a Prolog equivalent to rule (3.2).

$$p_0(t_1,t_2,...,t_i) :− p_1(t_1,t_2,...,t_j),...,p_n(t_1,t_2,...,t_k). \qquad (3.3)$$

Finally, sometimes we write rule (3.3) simply as:

$$p_0 :− p_1,...,p_n. \qquad (3.4)$$

where $p_0, p_1, ..., p_n$ represent atomic formulas.

To illustrates notions from Definition 3.1, let us consider an example definite program P shown in Figure 3.1. We observe a simple supply chain scenario where goods are shipped from one site to another – denoted by shipment(s_i, s_j) – and we are interested to find out all delivery paths, dlvPath(X,Y), where goods are shipped.

Figure 3.1 gives an example of a definite program based on a Horn signature with a set of constant symbols $\mathbf{C} = \{s_1,s_2,s_3\}$ and a set of predicate symbols $\mathbf{P} = \{$shipment, dlvPath$\}$. Formula (1) and Formula (2) in Figure 3.1 are facts, represented as ground atoms. Additionally, there are two rules in the example. Rule (3) states that "every shipment from site X to site Y passes through a delivery path from X to Y". Rule (4) declares that "for every shipment from site X to site Z, and an existing delivery path from Z to Y, we may conclude that there exist an additional delivery path from site X to site Y".

We can extend the rules from Figure 3.1 by adding two non-equality built-in predicates, see Figure 3.2. The purpose of the built-in predicates is to disqualify a shipment within a single site as a valid shipment. The example from Figure 3.1, extended with two non-equality predicates, is not a definite program any more. Note, however, that the built-in predicates are bound by ground atoms (1) - (2) (see Figure 3.1), and therefore these built-in predicates still represent finite relations. In the remaining parts of this work we will consider definite programs with function symbols with variables limited in range (hence those with fixed interpretations).

In the next section we discuss the proper formal meaning of definite programs. That is, we discuss based on what evidences an inferred delivery path may be considered indeed as a valid delivery path – as it is specified by the *logical semantics*.

(1) dlvPath(X,Y) :− shipment$(X,Y), X \neq Y$.
(2) dlvPath(X,Y) :− shipment(X,Z),dlvPath$(Z,Y), X \neq Z$.

Figure 3.2: Example definite rules with built-in predicates

3.2.2 Semantics of Definite Programs

The meaning of logic rules – that are written in a particular logic – depends on *semantics* of that logic. In this section we will introduce semantics of *definite programs*. We give the semantics of definite programs in a *model-theoretic* way. In this viewpoint, formulas of a logic program are used to define possible worlds or *models*. A model describes a world of interest, and can be used for examining what is *true* and what is *false* in that world. For instance, given a set of logic formulas that describes an intended model, we can ask the computer whether a certain conclusion – expressed as another logic formula – can be drawn from that model. If yes, we say that this formula is a *logic consequence* of our intended model. In general, the set of logical consequences of a logic program is infinite. Hence an intended model of a logic program gives the user possibility to query the program selectively for various aspects of the model.

Essentially, that is intuition behind representing worlds as models – it is a powerful mechanism for automated computation of correct conclusions from logic programs. However a logic program – that describes an intended model – may have other unintended (valid) models too. By writing a logic program, the programmer attempts to describe the intended model. But in general, this program may have many models. The programmer will use the computer to draw conclusions about the intended model. But again, since the computer does not know the programmer's intention, to draw a conclusion from a logic program it must prove the truth of the conclusion in any model of the program (including the intended and unintended ones). Sometimes this may be a computationally intensive task. However it is important to define what an intended model is. Therefore, in this section we discuss this topic in the scope of definite programs, and in the next section we show how an intended model can be computed.

Logic rules represent declarative statements about individuals, by establishing relations and functions on individuals. Thus the mathematical abstraction of a world – modelled by rules – is a non-empty set of individuals called a *domain*. In the scope of definite programs, domains consist of the set of all variably-free terms. Given an alphabet $\mathscr{A}$[1] the set $U_\mathscr{A}$ of all ground terms is called the *Herbrand universe* of $\mathscr{A}$. The set $B_\mathscr{A}$ of all ground, atomic formulas over $\mathscr{A}$ is called the *Herbrand base* of $\mathscr{A}$.

Definition 3.2 *A Herbrand interpretation $\mathscr{I}$ of a definite program P is a non-empty* interpretation domain, *and an* interpretation function. *The domain of $\mathscr{I}$ is U_P. The interpretation function maps symbols from P into this domain as follows:*

---
[1] $\mathscr{A}$ is defined by strings of symbols that include all elements from the signature of definite programs, including an infinite set of variables, as well as symbols for the logical connectives, parentheses, brackets and other punctuation symbols.

3.2. The Logic in Logic Programs

- If $c \in \mathbf{C}$ is a constant, then $c_{\mathscr{I}}$ is defined to be c itself.

- If $f \in \mathbf{F}$ is a function symbol of arity $\text{ar}(f) = n$, then $f_{\mathscr{I}}$ is defined as
  $[f(t_1,...,t_n)]_{\mathscr{I}} := f_{\mathscr{I}}(t_{1\mathscr{I}},...,t_{n\mathscr{I}})$
  That is, the meaning of a compound term is obtained by applying the function denoted by its function symbol f to the meanings of its principal subterms $t_1,...,t_n$, recursively.

- If $p \in \mathbf{P}$ is a predicate symbol of arity $\text{ar}(p) = n$, then $p_{\mathscr{I}}$ is defined as an n-ary relation over the domain. That is, $p_{\mathscr{I}}$ is a subset of U_P^n, which contains all n-tuples of ground terms.

◇

Constants, function symbols, and predicates represent building blocks of more complex formulas of the language. Therefore the interpretation of them provides a basis for assigning true values to definite clauses in general.

The Herbrand universe consists of ground terms, but definite programs may contain variables too. Hence we need a function to map variables of the alphabet to the domain of an interpretation. Such a function can be also extended to map constants and function symbols to the domain of an interpretation too.

A *variable assignment* is a mapping $\mu : \mathbf{V} \to U_P$ assigning a value from the interpretation domain to every variable. We let μ^* denote the canonical extension of μ to terms defined in the following way:

$$\mu^* : \begin{cases} v \mapsto \mu(v) & \text{if } v \in \mathbf{V}, \\ c \mapsto c & \text{if } c \in \mathbf{C}, \\ f(t_1,...,t_n) \mapsto f(\mu^*(t_1),...,\mu^*(t_n)) & \text{if } f \in \mathbf{F}. \end{cases}$$

Definition 3.3 *Given an interpretation $\mathscr{I}$ and a variable assignment μ for $\mathscr{I}$, the truth value of a definite clause is defined as follows:*

- *For an atom $p(t_1,...,t_n)$, $\mathscr{I} \models_\mu p(t_1,...,t_n)$ iff $\langle \mu^*(t_1),...,\mu^*(t_n) \rangle \in p_{\mathscr{I}}$;*

- *For a conjunction $p_1 \wedge ... \wedge p_n$ of atoms $p_1,...,p_n$, $\mathscr{I} \models_\mu (p_1 \wedge ... \wedge p_n)$ iff $\mathscr{I} \models_\mu p_1$ and ... and $\mathscr{I} \models_\mu p_n$;*

- *For a definite rule $p_0(t_1,t_2,...,t_i) \leftarrow p_1(t_1,t_2,...,t_j) \wedge ... \wedge p_n(t_1,t_2,...,t_k)$, $\mathscr{I} \models_\mu p_0(t_1,t_2,...,t_i)$ whenever $\mathscr{I} \models_\mu p_1$ and ... and $\mathscr{I} \models_\mu p_n$.*

◇

Definition 3.4 *A Herbrand interpretation $\mathscr{I}$ is said to be a Herbrand model of a definite program P iff every clause in P is true in $\mathscr{I}$. That is, a Herbrand interpretation is a Herbrand model iff it satisfies all definite rules in P for all variable assignments μ.* ◇

If a definite program P has a model, we say that P is *satisfiable* or *consistent*. We can derive conclusions from satisfiable programs by checking whether a conclusion – represented as a definite clause – is satisfied in all models of P.

To illustrate the above definitions, let us go back to an example program from Figure 3.1.

The alphabet of a program consists of exactly those symbols which appear in the program. Hence the Herbrand universe and Herbrand base can be determined from the program itself. The Herbrand universe is defined as the following set:

$$U_P = \{s_1, s_2, s_3\}$$

The Herbrand base of the program's alphabet is the set:

$$\begin{aligned} B_P = \{&\texttt{shipment}(s_1,s_1), \texttt{shipment}(s_1,s_2), \texttt{shipment}(s_1,s_3), \\ &\texttt{shipment}(s_2,s_1), \texttt{shipment}(s_2,s_2), \texttt{shipment}(s_2,s_3), \\ &\texttt{shipment}(s_3,s_1), \texttt{shipment}(s_3,s_2), \texttt{shipment}(s_3,s_3), \\ &\texttt{dlvPath}(s_1,s_1), \texttt{dlvPath}(s_1,s_2), \texttt{dlvPath}(s_1,s_3), \\ &\texttt{dlvPath}(s_2,s_1), \texttt{dlvPath}(s_2,s_2), \texttt{dlvPath}(s_2,s_3), \\ &\texttt{dlvPath}(s_3,s_1), \texttt{dlvPath}(s_3,s_2), \texttt{dlvPath}(s_3,s_3)\} \end{aligned}$$

Herbrand interpretations for constants and function symbols have predefined meanings. That is, constants are mapped to themselves, and functions symbols are interpreted as compound terms with the same principal function symbol. Hence to specify a Herbrand interpretation, it suffices to list the relations associated with the predicate symbols. For an n-ary predicate symbol $\texttt{p}$ and an Herbrand interpretation $\mathscr{I}$, the interpretation of $\texttt{p}$ consists of the following set of n-tuples: $\{\langle t_1,...,t_n\rangle \in U_P^n \mid \mathscr{I} \models_\mu \texttt{p}(t_1,...,t_n)\}$ for some variable assignment μ.

Let us consider few possible Herbrand interpretations of our example program P as shown in Figure 3.3.

To be a Herbrand model, a Herbrand interpretation needs to satisfy all clauses in the program. Clearly, $\mathscr{I}_1$ is not a model of our example program as it does not satisfy ground atomic formulas (1) and (2). In contrast to $\mathscr{I}_1$, $\mathscr{I}_2$ does satisfy atomic formulas (1) and (2), but does not satisfy rule (3). Namely there exist two ground instances ($\texttt{shipment}(s_1,s_2)$, and $\texttt{shipment}(s_2,s_3)$) that make the rule premiss true with no true conclusion.

$\mathscr{I}_3$ is a Herbrand model of our program P as it satisfies all four clauses from the program. Ground atomic formulas (1) and (2) are true in this model, and it is not difficult to show that rules (3) and (4) are satisfied too. Intuitively, the meaning of a rule we can get by substituting variables in the rule body, and if the substitution makes the premise of the rule true, the rule head must be true too. For instance, rule (3) and rule (4) in Figure 3.1 define the true instances of atom $\texttt{dlvPath}(X,Y)$ in terms of other true atoms. One such a *true* instance is $\texttt{dlvPath}(s_1,s_2)$ which we get by substituting X and Y in rule

3.3. The Control in Logic Programs   33

$\mathscr{I}_1 := \emptyset$
$\mathscr{I}_2 := \{\text{shipment}(s_1,s_2), \text{shipment}(s_2,s_3)\}$
$\mathscr{I}_3 := \{\text{shipment}(s_1,s_2), \text{shipment}(s_2,s_3),$
         $\text{dlvPath}(s_1,s_2), \text{dlvPath}(s_2,s_3), \text{dlvPath}(s_1,s_3)\}$
$\mathscr{I}_4 := B_P$

Figure 3.3: Example Herbrand interpretations of the program P

(3) with constants s_1, s_2 from a true atom $\text{shipment}(s_1,s_2)$. Other two instances are $\text{dlvPath}(s_2,s_3)$ and $\text{dlvPath}(s_1,s_3)$, obtained from rule (3) and rule (4), respectively.

Finally, $\mathscr{I}_4$ is a model of the program too. Applying the similar reasoning as in previous cases, we can prove that any substitution of true atoms from B_P – that make premises of a rule in P true – will produce a true conclusion contained by B_P.

In general, a Herbrand base B_P of a definite program P is always a Herbrand model of the program. However such a model is uninteresting, since every n-ary predicate of the program is interpreted as the full n-ary relation over the domain of ground terms. Rather we are interested in a model that reflects only information expressed by the program and nothing more – it includes minimum number of ground atoms which follow from the program. Such a model is called a *minimal* (or *least*) model, since we cannot make any ground atom false and still have it as a model.

$\mathscr{I}_3$ is a minimal Herbrand model of our example program P. It includes only those ground atoms that follow as logical consequences of the program. Moreover, $\mathscr{I}_3$ is the *unique* minimal model, as no other minimal model exists for P. Every definite program has a unique minimal model [Lloy87].

A minimal model also corresponds to the intended model of a definite program. As pointed out in [NiMa95], the intended model is an abstraction of the world that is described by the program. The world may be richer than the minimal Herbrand model. However, the information not included explicitly (via facts) or implicitly (via rules) in the program cannot be obtained as an answer to a goal. The answer corresponds to logical consequences of the program.

The question arises how a minimal Herbrand model can be computed. This is a topic of the following section.

3.3 The Control in Logic Programs

In the previous section we have discussed the model-theoretic semantics of definite programs, and in this section we discuss how to find a reasonable way to turn the logic (definite) program into a sequence of steps that compute the answer. The *operational semantics* explains how to draw correct conclusions from logic programs. This section gives only a brief introduction to the control in logic programs. For a detailed, formal

$$T_P \uparrow 0 := \emptyset$$
$$T_P \uparrow (i+1) := T_P(T_P \uparrow i)$$
$$T_P \uparrow \omega := \bigcup_{i=0}^{\infty} T_P \uparrow i$$

Figure 3.4: Iterative generation of immediate consequences

discussion on this matter, the interested reader is referred to textbooks [Lloy87, Apt90, NiMa95, vEKo76].

3.3.1 Immediate Consequence Operator

A minimal Herbrand model for a definite program can be constructed by following an approach given in the *fixpoint* theory. A fixpoint (or fixed point) of a function $T : \mathscr{D} \to \mathscr{D}$ is a point $x \in \mathscr{D}$ that is mapped to itself by the function, that is $T(x) = x$. The intuition behind the fixpoint theory is to use a fixpoint function T to construct a minimal Herbrand model. The domain $\mathscr{D}$ of T is a Herbrand interpretation $\mathscr{I}$. The function takes ground instances of rules from a definite program P, and produces true conclusions. These conclusions are elements of every model of P. The function is applied iteratively until no more true conclusions are produced – that is, until a fixpoint is reached.

Consider a definite program P, and one its interpretation $\mathscr{I}$ which includes all facts from P. Since all facts from P must be included in every model of P, $\mathscr{I}$ is a subset of a minimal Herbrand model[2]. Let us further consider a rule of type $a_0 :- a_1,...,a_n$ $(n > 0)$ in P. Every (ground) instantiation that makes the rule body $a_1,...,a_n$ true – with respect to $\mathscr{I}$ – yields a true conclusion, which is an instance of the rule head a_0. It is now possible to construct an interpretation $\mathscr{I}'$ that includes all elements from $\mathscr{I}$, plus true conclusions obtained from every instantiation of each rule in P. We can write $\mathscr{I}'$ formally as follows:

$$\mathscr{I}' = \{a_0 \in B_P \mid a_0 :- a_1,...,a_n \text{ is a ground instance of a rule in } P \text{ and } a_1,...,a_n \in \mathscr{I}\}$$

The function T_P such that $T_P(\mathscr{I}) = \mathscr{I}'$ is said to be the *immediate consequence operator*. For a definite program P it can be shown that there exists a minimal interpretation $\mathscr{I}_n$ such that $T_P(\mathscr{I}_n) = \mathscr{I}_n$, and that $\mathscr{I}_n$ is the minimal Herbrand model of P.

A common notation, used to represent elements iteratively produced by this operator, is shown in Figure 3.4. To illustrate how the immediate consequence operator constructs the minimal Herbrand model, let us consider again our example definite program from Figure 3.1. In the 0th iteration $\mathscr{I} = \emptyset$ and $T_P \uparrow 0 = \emptyset$. The following three iterations are shown in Figure 3.5. Computing $T_P \uparrow 4$ would produce the same set as the one generated by $T_P \uparrow 3$. This means that no more true conclusion can be produced, and the fixpoint has been reached.

Note that $T_P \uparrow i \subseteq T_P \uparrow (i+1)$. That is, the immediate consequence operator recomputes elements in every iteration. Such a computation is wasteful – known as *naive evaluation*.

---
[2]If P has only facts with no rule, $\mathscr{I}$ is further a minimal Herbrand model of P.

3.3. The Control in Logic Programs

$T_P \uparrow 0 = \emptyset$
$T_P \uparrow 1 = \{\texttt{shipment}(s_1,s_2), \texttt{shipment}(s_2,s_3)\}$
$T_P \uparrow 2 = \{\texttt{shipment}(s_1,s_2), \texttt{shipment}(s_2,s_3)$
$\phantom{T_P \uparrow 2 = \{}\texttt{dlvPath}(s_1,s_2), \texttt{dlvPath}(s_2,s_3)\}$
$T_P \uparrow 3 = \{\texttt{shipment}(s_1,s_2), \texttt{shipment}(s_2,s_3)$
$\phantom{T_P \uparrow 3 = \{}\texttt{dlvPath}(s_1,s_2), \texttt{dlvPath}(s_2,s_3), \texttt{dlvPath}(s_1,s_3)\}$

Figure 3.5: Example construction of the minimal Herbrand model

We can calculate only the difference $\Delta T_P \uparrow (i+1) = T_P \uparrow (i+1) - T_P \uparrow i$ between the sets computed in two successive iterations. This strategy is known as *semi-naive evaluation*.

Both strategies however start from existing facts, and use clauses to derive new facts. That is, to prove a goal we need to compute *all* true consequences of a given program (possibly including those expressed as instantiations of the goal). Therefore, these strategies are known as *bottom-up* evaluations. Alternatively, a *top-down* evaluation would start from a particular goal, and check whether the goal is true in a world described by a logic program. In the next section we briefly introduce such a strategy, known as *SLD-resolution*.

3.3.2 SLD Resolution

The resolution principle – introduced by J. A. Robinson in [Robi65] – is a general rule of inference for propositional logic and first-order logic. This principle has become the basis of most logic programming systems. A refinement of resolution for definite programs (the Horn fragment) was first described by R. A. Kowalski [Kowa74], and termed as Selective Linear Definite clause resolution (SLD-resolution) by M. H. van Emden.

SLD-resolution is a refutation technique. That is, to prove a goal SLD-resolution starts from a goal which is the negation of the initial goal, and tries to prove that the goal is false in every model of a given logic program. SLD-resolution is both sound and refutation complete for definite clauses [Clar79]. In this section we will informally introduce SLD-resolution. For a formal discussion and theoretical properties of SLD-resolution, the interested reader is referred to [ApvE82, Lloy87, Apt90, vEKo76, NiMa95, Clar79].

As said in Subsection 3.2.1, a definite program is a set of clauses of type:

$$a_0 :- a_1, ..., a_n \quad (n \geq 0)$$

where $a_0, ..., a_n$ are atomic formulas (subgoals). If a_0 is absent, the clause is said to be a goal. Considering a definite program P and a goal:

$$:- a_1, ..., a_n \quad (n > 0)$$

the question is whether the goal holds in a world described by P. Since in definite clauses all variables are universally quantified, the goal is equivalent to:

$$\forall X_1,...,\forall X_m \neg(\mathsf{a}_1,...,\mathsf{a}_n) \quad (n>0)$$

which is by DeMorgan's law logically equivalent to:

$$\neg\exists X_1,...,\exists X_m(\mathsf{a}_1,...,\mathsf{a}_n) \quad (n>0)$$

SLD-resolution starts from this negated goal, and aims to prove that such a statement is false in every model of P (including the intended model too). If that is provable, then it also true that there exist some $X_1,...,X_m$ for which the goal $\mathsf{a}_1,...,\mathsf{a}_n$ $(n>0)$ is a logical consequence of the program P, that is:

$$P \models \exists X_1,...,\exists X_m(\mathsf{a}_1,...,\mathsf{a}_n) \quad (n>0)$$

If that is a case, we are interested to substitute variables $X_1,..,X_m$ with ground terms from a given interpretation domain of P, and to get the final answer. Let us denote such a substitution with θ, and define it as a finite set of pairs of terms $\{X_1/t_1,...,X_m/t_m\}$ where each t_i is a ground term and X_i is a variable such that $t_i \neq X_i$ and $X_i \neq X_j$ if $i \neq j$. The application $X\theta$ of substitution θ to a variable X is defined as follows:

$$X\theta := \begin{cases} t & \text{if } X/t \in \theta, \\ X & \text{otherwise} \end{cases}$$

SLD-resolution checks whether the goal $\mathsf{a}_1,...,\mathsf{a}_n$ $(n>0)$ is a logical consequence of P in few steps. In each step, it selects an atomic formula $\mathsf{p}(t_1,...,t_n)$ (which represents a subgoal a_i in the goal) and a definite clause $\mathsf{p}(s_1,...,s_n) :- \mathsf{a}'_1,...,\mathsf{a}'_m$ $(m \geq 0)$ from P. It constructs a substitution θ such that $\mathsf{p}(t_1,...,t_n)\theta$ and $\mathsf{p}(s_1,...,s_n)\theta$ are identical. In this way, a new goal is constructed in which the subgoal a_i is substituted by $\mathsf{a}'_1,...,\mathsf{a}'_m$, and a substitution θ is applied to the atom p of arity n. We say that a subgoal a_j is proved if, by applying a substitution θ_j, $\mathsf{a}_j\theta_j$ is identical to a fact from P. Such a subgoal may therefore be removed from the goal.

We see that, in each step, SLD-resolution tries to eliminate a subgoal from the goal by replacing it with a clause from P, and generating a substitution. If the last step turns to be an empty goal (corresponding to falsity), the final conclusion is the negation of the initial goal. That is, if we reached the conclusion that $:- \mathsf{a}_1,...,\mathsf{a}_n$ $(n>0)$ is false with respect to P after k steps, then it means that:

$$P \models (\mathsf{a}_1,...,\mathsf{a}_n)\theta_1,..,\theta_k$$

To demonstrate SLD-resolution principle of inferencing, let us consider our example program from Figure 3.1 again. Suppose the goal is to find all existing delivery paths starting form site s_1. This query can be expressed as:

3.3. The Control in Logic Programs

$$:- \text{dlvPath}(s_1, Y).$$

which is an abbreviation for $\forall Y \neg \text{dlvPath}(s_1, Y)$, and equivalent to:

$$\neg \exists Y \text{dlvPath}(s_1, Y).$$

Hence the starting point of reasoning is that there is no Y such that the delivery path between s_1 and Y exists. If that turns not to be true, the inference procedure will lead to a refutation.

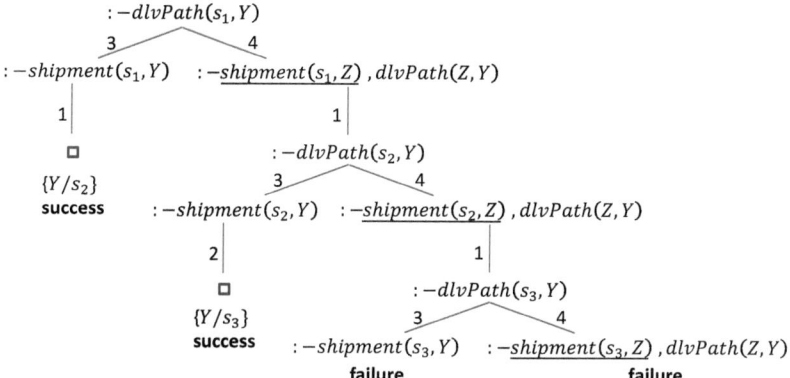

Figure 3.6: An SLD tree for our example definite program

Figure 3.6 shows an SLD-tree for the example program. We see that rule (3) and rule (4) – from Figure 3.1 – provide two definitions of the delivery path, which are represented by two corresponding labelled branches in Figure 3.6. The left branch says that shipment(s_1, Y) does not exists, i.e., the goal is unsatisfiable with P. This is obviously false, as there exists a fact shipment(s_1, s_2) in P (see clause (1) in Figure 3.1). Hence this branch leads to a refutation denoted by □, and it is possible to find a substitution θ, for which shipment(s_1, Y) and shipment(s_1, s_2) are identical – that is, when Y is substituted by s_2. This refutation leads to *success* as the branch proves that there is Y such that the delivery path between s_1 and Y exists, namely s_2. Hence we can conclude that:

$$P \models \text{dlvPath}(s_1, s_2).$$

The right branch is obtained when the initial goal dlvPath(s_1, Y) is replaced by rule (4), and a substitution $\{X/s_1\}$ is applied. By using clause (1) and applying a substitution $\{Z/s_2\}$, this subgoal can be reduced to dlvPath(s_2, Y). Here we get a situation that is similar to our initial goal. That is, we can construct again two branches from rule (3) and rule (4). The left branch succeeds with a substitution $\{Y/s_3\}$, while the right branch will fail as $\text{shipment}(s_3, Y)$, as well as $\text{shipment}(s_3, Z)$ are not true in P.

In conclusion, we have derived two answers for our initial goal, $\text{dlvPath}(s_1, s_2)$ and $\text{dlvPath}(s_1, s_3)$.

As we have seen, SLD-resolution is a goal-directed strategy. The strategy aims to be more effective than the bottom-up computation since it constrains the computation to a given goal. On the other hand, SLD-resolution may create infinite SLD-trees in some cases for which the bottom-up strategy ensures the termination [NiMa95]. There exist considerable amount of work in the area of combining the two strategies – most notably the work on query-sub-query [Ullm89, AbHV95], and magic sets [BMSU86, Chen97] – and further to improve termination by tabling (or memorization) [Warr92].

4
State of the Art

The field of EP has recently gained considerable attention in research as well as in industry. For general introduction to EP and its ground concepts, the interested reader is referred to textbooks [Luck02, ChSc10, EtNi10]. These textbooks – in particular the latter one – also present the state of the art with respect to common and advanced features in EP systems. Nevertheless, in this section we will survey the state of the art in EP from the point of view of specific features and the scope of this work. The work related to ours mainly fits into following areas: active databases as predecessors of EP systems; general EP systems and Data Stream Management Systems (DSMS), including approaches for retractions in EP and out-of-order EP; logic-based approaches for EP; and approaches related to data streams and the *Semantic Web*.

4.1 Active Databases

In order to capture relevant changes in a system and respond to those changes adequately, a number of formal reactive frameworks have been proposed. Work on modelling *behavioural* aspects of an application (using various forms of reactive rules) started in the active database community a long time ago. Different aspects have been studied extensively, ranging from language specifications to discussions about architectural issues [PaDi99]. Active database languages use event specifications to facilitate database *triggers*, which do not only listen to simple events but observe complex combinations of events too.

Simple events carry a type, their occurrence time, and possibly other parameters that can be used in data analysis to help in detecting event patterns, or to be part of a computation after detection. Complex event specifications are patterns of events which are matched against the streams of events that occur during the run time of the system. These patterns consist of simple event types and event operators. Simple events are the basic (or atomic) events the system can detect. Complex events are detected from occurrences of one or more of them. All simple events have a simple event type, which for a database application might be *insert*, *update*, and *delete*. The types are used as placeholder in event patterns.

Event patterns are structured by event operators. A given operator might have several event types as arguments and, for example, to stipulate that the constituent events must occur in a sequence. An event detector for the given pattern acts as a stream pattern matcher and listens for events that satisfy the type constraints and the semantics of the given operator. Many operators were proposed in the past, hence in the following paragraphs we discuss several event pattern languages and their operators. Common operators offered by many languages include conjunction (AND), disjunction (OR), sequence (SEQ) and accumulation.

One early active database system is *HiPAC* [McDa89]. It is an object-oriented database with transaction support. HiPAC can detect events only within a single transaction. Global event detectors are proposed, which detect complex events across transaction boundaries and over longer intervals. *Ode* [GeJS92b] is another active database system with a language for the specification of event expressions. The language is also referred to as *Compose*. Ode proposes several basic event operators and a number of derived operators for ease of use and shorter syntax. The last of the classical event specification languages discussed here is *Snoop* [CKAK94, ChMi94] and its successor *SnoopIB* [AdCh06]. Snoop provides the well supported operators: AND , OR and SEQ , as well as additional operators such as: negation (NOT), conjunction with specified number of conjunctions (Any), an operator which captures the occurrence of an aperiodic event bounded by two arbitrary events for providing an interval (A), an operator which allows one to express the occurrence of unbound number of occurrences of certain event in an interval (A*), an operator which triggers a periodic event (P), an operator which repeats triggering of a periodic event (P*), and an operator which triggers an event after certain event occurred plus certain time elapsed (Plus), for more details see [CKAK94, ChMi94]. Early work on Snoop defines events as instantaneous occurrences. This also holds for complex events, even in cases when their constituents span over an interval of time. As a result, a complex event is defined on a time point too (instead of being defined on a time interval, delimited by the start of the first constituent event and the end of the last constituent event of that complex event). Consideration of only a time point of detection of an event is termed as the point-based semantics. It poses problems with nested sequences as pointed out in [GaAu02]. Interval-based semantics for Snoop is called SnoopIB and was first published in [AdCh06]. The issue of point-based versus interval-based semantics is further discussed in Section 5.2.

4.1. Active Databases

Many of active database languages belong to their respective database management systems, or to prototypes thereof. Three of them, which have noteworthy implementation details, are described here: the Ode approach conducts complex event detection by using automata, SAMOS uses coloured Petri nets and Sentinel uses a graph based approach.

Complex event detection in Ode [GeJS92a] is implemented using automata. Input for the automata is a stream of simple events. Ode thus transforms complex event expressions into deterministic finite automata. For sub-expressions which are complex events themselves, the process is done recursively. Atomic simple events are ultimately represented as automata of three states: a start state, an accepting state (entered upon detection of the simple event occurrence) and a non-accepting state (entered upon detection of any other simple event). Apart from providing the implementation, automata are a convenient model to define semantics of complex event operators. A downside of automata is that an automaton cannot accept overlapping occurrences of the same complex event. Also event parameters pose a problem. They are either stored outside of the automaton, or the automaton is increased greatly in the number of states to accommodate the different parameters and possible values thereof.

Complex event detection in SAMOS [GaDi94] is implemented using Petri nets. Each primitive event type is represented by a Petri net place. Primitive event occurrences are entered as individual tokens into the network. Complex event expressions are transformed into places and transitions. When constituent events are part of several expressions, duplicating transitions are used to connect the simple event with the networks requiring it. This results in a combined Petri net for the set of all event expressions. Petri nets, like automata provide a model of the semantics of event operators. Also the detection of overlapping occurrences is possible. Event parameters are stored in tokens and flow through the network. Although the tokens are individual, there is no mechanism to deterministically choose a token if there is more than one token in a single place.

Sentinel [Chak97] is an active object-oriented database implementing complex event detection for the Snoop operators. Event detection follows a graph based approach. The graph is constructed from the event expressions. Complex expressions are represented by nodes with links to the nodes of their subexpressions, down to nodes of simple events. Event occurrences enter the bottom nodes and flow upwards through the graph, being joined into composite occurrences. The graph is a directed acyclic graph and generally does not form a tree for two reasons: nodes may have several parents, when their represented expression is a part of more than one complex events. Secondly there is no single root node as a single most complex event. A possibly conceived drawback of Snoop, compared to the previously mentioned implementations, is that the data structures of Snoop do not represent and even clarify the semantics of the event expressions. The logic of Snoop is hidden in the implementation of each graph node. However the semantics of Snoop is defined externally, using event histories and describing the operators as mappings from simple event histories to complex event histories. Furthermore Snoop defines the selection and consumption of simple events for the concurrent detection of overlapping complex events. The four alternative definitions were proposed: recent, chronicle, continuous and cumulative consumption polices (event contexts). We will give more details about consumption polices and their implementation in our EP framework in Section 7.4.

4.2 Event Processing Systems

We start this section by surveying related work in DSMS. Initially, DSMS have operated on streams as *temporally totally ordered* data sets. This characteristic was a discriminator between DSMS and general EP systems (which have operated on *event clouds* as *partially ordered* sets of events). However this border is not clear any more, and nowadays some of DSMS do not operate strictly on ordered streams. On the other hand – given a broad definition of EP in Section 2.3 – DSMS can be considered as EP systems too.

Work in the area of DSMS started by introducing languages that are reminiscent of SQL, but operate on streaming data. Database execution models were also adapted to process streams of data. Two examples are StreamSQL with a corresponding StreamBase system[1], and the Continuous Computation Language (CCL)[2] which is implemented in the Coral8 CEP Engine. Queries in these languages match patterns in streams instead of database tables. Queries are long-running and produce incremental results in contrast to SQL queries. In CCL sliding windows are supported, as well as joins of events. Additionally, patterns may be specified using the operators AND, OR, SEQ and NOT. All operators can only be applied to events limited by windows. Complex events have to adhere to SQL schemata which prohibits nested sets (for example an event that includes a previously unknown number of constituents). Similarly, StreamSQL offers common operators AND, OR, SEQ and NOT, as well as customizable time-based and count-based windows.

TelegraphCQ [CCDF+03] is yet another system which derives relational operators from SQL, including aggregates too. The system was developed as an extension of PostgreSQL database, hence it naturally supports the analysis of historical data. TelegraphCQ features continuously adaptive query processing, dynamic data routing, and operators reordering. These features enable TelegraphCQ to be distributed over multiple machines.

Work in [KrSe09] accounts for a sliding window semantics that is equivalent to the traditional relational database semantics (tailored for continuous queries). The work also introduces efficient online algorithms for the stream algebra, and provides the adaptive runtime environment. Instead of adapting view maintenance techniques, the work carries over enhances and findings from temporal databases to meet challenges of the data stream computation model [KrSe09].

Complex Event Detection and Response (CEDR) [BGAH07] is a general purpose DSMS. Design of the CEDR system is focused on a declarative query language capable of expressing a wide range of event patterns with temporal and value correlation, negation

---

[1] http://streambase.com/developers/docs/latest/streamsql/index.html
[2] http://www.coral8.com/system/files/assets/pdf/5.2.0/Coral8CclReference.pdf

4.2. Event Processing Systems

(non-occurrence of events), along with query directed instance selection and consumption policies – where selection specifies which event instances will be involved in producing output, and consumption specifies which instances will never be involved in producing future output, and therefore can be effectively "consumed" [BGAH07].

An interesting aspect of CEDR design are *correctness* guarantees, which are defined in the semantics of its operators even in the presence of out-of-order events. The authors start from an assumption that a system needs to deal with stream imperfections, such as latency (or out-of-order events), and provide a design which is a trade-off between insensitivity to event arrival order and the system performance. We will further discuss the correctness guarantees in the CEDR system, in Section 4.3, where we talk about retraction in EP. Finally, let us mention that Microsoft StreamInsight[3] is a commercial DSMS, which is based on the CEDR system.

Amit [AdEt04] has been introduced as a pioneer tool aimed at reducing the complexity of active applications. The tool includes both an expressive language and an efficient run-time execution mechanism. Amit introduces the notion of an *inferred* event, which is the occurrence of a significant *situation* that does not happen explicitly in the physical reality. Instead, it can be logically inferred by viewing the world's state and the history of concrete event occurrences.

Situations are detected through the detection process, which may have different *detection modes*. Three modes are distinguished: immediate, delayed, and deferred – depending whether incoming events are immediately processed, or the conditions for situation detection are evaluated at the end of the situation lifespan. Also, six different selection strategies have been identified: first, strict first, last, strict last, each, and strict each, see [AdEt04] for details.

EP in Amit is based on the notion of *lifespan*, that is the temporal context during which situation detection is relevant. The underlying formalism specifies various event operators defined on the lifespan. In particular, Amit supports joining operators (SEQ , AND); counting operators (*atleast, atmost, nth* – that are a sort of AND operators coupled with OR and conditions to weight occurring "at least", "at most", and "the exact" number of disjuncts, respectively); absence operators (NOT, *unless*); and temporal operators (*at, every, after* – used for detection of situations upon occurrence of *periodic* events generated by the tool. A situation may be detected "at" the lifespan, during "every" periodic lifespan, or "after" the lifespan defined by a tool periodic event.

Amit enables a situations to be used as operand in definition of other situations, which is the basic mechanism for defining nested situations (complex events).

An interesting aspect of Amit is its capability to perform *semantic matching* of different events. As stated in [AdEt04], a *key* denotes a *semantic equivalence* among attributes that belong to different events. For example, the stock-exchange attribute in the stock-quote event, the stock-exchange attribute in the trade-start event, and the stock-exchange attribute in the trade-end event are semantically equivalent in the sense that they refer to

---

[3]http://msdn.microsoft.com/de-de/library/ee362541.aspx

a stock exchange symbol. Keys are used to match different event instances that refer to the same entity. Amit, therefore, enables *mapping* between attributes with semantically equivalent names. Although the notion of a key in Amit is a simple mechanism to establish the semantic matching, it is clearly pointed out that such a requirement is needed in EP applications.

Finally, it is worth mentioning that Amit has served as a predecessor of the E-business Management Service[4] of IBM Global Services.

ZStream [MeMa09] is a general EP framework. The framework unifies the evaluation SEQ, AND, OR, NOT, and Kleene closure[5] as variants of the *join* operator. ZStream uses tree-based query plans to represent and evaluate query patterns. The framework puts a considerable emphasise on query plan optimisations. Since a single pattern in ZStream may have several equivalent execution plans (with different evaluation costs), ZStream features a cost model to estimate the computation costs, and chooses the optimal plan with respect to the actual runtime behaviour. In particular, if we consider that the join of two events has its left and right node, [MeMa09] proposes few possible strategies. A left-associative join couples events from left to right. This strategy is a good choice when the rightmost event(s) in a pattern have a higher occurrence rate than the others. By analogy, the right-associative coupling is beneficial when the leftmost event(s) have a higher rate of occurrence(s). Other combinations, like for example bushy plan and inner plan, are possible too [MeMa09]. ZStream is able to adaptively adjust the order in which it executes patterns on the fly, and features a dynamic programming algorithm to efficiently search for an optimal query plan.

SASE [WuDR06, GADI08, ADGI08] is likewise a general EP framework. The focus is given to the realisation of a pattern language with efficient evaluation of pattern queries. The authors argue that the conventional stream query processing, based on selection-join-aggregation patterns, is inadequate. Instead, [ADGI08] proposes a formal query evaluation model, NFA^b, which is a combination of a non-deterministic finite automaton (NFA) with a match buffer (^{b}). A non-deterministic finite automata is used to realise a state-changing mechanism in the process of the pattern detection. The purpose of a match buffer is to keep events selected by an NFA.

The SASE language has initially supported SEQ, NOT, and time-based sliding windows [WuDR06]. Later on, it has grown in an expressive language supporting aggregations and Kleene closure [ADGI08]. The work in [ADGI08] provides contribution with respect to the event selection strategy, i.e., how to select the relevant events from an input stream mixing relevant and irrelevant events. There are four different event selection strategies defined. In the most stringent strategy, two selected events must be contiguous in the input stream, while in the most relaxed strategy, contiguity requirements are removed and non-deterministic actions on relevant events are allowed [ADGI08]. Additionally, the work on SASE accounts for the formal analysis of the expressive power of the language,

---

[4]http://www-935.ibm.com/services/us/en/it-services/gts-it-service-home-page-1.html
[5]Kleene closure extracts from the input stream a finite yet unbounded number of events with a particular property.

4.2. Event Processing Systems

as well as for the complexity of its detecting algorithm. Finally, the more recent work on SASE argues that the occurrence time of events are often not known precisely, and the events from various sources cannot be easily merged into a single stream with a total (or partial) order. Therefore the authors in [ZhDI10] have proposed a temporal model for unknown or imprecise event occurrence times.

Esper[6] is a state of the art, open source engine for EP. The engine is based on the Event Processing Language (EPL) – a SQL-like language with SELECT, FROM, WHERE, GROUP BY, HAVING and ORDER BY clauses. In EPL, the notion of a table is replaced by the notion of a stream (as the source of data), and rows as the basic unit of data are replaced by events. EPL is an expressive language to specify expression-based event pattern matching (including AND , SEQ , OR , and NOT). The language provides constructs to realise the windows (time windows, batch windows, and time batch windows), aggregations, joining (including inner, outer, left, right, and unidirectional joins), grouping, filtering, and built-in functions for use with streams of events. Finally, Esper supports access to relational and non-relational data conjunctively used with stream processing.

Esper supports different event type representations, ranging from plain-old Java object events, event types specified in a map, and Extensible Markup Language (XML) events. The map specification of event types is an interesting approach – it can eliminate the need to use Java classes as event types, thereby making it easier to change types at runtime or generate type information from another source. XML events are also useful in many practical applications. If an XML schema document (XSD file) can be made available as part of the configuration, then Esper can read the schema and appropriately present event type metadata and validate statements that use the event type and its properties.

Underlying the Esper pattern matching engine is a state machine implementation. Esper outputs detected events either in a push-based mode or in a pull-based one using iterators. Esper engine can be integrated into other applications either as a Java or .Net library. Finally it is worth mentioning that both centralized and clustered deployments of Esper are possible.

Afore mentioned EP and DSMS approaches [ADGI08, WuDR06, GADI08, MeMa09, AdEt04, BGAH07, ArBW06, KrSe09, CCDF$^+$03, CBBC$^+$03] are capable to handle large volumes of streaming data with low latency. Most of them are based on languages with well adopted SQL-like syntaxes. As such these approaches are widely used today in automated stock trading, logistic services, transaction management, business intelligence and so forth. However they are not well suited for knowledge-rich applications including structured data, ontologies, and other forms of formally represented knowledge where support for *knowledge-based EP* and *stream reasoning (SR)* is required.

In this section we have referred only to some of the most remarkable work in this area. This is by no means a complete overview of related work. A recent and comprehensive survey of EP and related areas can be found in [CuMa11].

---

[6] http://esper.codehaus.org/esper/documentation/documentation.html

4.3 Approaches for Retraction in Event Processing

EP finds its use in areas where relevant changes need to be captured under time constraints (at near real time), and possibly appropriate decisions need to be made upon detected events. If certain events (that justified decision) are *revoked*, in some cases the decision should be *reconsidered* too. Also if an event had triggered an action, and got retracted later, the action may need to be nullified, e.g., by executing a compensation action or amended in another way (depending on the application domain). A typical example of these scenarios include a facility that enables either humans to cancel their orders, or machines to abort actions or processes (e.g., transaction processing).

This conceptual framework is similar to that of truth maintenance systems in Artificial Intelligence systems [Doyl87]. A truth maintenance system (TMS) [Doyl87, Doyl78] is a knowledge representation method for formalizing both beliefs, and their mutual dependencies. The name truth maintenance is due to the ability of these systems to restore *consistency*. The topic of retraction in EP deals with a sort of truth maintenance, but specifically focused to the EP domain.

Retraction (or revision) in EP is not a common feature in general EP systems. For example in [EtNi10], retraction and out-of-order EP are considered as challenging topics in today's EP. However since they are in the scope of our work, this section and the following one are devoted to the work related to these specific features.

Events and transactions are normally used together to facilitate monitoring and analysis of transaction applications. Transaction instances generate log events and error information. When analysing the logs, we usually want to collect and correlate only the *relevant* events to a single transaction instance. But in most cases, transaction processing is a distributed processing, and these log events are distributed over many machines and applications. Therefore EP seems to be a natural approach to perform such a processing. Also in most cases the log events are analysed periodically (e.g., every night). EP aims to push such an analysis toward continuous and (near) real time processing.

However since transactions may fail during execution, we may need to retract certain events which were triggered before the failure. For example, it is essential to know if errors, faults, and time-outs have occurred during a transaction. Commercial systems, such as the WebSphere Message Broker from IBM[7] and a transaction programming model for events from Microsoft[8], offer tools for transaction monitoring and auditing. There, transaction events are triggered during transactions executions, and certain actions are triggered by events when a transaction is committed, or aborted and rolled back. However, in both systems, there is no possibility to retract triggered events, and further, to examine consequences of these retractions. All events published during execution remain published.

In [DoFl06], so called *dubbed transactional* events were introduced. Transactional events are used to manage complexity of concurrent programs. They combine first-class syn-

---
[7] http://www.ibm.com/developerworks/websphere/library/techarticles/0911_fan/0911_fan.html
[8] http://msdn.microsoft.com/en-us/library/aa480462.aspx

4.3. Approaches for Retraction in Event Processing

chronous message passing events with all-or-nothing transactions. The use of transactional events was motivated by a more efficient implementation of special constructs in concurrent programs such as guarded synchronous or three-way rendezvous.

The work in [CGSP$^+$09] introduces a publish/subscribe communication system that is based on an optimistic transactional EP scheme. The system provides efficient coordination between time-critical, low-latency Java tasks.

Transaction compensation in Web Services were proposed in [StKa02]. It is an event-based approach for managing compensation policies. Transaction compensation is built as a trigger mechanism that allows a web service designer to specify compensation rules. Events are used there to dynamically generate compensating transactions during runtime.

Borealis [CcCC$^+$02] features a mechanism for revision processing. The mechanism handles erroneous input events by generating corrections of previously output query results on data streams. The work is motivated by financial data stream sources that issue "revision tuples", amending previously issued tuples. Two strategies are proposed: upstream and downstream processing. The former strategy "replays" previously processed input events that were involved in the same computations as the event being revised (i.e., a sort of bottom-up approach). The latter one "retrieves" all previously produced complex events to which the event being revised originally contributed, and modifies these complex events according to the revision (i.e., top-down approach).

This work has been extended in [MaCh08] by proposing a revision model based on "replay" of the event history. The technique assumes that a stream engine maintains an archive of recent data seen on each of its input streams. These archives are revised when revision tuples occur, and reprocessing (replaying) the sequence of input tuples then generates any of the query results invalidated by the revision.

While this technique is general and works well for all classes of patterns supported by the Borealis system [CcCC$^+$02], it requires the event history to be kept (persisted). The history is kept as long as revision needs to be guaranteed.

In Chapter 9 we will also present an approach for revision in EP. There we also need to keep extra data in order to enable revision. However we will see (in Section 9.2) that we do not need to keep the *whole* event history (i.e., during the period of time in which revision is guaranteed). Instead, we keep only intermediate results (goals) relevant with respect to detected complex events. Moreover we do not need to *replay* the whole history when computing revisions. The intermediate results (goals) represent partial results, hence they enable us to obtain revisions without re-computing them from scratch.

In [BGAH07] revision is considered as a problem caused by out-of-order events. That is, due to out-of-order (late) events it is possible to revise their occurrence time as well as the time when events are reported to the system. In contrast, we consider a general case where not only times can be revised, but an event itself can be retracted too. Moreover, the consequences of that retraction are amended not only on detected patterns but also on complex patterns that are built out of them (i.e., hierarchies of complex events).

Further on, the work in [BGAH07] is based on *buffering* and synchronization points. An input stream may be *blocked* in between synchronization points until events are reordered. On the other hand, we propose an approach that never blocks the input events, i.e., we never buffer the input stream and reorder it.

An out-of-order EP with Software Transaction Memory is described in [BFSF08]. The authors propose to use *speculative execution* enabling events to be processed optimistically but does not output them until all preceding events have been completed (as some of them may be out-of-order). Here event revision, possibly caused by out-of-order events, is avoided at the expense of having delays (and again buffers are used to cope with late events).

In [ZhDI10] the authors observe that in real-world applications event occurrence times are often *unknown* or *imprecise*. Therefore, they proposed a temporal model that assigns a time interval to each event to represent all of its possible occurrence times and *revisit* pattern evaluation under this model. The authors argue that existing EP approaches assume the occurrence time of each event is always known precisely. They relax this assumption by allowing an interval of possible time occurrences to be assigned (instead of a fixed, precise timestamp). Their approach is capable to efficiently detect correct complex events regardless of which timestamp (from that interval) appears to be correct. Although this approach does not directly deal with revision per se, it can be seen as a related work. The timestamp interval effectively ensures the correctness of results in the same vein as revision guarantees correct computation of complex events (for a given interval in which the event history or intermediate results are kept). However revision as considered in our approach (in Chapter 9) is a more general problem in the sense that it deals also with possible retraction of events themselves, i.e., not only corrections of their timestamp.

Finally, there exist approaches based on *updates* [GHMA$^+$05, GoÖ5]. Revisions invalidate previously processed inputs, and correct all pattern (query) results that were produced from them. However updates do not invalidate previously processed inputs but simply end the interval during which they were valid.

4.4 Approaches for Out-of-Order Event Processing

The field of EP has the task of processing streams of (atomic) events with the goal of detecting derived (complex) events according to meaningful event patterns[9]. However, in most cases it is typically assumed that events in an event stream are *totally ordered*: the order in which events are received by the system is the same as their timestamp order. This assumption is called *total order assumption* [LLDR+07]. In reality events may arrive *out-of-order* due to network latencies or even machine failures. State of the art event stream processing technology experiences significant challenges when faced with out-of-order data arrival including output blocking, huge system latencies, memory resource overflow, and incorrect result generation [LLGR+09]. Indeed, many approaches for EP [ADGI08, Alve09, MeMa09, CCDF+03, DeJG07] cannot handle out-of-order events properly. They process events at the time when they come. Hence, a late event will have a larger timestamp than the events which have already arrived earlier. As a consequence, systems not considering out-of-order arrival will disregard the timestamp and may either detect incorrect complex events or fail to detect some valid patterns that occurred [LLDR+07].

To solve this problem, other systems [LLDR+07, BGAH07, BFSF08] propose to use *buffers* to keep the event history for a certain time window. If out-of-order events occur, they will be *reordered* in the buffer so that the event stream afterwards can be treated (and processed) as an in-order stream. While this approach works in general, it causes high latency in EP, and the main requirement of EP systems is to process data (events) with the least latency possible. So the question, how much history of events is sufficient to be kept in memory to ensure correct processing, remains an optimisation challenge.

Work in [LLGR+09] presents two solution for processing out-of-order event streams: aggressive and conservative strategies. The aggressive strategy works under the optimistic assumption that out-of-order event arrival is rare. To tackle the unexpected occurrence of an out-of-order event and with it any premature erroneous result generation, appropriate error compensation methods are designed for the aggressive strategy. The conservative method works under the assumption that out-of-order data is prevalent, and thus produces output only when its correctness can be guaranteed. Authors propose a partial order guarantee model, under which such correctness can be guaranteed. The aggressive strategy output results immediately without waiting for out-of-order events, but guarantees only delayed correctness. A compensation technique is utilized to correct erroneous results [LLGR+09]. The conservative strategies introduces delays in producing output results, and exploits partial order guarantees to produce permanently correct results.

In this work (in Chapter 10) we present a solution for out-of-order EP which does not delay events – similarly as the aggressive strategy in [LLGR+09]. Our strategy, however, is designed so that it is well integrated with the other parts of our logic-based EP approach, i.e., to support both EP and stream reasoning. Moreover our approach is general in

---

[9]Apart from this task (also known as pattern matching), EP further addresses other issues like event filtering, splitting, aggregation, translation and so forth, see Section 2.3.

sense that does not require an assumption about frequency of out-of-order events to be specified.

4.5 Logic-Based Approaches in Event Processing

EP formalisms based on *deductive* or *logic rules* [BrEc07a, PaKB10, FSSB05, MoZa95, APPS10, LaLM98] have been attracting considerable attention as they feature formal, declarative semantics and inference capabilities. *Declarative semantics* of an EP system prescribe *what* the system needs to detect, i.e., a user does not need to worry *how* that will be detected. Also, EP systems based on deductive rules have capability to process not only events, but also any additional *background knowledge* relevant with respect to detection of complex situations in real time. Hence a rule-based approach enables a high *abstraction* level and a *uniform* framework for programming knowledge-based EP applications (i.e., specification of complex event patterns, contextual knowledge, and their interaction). Such applications can be further supported by *machine learning* tools, to automate the construction and refinement of event patterns (see, for example [Ray09]).

However one significant difficulty encountered with logic rule-based systems is that most of them are inherently *request-response* systems, i.e., not *event-driven*. For a given query (request), an inference system typically evaluates available knowledge and returns response. When used for EP, these systems *cannot* detect a complex event as soon as it happens. Instead, they detect a complex event at the moment when the request is posed. Such a behavior is not adequate in EP as we expect the system to detect a complex event as soon as it occurs (not at the moment when a request for proving that complex event is posed). Existing approaches [LaLM98, PaKB10, FSSB05] do not implement an event-driven mechanism. We address this issue and propose an execution model, featuring the *event-driven execution* while still retaining the favorable characteristics of logic-based approaches, including inference capabilities too.

To achieve the aforementioned aims, these approaches all represent complex events as rules (or queries). Rules can then be processed either in a bottom-up manner [Ullm90], a top-down manner [ChWa96, AbHV95], or in a manner that combines both [BMSU86]. However, all these evaluation strategies have not particularly been designed for event-driven computation. They are rather suited for a *request-response* paradigm. That is, given (and triggered by) a request, an inference engine will search for and respond with an answer. This means that, for a given event pattern, an event inference engine needs to check if this pattern has been satisfied or not. The check is performed at the time when such a request is posed. If satisfied by the time when the request is processed, a complex event will be reported. If not, the pattern is not detected until the next time the same request is processed (though it can become satisfied in between the two checks, being undetected for the time being). For instance, [PaKB10] follows the mentioned request-response (or so called *query-driven*[10]) approach. It proposes to define queries

---
[10]If a request is represented as a query (what is a usual case).

4.5. Logic-Based Approaches in Event Processing

that are processed repetitively at given intervals, e.g., every 10 seconds, trying to discover new events. However, generally events are not periodic or if so might have differing periods, and nevertheless complex events should be detected as soon as they occur (not in a predefined time window). This holds in particular for time-critical scenarios such as monitoring stock markets or nuclear power plants.

To overcome this issue, in [BrEc07a, Ecke08], an expressive language XChange^{EQ} was proposed. The language features deductive and reactive rules for events, as well as event queries, event composition capabilities, event accumulation, possibilities to express temporal (and other) relationships between events and so forth. The language is accompanied with an incremental evaluation that avoids recomputing certain intermediate results every time a new event arrives. The authors use relational algebra evaluation techniques based on incremental maintenance of materialized views [GuMu99] and finite differencing [Ecke08, BrEc07a].

In Chapter 7 we propose an alternative evaluation strategy to this one. In comparison to [BrEc07a, Ecke08], our goal is to target a broader class of EP features. In particular, we cover iterative rules with sliding windows, event retractions and out-of-order EP.

Prova [KPNR+06] is a language, accompanied by a system implementation, for reactive agents and EP. Prova is close to our approach in sense that it supports declarative rules. On the other hand it is a reactive system, supporting agent programming. Complex event patterns can be created in Prova as event-condition-action (ECA) rules. The Prova language however does not provide event operators (e.g., SEQ , AND , OR , and so forth); they rather need to be encoded as ECA rules. Prova combines imperative, declarative and functional programming styles, and is implemented in Java.

A big portion of related work in the area of rule-based EP is grounded on the RETE algorithm [Forg82]. RETE is an efficient pattern matching algorithm, and it has been the basis for many production rule systems. The algorithm creates a decision tree that combines patterns from all rules in a knowledgebase. RETE was intended to improve the speed of forward chained production rule systems at the cost of space for storing intermediate results. Production rules can be utilized to form complex event patterns, in which case a RETE-based production rule system is used as an EP system. Thanks to forward chaining of rules, RETE is also event-driven (data-driven).

The RETE algorithm was primary designed for condition action (production) rules. Complex conditions from many such rules can be structured through a RETE network, and some of them may be shared throughout the network. By *sharing* complex conditions a more efficient evaluation is gained (in comparison when each condition, for each rule, is evaluated separately). Our approach – based on event-driven backward chaining (EDBC) rules – is designed for matching complex events (not complex conditions). This means that we have one model which fits for pattern matching, as well as for other aspects of EP (e.g., iterative rules, sliding windows, aggregates, retraction in EP, and out-of-order events. See also Section 1.3 for further discussion on event consumption policies and the RETE algorithm.). In order to address some of these issues (e.g., sliding windows and aggregates) systems based on the RETE algorithm implement additional components, however the RETE algorithm itself does not provide support for these aspects. On the other hand, the goal of our work is to provide a uniform approach that naturally accommodates all the mentioned aspects related to EP.

Similar to the RETE algorithm, our approach utilises both, computation sharing and a forward chaining inference. However, unlike RETE-based approaches (e.g., Jess[11] and Drools[12]) that cannot handle function symbols [LFWK09], our approach which is based on LP can handle them (as LP systems, e.g., Prolog systems can deal with function symbols).

Close to our approach is [Hale87]. It is an attempt to implement production rules also with a RETE-like algorithm. However, the work proposes the use of subgoals and data-driven backward chaining rules. It has deductive capabilities, and detects satisfied conditions in business rules (using backward chaining), as soon as relevant facts become available. In our work, we focus on an EP language and a corresponding EP system (not on production system), and the same argumentation as for a pure RETE approach applies here too.

Concluding this section, many mentioned studies aim to use more formal semantics in EP. Our approach based on ETALIS Language for Events may also be seen as an attempt towards that goal. It includes features from general EP systems, as well as some advanced features not found in state of the art EP systems. In its essence it is still a rule-based inference system. Therefore it retains afore mentioned advantages of logic-based approaches in EP. It does data-driven computation and features deductive capabilities.

4.6 Semantic-Based Approaches

While existing semantic technologies and reasoning engines are constantly being improved in dealing with *time invariant* domain knowledge, they lack in support for processing *time sensitive* data. The work in [AdBE00] has raised the importance to express the *event semantics* and relationships (e.g., subclass relationships) between events and other entities. The authors in [AdBE00] describe the semantic abstractions and the implied knowledge representation scheme for events. Moreover, they provide a comprehensive event model with a number of semantic properties for events.

More recently few approaches have emerged to address issues from this area, recognising time as an important dimension in processing knowledge. In the following we review few of them.

4.6.1 Temporal RDF

The Resource Description Framework (RDF) [KlCa04] has been widely used for expressing graph-structured data. The work in [GuHV07] introduces *time* as a new dimension in

---
[11]Jess: http://www.jessrules.com/
[12]Drools: http://www.jboss.org/drools

4.6. Semantic-Based Approaches

RDF graphs. The authors provide a semantics for temporal RDF graphs and a temporal query language for RDF, following concepts of temporal databases. They are concerned with evolution of RDF graphs through time, and provide a framework for temporal entailment and *querying* over changing graphs.

Our work differs from this approach in that our aim is to detect temporal complex patterns under time constraints, rather than just once posing a query and getting a singular response. We want to detect situations of interest *continuously* as soon as they happen. Hence patterns need to be continuously evaluated in order to process occurrences of relevant triples, and further to recognise complex events.

SPARQL-ST [PeSJ11] is an extension of SPARQL language [PrSe08] for complex spatial and temporal queries. The language, and a corresponding implementation, deal with temporal data (and possible reasoning about that data). However as in [GuHV07], SPARQL-ST queries are evaluated when invoked, i.e., they are not continuously active. The same argumentation also applies to other SPARQL approaches like Temporal SPARQL [TaBe09], stSPARQL [KoKy10], and T-SPARQL [Gran10].

The work in [RoMM09] motivates the need for a semantic management of streaming data. Streaming data are represented in RDF format with the purpose of its exploitation in semantic-web applications (semantically annotated data and reasoning services). For this purpose, they propose a Time-Annotated RDF model and Time-Annotated SPARQL. However the authors explicitly mention that continuous queries, as one typical requirement of streaming data management systems, are not considered in that work.

4.6.2 Stream Reasoning Approaches

Continuous SPARQL (C-SPARQL) [BBCG10] is a language for continuous query processing and Stream Reasoning. It extends the SPARQL language by adding support for window and aggregation operations. In C-SPARQL, the set of currently valid RDF statements is determined based on a query (including its window specification), and classical reasoning on that RDF set is performed as if it were static. In our work presented in Chapter 11, we focus more on detection of RDF triples in a specific *temporal* order (e.g., sequence versus conjunction). We strongly believe that temporal relatedness between events (e.g., a certain event happens before another event inside a sliding window) as defined in DSMS [ADGI08, CCDF$^+$03, CBBC$^+$03] is required to capture more complex patterns over RDF streaming data. Additionally, in C-SPARQL queries are divided into a static and dynamic part. The static part is evaluated by a separate RDF triple storage, while a stream processing engine evaluates the dynamic part of the query. In such settings, these two parts act as "black boxes" and C-SPARQL cannot take advantage of a query pre-processing and optimizations over the unified (static and dynamic) data space. We propose an approach based on logic rules where the both parts are handled in a uniform framework.

Streaming Knowledge Bases [WJFY08] is a reasoning tool dealing with streaming RDF triples and computation of RDFS closures with respect to an ontology. For instance, the tool can identify a triple from a stream having a subject that is an instance of a certain class (or any of its subclasses that are defined in an ontology). The approach is based on TelegraphCQ [CCDF+03] that is an efficient DSMS (see Section 4.2). In order to speed up stream reasoning, the authors propose to pre-compute all inferences in advance, and to store them in a database. Although this is an interesting approach, we believe that stream reasoning demands both, on-the-fly inference capabilities and run time performance.

The work in [BoGJ08] introduces Streaming SPARQL. The approach is built on temporal relational algebra, and the authors provide an algorithm to transform SPARQL queries to the algebra. Similarly as in [BBCG10], the approach does not detect sequences of RDF triples occurring in a specific order. The same holds for [BBCV+10], where the authors propose stream reasoning based on incremental maintenance of materializations. Streaming RDF triples (as they occur) trigger an inference procedure that maintains materializations. Although promising, it is not clear how this approach works for multiple queries with different time window definitions (materializations in [BBCV+10] are maintained only for one query).

In Chapter 11 we provide Event Processing SPARQL (EP-SPARQL) which is a new language to address dynamic aspects in the realm of the Semantic Web. It is as an extension of the commonly used SPARQL language [PrSe08]. We provide the syntax and formal semantics of the language and devise an effective execution model for the proposed formalism. The execution model is event-driven (data-driven) and features SR capabilities.

Part II

ETALIS Language for Events

5

Logic-Based Event Processing: Design Principles and Requirements

In Chapter 2 and Chapter 3 we have introduced Event Processing (EP) and logic programming (LP). One of the main goals of this work is to combine these two areas, thereby providing a logic-based EP. Hence, before we propose a formalism to fulfil this goal, let us first draw basic design principles and requirements that such a formalism needs to adhere to.

5.1 Formal Declarative Semantics

In Section 2.2 we have discussed events as means to declare changes, and draw a parallel between event-driven programming and declarative programming. Indeed, occurrence of an event can be treated as a declaration about something that has occurred, or changed the current state of affairs. *Who* may use what, and *how* is that used, is not specified. Instead, we specify rules (patterns) which define complex matters of interests. Whenever premises of such a rule can be proved – based on occurring events and another available knowledge – a complex event will be derived. This means that we also declare statements about complex events. They may involve temporal, semantic, and other relations between events. However they are *declarative* in their nature, i.e., these rules describe what patterns in their essence are, and do not specify possible ways of detecting them, the order in which rules need to be evaluated and so forth.

There exist well-known examples of declarative languages in query processing. For example, a subset of SQL with SELECT queries is declarative. In EP both, declarative and imperative languages, are equally popular.

In this work we will consider declarativeness as an important property, and devise a formalism for EP that holds this property. Further on, we will pay attention that our declarative formalism features a mechanism which guarantees *predictability* and *repeatability* of results produced by an EP system.

Recognition systems with a logic-based representation of event structures, in particular, have been attracting considerable attention because, among others, they exhibit a formal, declarative semantics, and they are supported by *machine learning* tools automating the construction and refinement of event structures [APPS10].

Machine learning support per se is out of scope of this work, however we want to emphasize importance of the *declarative, rule-based semantics* as a crucial principle in designing an EP language. This property can further enable automated construction of both, event patterns (queries) and a background knowledge. These features are beyond capabilities of existing EP approaches [ADGI08, BGAH07, ArBW06, KrSe09, CCDF$^+$03], and this is one important benefit of formal rule-based approaches in EP.

Declarative programming has become of particular interest recently, as it may greatly simplify writing *parallel* and *distributed* programs [ACCE$^+$09, CCHM08]. Since in EP we also often need to write parallel and distributed programs, this is one reason more to believe that declarative programming will prevail in EP too.

On the other hand, *consumption policies*[1] is a subject in EP that is not in-line with declarative principles. A consumption policy typically selects one, out of several events occurrences, and defines how multiple occurrences of the same event are consumed. This, however, has a direct impact on event pattern rules. For instance, if an event occurrence is consumed by rule A, it may not be available to rule B, and vice versa. As a consequence the *order* in which rules A and B are evaluated matters (what is against the principle of declarative programming).

The EP language that we will propose in Chapter 6 is declarative. We will further provide common consumption policies as an optional feature of this formalism in Section 7.4. It should be therefore noted that event programs – written in the proposed language – may lose this property when interpreted under a certain consumption policy. However, the language semantics under unrestricted policy, which is also provided in Section 7.4, ensures the declarative property of our formalism.

Further to this topic, it is worth of mentioning that we (in Chapter 12) provide an implementation of the language. The implementation is realised in Prolog, and enables a programmer to extend event programs with Prolog specific features (some of which are

---

[1] In EP, consumption policies [CKAK94] deal with the issue of *selecting* particular event occurrences when there is more than one event instance applicable, and *consuming* events after they have been used in patterns. We will discuss different consumption policies in Section 7.4.

not declarative). We have adopted this design principle since Prolog – as general programming language – offers many advanced features. However again, a programmer needs to take care when writing event programs with non-declarative features, as in that case the overall system may behave in a non-declarative manner too.

5.2 Point-Based Versus Interval-Based Temporal Semantics

Time plays a central role in EP, and EP languages are designed to express rich *temporal relations* between events. For example, events A and B have both occurred but A has occurred *before* B, or A has occurred *simultaneously* with B, are examples of temporal relations. To detect such and similar relations, an event is characterised by a *timestamp*. A timestamp that denotes an event occurrence can be defined either as a time *point* or a time *interval*. Point-based events are instantaneous, i.e., they happen at one specific point in time and have a duration of zero. An example of such an event is a stock market event denoting the current stock price of a certain company.

We also refer to point-based events as *atomic* events. Atomic events build *complex* (derived) events. It is our design principle to endow complex events with a time interval, denoting when the event *started* and when it *ended*[2]. An example of an (interval-based) complex event is an event that represents a stock market working day. This event has *duration*, starting when the market opens and ending when the market closes. It is said that – languages with interval-based events – are founded on *interval-based semantics*, as oppose to languages with *point-based semantics*.

We have adopted an interval-based semantics for two reasons. The first reason is that an interval-based semantics enables richer semantics. Note that if we consider events as instantaneous, the only possible (temporal) relations between two events are *before*, *after*, and *simultaneously*. In addition to those, events defined on time intervals enable all existing temporal relations as defined by Allen's interval algebra [Alle83]. These temporal relations include: *before, meets, overlaps, starts, during, finishes, equals to* (simultaneous). We will discuss these relations in more details in Chapter 6.

The second reason for adopting an interval-based semantics is related to possible inconsistencies encountered with point-based events [GaAu02, PaKB10, AnSt08b]. To illustrate this, let us consider a complex event e that is a sequence of events e_1, e_2, and e_3 in the following pattern e_1 *before* (e_2 *before* e_3).

If events were not regarded to occur in a time interval, the detection time of the terminating event is used as an occurrence time of the complex event. Consequentially, it would be possible to detect e with a sequence: e_1 *before* e_2 *before* e_3 as well as with a sequence: e_2 *before* e_1 *before* e_3. In order to prevent such an unintended semantics, we use the interval-based semantics. For example, consider an intermediate event e_i which

---

[2]This principle is however not a norm. A number of EP systems define both, atomic and complex events as instantaneous.

is detected when an occurrence of $e_2(T_3, T_4)$ is strictly followed by an occurrence of $e_3(T_5, T_6)$[3]. That is, event e_1 is defined on a time interval (T_3, T_6), for some time points $T_3 \leq T_4 < T_5 \leq T_6$. In this case e will never be detectable by a sequence: e_2 *before* e_1 *before* e_3, as $e_1(T_1, T_2)$ has not happened strictly before $e_i(T_3, T_6)$ (i.e., $T_2 < T_3$ is not satisfied).

5.3 Seamless Integration of Events with Queries and Domain Knowledge

5.3.1 Query Processing

EP applications often involve query processing coupled with EP. Database information may serve in *enriching* an event with additional data. For instance, a sensor event may carry an *ID* which can be matched with a database relation to enrich the event with information about the sensor source (e.g., sensor measurement units, information about sensor precision etc.). We will see an implementation of this and similar examples in the remaining parts of this work. However at this point, we want to raise importance of query processing which needs to be coupled with EP.

We propose a language which integrates query processing with EP in an easy and natural way. Since our approach is based on deductive rules, query processing is performed similarly as in deductive databases (enabling *recursive* queries too).

5.3.2 Knowledge Processing

In Chapter 1, we have already tried to raise importance of background (static) knowledge in the context of EP. Events and event pattern rules represent *temporal* knowledge, based on which it is possible to derive more complex dynamic matters. Apart from this knowledge, there may exists *static* (or evolving) knowledge (i.e., facts, rules and ontologies, constituting the *domain* knowledge). For instance, suppose an event processing applications provides real time information about air pollution in a certain geographic area. Then event pattern rules will calculate pollution from streaming sensor data, while physical locations of sensors, their density, and other relevant information are represented as a static knowledge. Note that for detection of some environmental phenomena (e.g., gust front tornado) we need to process the background knowledge on the fly, that is, to process it while processing real time data (events).

A considerable amount of (static or slowly evolving) knowledge has been made available through the Linked Open Data (LOD) initiative and other on line information sources (see Section 1.2). Since this knowledge is structured, it can be used by machines, and more importantly, it can be used in conjunction with EP. Therefore an important design

---
[3]To follow *strictly*, means that $T_4 < T_5$, and not $T_4 \leq T_5$.

decision – which underlines our approach – is to propose a formalism capable to define real time situations detectable upon events as well as on domain knowledge.

Note that databases and knowledgebases both contain additional information required in EP. Knowledgebases are however a special kind of databases for knowledge management. While it is possible to query databases to get explicitly stated information, knowledgebases, in addition, enable derivation of implicitly stated information too.

5.4 Event-Driven Incremental Reasoning

EP – as a real time processing – needs to ensure detection of derived events in a *timely* fashion and in the asynchronous *push* mode (see Subsection 2.2.2). Our approach to EP is founded on deductive rules. As said, deductive systems are rather suited for a *request-response* computation. That is, for given a *request*, an inference engine will evaluate available knowledge (i.e. rules and facts) and *respond* with an answer. This means that the event inference engine needs to check if this pattern can be deduced or not. The check is performed at the time when such a request is posed. If satisfied by the time when the request is processed, a complex event will be reported. If not, the pattern is not detected until the next time the same request is processed (though it can become satisfied in-between the two checks).

In Section 3.3 we have discussed bottom-up and top-down strategies for logic programs. There exist also other strategies aiming to improve the basic evaluation strategies [Ullm89, AbHV95, BMSU86, Chen97, Warr92]. Forward chaining reasoning methods (e.g., implemented in RETE-based deductive systems) give a solution to the issue of data-driven computation. However other issue, as pointed out in Section 1.3 and Section 4.5 remain (since this strategy was not initially designed for EP).

EP demands an *event-* or *data-driven* computation strategy as found in various approaches such as non-deterministic finite automata (NFA) [ADGI08], Petri Nets [GaDi92], and RETE algorithm [Forg82]. Additionally, this strategy needs to satisfy all other requirements and design principles as discussed in this and other sections (including knowledge processing, reasoning, consumption policies, time windows, event aggregations, and so forth).

In Chapter 7 we devise such a strategy, and discuss its implementation in Chapter 12.

5.5 Expressivity

An event processing network (EPN) comprises of event processing agents (EPAs). Capabilities of an agent to processes events depends on capabilities of an underlying formalism used to program that agent. Therefore *expressivity* of an EP language is an important aspect in building EP applications. In Section 2.3 we have given a list of common agents, explaining operations on events each of them performs. In the remaining parts of this work, we will propose a language capable to express event operations of all those agents, i.e., filtering, pattern detection, event transformation, splitting, aggregations, composition, translation, enrichment and projection. Moreover the language can express all temporal relations from Allen's interval algebra [Alle83], and supports negation (where a negated event is understood as absence of that event in an interval).

5.6 Set at a Time Versus Event at a Time Processing

An event processing agent (EPA) takes one or more events as input, and creates one ore more events as output. When creating an output, an EPA may commonly process events either in *set at a time* or *event at a time* fashion.

In so called *set at a time* processing, see [ArBW06, KrSe09, CCDF+03, CBBC+03, MWAB+02], event patterns are matched against *sets* of events. Similarly as in relational algebra, event operations are represented by operations on sets of events (relations). Operations are executed as events occur, but events are not processed individually. Instead, they are handled in snapshots created by sets.

In EP, input events of an EPA are very often determined by means of a *sliding window*. A sliding window serves to constrain the processing of an unbound event stream to a finite window (collection) of events that "slide" either over time or individual events. EP systems, that are based on set at a time processing, process events from a sliding window in *snapshots* (i.e., as sets), and output results with a certain *time granularity*. Time granularity of snapshots influences directly computational costs, memory consumption, stream rates in downstream operators and the entire cost model [KrSe09].

In so called *event at a time* processing, the computation is done whenever a relevant event occurs. That is, each event is processed *individually* with respect to the current state of the computation. Occurrence of an event changes the state if the event furthers the detection of one or more of monitoring event patterns. In this respect, the event at a time processing is a *stateful* processing[4] and it assumes processing of a single event, or processing of a single event with respect to other individual event (i.e., not a set of events).

Event consumption policy is a common feature in EP that is naturally supported by the event at a time processing. As a consumption policy specifies how to remove unused events from memory, individual selection of events, provided by the event at a time processing, offers a fine-grained way to implement various policies (see for example polices in [ADGI08] and [CKAK94]).

Furthermore, consider the detection of a sequence of events. In the set at a time processing two event snapshots (or streams) need to be *synchronised* in order to detect that an

---

[4]This does not imply that with this processing, stateless operations (e.g., filtering) cannot be performed or combined with stateful operations (e.g., pattern matching).

5.7. Simplicity and Ease-of-Use

event from the second snapshot occurred after an event from the first snapshot[5]. Additionally, it is important whether an event belongs to a certain snapshot, or to a snapshot that is right before or right after it. In the event at a time processing, events are also assumed not to be "late" (otherwise we talk about out-of-order EP, see Chapter 10). However the final result of detecting a (sequence) pattern does not depend on allocation of events in a particular snapshot. As a result, synchronisation in the set at a time processing is more sensitive and error prone (specifically this issue may be indicative with *iterative* rules when the output of a rule is the input of the same rule, see Section 7.3).

Based on the above argumentation, our design decision – regarding the proposed formalism in this work – is to use event at a time processing.

5.7 Simplicity and Ease-of-Use

As noted in [BrEc07c, BrEc07b], expressive event languages should cover at least the four dimensions of data extraction, event composition, temporal and causal relationships, and event accumulation for non-monotonic features such as negation (absence of events) and aggregation.

In general, the value of events – with respect to an application – comes from two aspects. The first aspect is related to *time* (as events enable real time processing), and the second aspect is related to *data* (carried by events). While the time aspect – in real time processing – is important for obvious reasons, in the following we want to emphasise the importance of the event data too.

For example, events may be filtered out based on a filtering condition, which operates on event data; an event pattern may be derived from few simpler events that pass certain event data to the derived event; an aggregation function may be applied over data of input events to generate an event with an aggregated value; event streams may be joined on common data, similarly as two relations are joined in databases; an event may be enriched with data from an external information source (e.g., a database or an ontology) and so forth.

An EP language should therefore enable easy processing of data carried by events. We follow a rule-based approach which enables easy extraction of data, and passing it via *variable bindings*. Consequentially, operations such as filtering, aggregation, joining, enrichment, and so forth, are easily expressed in this approach and have a compact representation in event patterns.

On the other hand, since our formalism is founded in LP its use in practise demands LP skills too. For some users, this can be a burden from the usability point of view. However one of the main goal of our work is to enable seamless integration of EP with

---

[5]Otherwise events from different event snapshots or streams cannot be compared with respect to their time occurance.

stream reasoning (SR) capabilities. Therefore we have decided to enable users of our EP formalism with the full power of LP too.

Rules can be considered as *patterns* of knowledge. From that point of view, it is natural to represent event patterns as rules. SQL-based syntax is widely spread out in today's EP systems [ADGI08, ArBW06, KrSe09]. It is considered to be easy to understand, as many programmers today are familiar with database concepts. We propose a *rule-based syntax* and argue that it is convenient for EP. We base our opinion gained on experience in implementation of the proposed language itself, as well as on experience gained in implementation of few use cases (see Chapter 13).

For example, let us consider the following simple pattern rules. The first pattern detects a sequence of two instances of event e, where only instances with the *Name* 'a' and the *Result* equals to 1 are selected. Similarly, the second pattern detects a sequence of two instances of complex event ce1 with the same filter condition for the *Result* attribute.

$$\text{ce1}(Result) \leftarrow \text{e}(Name, Result) \text{ SEQ } \text{e}(Name, Result)$$
$$\text{WHERE } (Name =' a', Result = 1).$$
$$\text{ce2}(Result) \leftarrow \text{ce1}(Result) \text{ AND } \text{ce1}(Result)$$
$$\text{WHERE } (Result = 1).$$

Their representation in an SQL-like language of Esper[6] based on [ArBW06] is shown below.

```
<Query name= "ce1" text="
insert into tmpE(ceName, Result)
select 'ce1' as ceName, e1.Result as Result
from pattern [every ( +
    e1=e(e1.Name='a' and e1.Result=1) ->
    e2=e(e2.Name='a' and e2.Result=1) )]"/>

<Query name= "ce2" text="
select 'ce2' as Name, e1.Result as Result
from pattern [every ( +
    e1=tmpE(e1.ceName='ce1' and e1.Result=1) and
    e2=tmpE(e2.ceName='ce1' and e2.Result=1) )]"/>
```

As we see, complex events detected by the first pattern need to be *re-inserted* in a temporal stream of events tmpE (using insert in the first Esper statement). If complex event ce2 was further used in building a more complex event we would need to insert instances of ce2 event in another temporal stream too. Consequently, very complex (nested) events in such a language become easily unreadable. On the other hand, with a

---

[6]Esper is a CEP system: http://esper.codehaus.org/.

rule-based syntax it is easy to nest (complex) events. Also it is easy to pass data within nested events via *variable bindings*, which in total gives a more compact and clear syntax of the language.

Finally it is worth mentioning that our prototype implementation – presented in Chapter 12 – consist of about 2500 lines of Prolog code, while Esper 3.3.0 has approximately 150000 lines of code. Hence, rule-based declarative programming additionally results in drastic *reduction* in code size.

5.8 Extensibility

Extensibility of an EP language is an important design principle. EP systems are in general used as a middleware technology, and as such, they need to be customisable to different specific domains. Therefore, we believe that an EP language and its underlying execution model need to be simple enough in order to enable possible extensions. We follow this principle, and will propose few extensions of the main formalism in Chapter 7.

6

ETALIS: A Rule-Based Language for Event Processing and Reasoning

In this chapter we introduce the ETALIS Language for Events (ELE)[1], see [AFRS+10], and [AFRS+11b]. We start the chapter by giving a high level introduction to the general problem for which the language can be used. We define formal syntax and semantics of the ETALIS formalism. Throughout this section, we use a number of examples to demonstrate the power of the introduced language, and demonstrate its usefulness in practical applications.

6.1 Introduction

Informally, an *event* represents something that occurs, happens or changes the current state of affairs. For example, an event may signify a problem or an impending problem, a threshold, an opportunity, an information becoming available, a deviation and so forth. Simple events are combined into complex (derived) events depending on their temporal, causal and semantic relations.

The task of EP and Stream Reasoning in Event-driven Transaction Logic Inference System (ETALIS) is illustrated in Figure 6.1[2], and it can be described as follows. Within some dynamic setting, events from multiple event sources take place (denoted as *Events*

---
[1] We sometimes refer to the ETALIS Language for Events as the ETALIS formalism or just ETALIS.
[2] The figure is inspired by a similar illustration created by Opher Etzion and Tali Yatzkar –IBM Haifa.

in Figure 6.1). These events are also known as atomic events, and they are instantaneous. Notifications about these occurred events together with their timestamps and possibly further associated data (such as involved entities, numerical parameters of the event, or provenance data) enter ETALIS in the order of their occurrence. The core engine of ETALIS is represented by the wheel in Figure 6.1. Later, in Section 12.1, we will give a system diagram for the ETALIS engine.

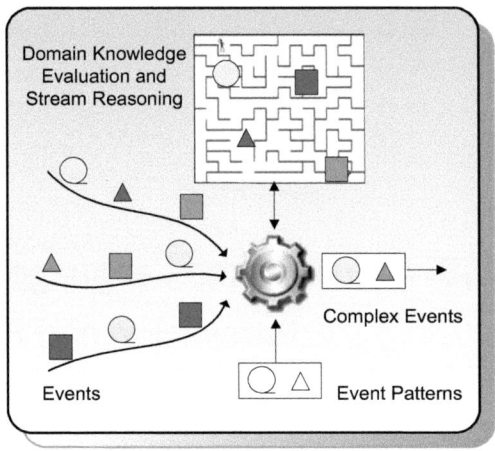

Figure 6.1: ETALIS Conceptual Architecture

Further on, ETALIS features a set of complex event descriptions – denoted as *Event Patterns* – by means of which *Complex Events* can be specified as temporal constellations of atomic events (see Figure 6.1). The complex events, thus defined, can in turn be used to compose even more complex events i.e., they can be turned back as input *Events*[3]. As opposed to atomic events, those complex events are not considered instantaneous but are endowed with a time interval denoting when the event started and when it ended.

Event Patterns in Figure 6.1 suggests that ETALIS Conceptual Architecture is used for the task of pattern matching only. This is not the case – namely in ETALIS, Event Pattern rules are used for pattern matching, as well as for all other EPN operations (e.g., filtering, splitting, translation etc.). Events derived by these rules are in general called Complex Events no matter whether a complex event is produced as a consequence of a filtering operation or pattern matching (see Figure 6.1).

Finally – when detecting complex events – ETALIS may consult a *Domain Knowledge*. For instance, consider a traffic management system that detects areas with slow traffic (in real time). Such an area is detected when events – denoting *slow* traffic in a particular area – subsequently occur within a certain time span. What is a "slow" traffic, and what is a "particular" area, for different events, roads and road subsections, is specified as a

---
[3] An edge, representing this possibility, is omitted to avoid cluttering the figure.

domain or background knowledge (a more detailed version of this example is described in Section 1.1). ETALIS can evaluate the background knowledge on the fly, possibly inferring *Complex Events* that involve new *implicit* knowledge. This knowledge is derived as a logical consequence from event driven deductive rules, thereby providing the *Stream Reasoning* capability (illustrated with the upper part of Figure 6.1).

A conceptual architecture – presented by Figure 6.1 – gives an informal introduction to basic notions formally defined in the following sections. In Subsection 6.4.1 we will show an implantation of the slow traffic example, and in Section 12.1 we will go into details of an internal architecture of ETALIS.

6.2 Syntax of the Language

In Subsection 3.2.1 we have introduced the syntax of definite logic programs. In this section – following a similar approach – we will introduce the syntax of ELE.

Formal syntax and semantics of ELE features:

- *static rules* accounting for static background information about the considered domain (denoted as *Domain Knowledge* in Figure 6.1);

- *event rules* that are used to capture the dynamic information by defining patterns of complex events (denoted as *Complex Events* in Figure 6.1).

Both parts may be intertwined through the use of common variables. Based on a combined (static and dynamic) specification, we will define the notion of entailment of complex events by a given event stream.

An ELE *rule base*[4] $\mathscr{R}$ is composed of a static part $\mathscr{R}^s$ and an event part $\mathscr{R}^e$. Thereby, $\mathscr{R}^s$ is a set of Horn clauses using the static predicates. Formally, a *static rule* is defined as $a : -a_1, \ldots, a_n$ where $a, a_1, \ldots, a_n$ are *static atoms*[5]. Every term that a contains is either a variable, a constant or a function symbol. Moreover, all variables occurring in any of the atoms have to occur at least once in the rule body outside any function application.

The event part $\mathscr{R}^e$ allows for the definition of patterns based on *time* and *events*. Time instants and durations are represented as nonnegative rational numbers $q \in \mathbb{Q}^+$. Events can be atomic or complex. An *atomic event* refers to an instantaneous occurrence of interest. Atomic events are expressed as ground event atoms (i.e., event predicates the arguments of which do not contain any variables). Intuitively, the arguments of a ground atom representing an atomic event denote information items (i.e. event data) that provide additional information about that event.

---

[4]or ETALIS rule base
[5]Static rules and static atoms are, in fact, Horn rules and atoms as defined in Subsection 3.2.1. We use here the prefix "static" only to distinguish these rules and atoms from *event rules* and *event atoms*, as defined in the remaining part of this section.

Atomic events are combined to *complex events* by *event patterns*. An event pattern is expressed as an *event rule*. Event rules describe temporal arrangements of events and absolute time points. They can be intertwined with static rules, thus combining the temporal arrangements of events with static relations from a knowledgebase (KB).

The following definition introduces formally central notions regarding the syntax of ELE.

Definition 6.1 *A* signature $\langle \mathbf{C}, \mathbf{V}, \mathbf{F}_n, \mathbf{P}_n^s, \mathbf{P}_n^e \rangle$ *for an ELE rule base consists of:*

- *a set* **C** *of constant symbols including true and false*
- *a set* **V** *of variables (denoted by capitals X, Y, ...)*
- *for* $n \in \mathbb{N}$, *sets* $\mathbf{F}_n$ *of function symbols of arity n*
- *for* $n \in \mathbb{N}$, *sets* $\mathbf{P}_n^s$ *of static predicates of arity n*
- *for* $n \in \mathbb{N}$, *sets* $\mathbf{P}_n^e$ *of event predicates of arity n, disjoint from* $\mathbf{P}_n^s$

Based on the signature for ELE, we define the following notions:

- *A* term *is defined by:*

$$t ::= c \mid v \mid f_n(t_1, \ldots, t_n) \mid p_n^s(t_1, \ldots, t_n)$$

- *The set of (static / event) atoms is defined as the set of all expressions* $p_n(t_1, \ldots, t_n)$ *where* p *is a (static / event) predicate and* $t_1, \ldots t_n$ *are terms.*

- *An ETALIS rule base* $\mathscr{R}$ *consists of a static part* $\mathscr{R}^s$ *and an event part* $\mathscr{R}^e$.

- $\mathscr{R}^s$ *is a set of Horn clauses using the static predicates* $\mathbf{P}_n^s$.

- $\mathscr{R}^e$ *allows for the definition of clauses (patterns) based on time and events. Time instants and durations are represented as nonnegative rational numbers* $q \in \mathbb{Q}^+$.

- *An atomic event is expressed as a ground event atom. An atomic event refers to an instantaneous occurrence of interest.*

- *A complex event is expressed as a ground event atom. A complex event refers to an occurrence with duration.*

- *The language P of event patterns – which allows the composition of events – is defined by*

$$P ::= p^e(t_1, \ldots, t_n) \mid P \text{ WHERE } t \mid q \mid (P).q \\ \mid P \text{ BIN } P \mid \text{NOT}(P).[P, P]$$

Thereby, p^e *is an n-ary event predicate,* t_i *denote terms, t is a term of type boolean, q is a nonnegative rational number, and* BIN *is one of the binary operators* SEQ, AND, PAR, OR, EQUALS, MEETS, DURING, STARTS, *or* FINISHES. *As a side condition, in every expression p* WHERE *t, all variables occurring in t must also occur in the pattern p.*

6.2. Syntax of the Language

- *An event rule is defined as a formula of the shape*

$$p^e(t_1,\ldots,t_n) \leftarrow p$$

where p is an event pattern containing all variables occurring in $p^e(t_1,\ldots,t_n)$.

Figure 6.2 demonstrates the various ways of constructing complex event descriptions from simpler ones in ELE. Moreover, Figure 6.2 also informally introduces the semantics of the language, which will further be defined in Section 6.3.

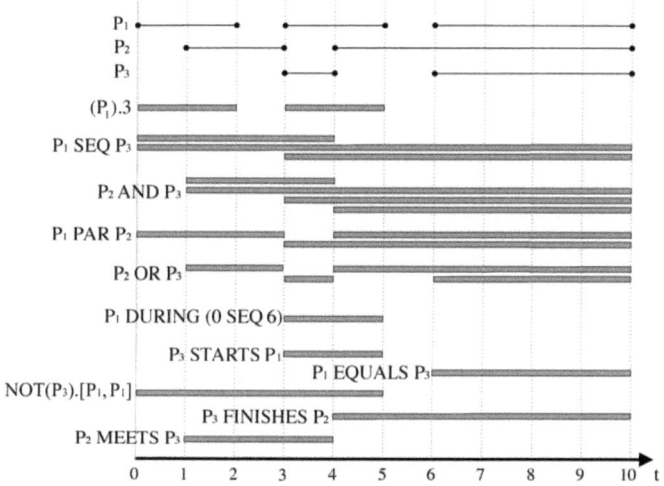

Figure 6.2: Language for Event Processing - Composition Operators

Let us assume that instances of three complex events, P_1, P_2, P_3, are occurring in time intervals as shown in Figure 6.2. Vertical dashed lines depict different time units, while the horizontal bars represent detected complex events for the given patterns. In the following, we give the intuitive meaning for all patterns from the figure:

- $(P_1).3$ detects an occurrence of P_1 if it happens within an interval of length 3, i.e., 3 represents the (maximum) time window.

- P_1 SEQ P_3 represents a sequence of two events, i.e., an occurrence of P_1 is followed by an occurrence of P_3; here P_1 must end before P_3 starts.

- P_2 AND P_3 is a pattern that is detected when instances of both P_2 and P_3 occur no matter in which order.

- P_1 PAR P_2 occurs when instances of both P_1 and P_2 happen, provided that their intervals have a non-zero overlap.

- P_2 OR P_3 is triggered for every instance of P_2 or P_3.

- P_1 DURING (0 SEQ 6) happens when an instance of P_1 occurs during an interval; in this case, the interval is built using a sequence of two atomic time-point events (one with $q = 0$ and another with $q = 6$, see the syntax above). In general, the interval may consist of other (derived) events too.

- P_3 STARTS P_1 is detected when an instance of P_3 starts at the same time as an instance of P_1 but ends earlier.

- P_1 EQUALS P_3 is triggered when the two events occur exactly at the same time interval.

- NOT(P_3).[P_1, P_1] represents a negated pattern. It is defined by a sequence of events (delimiting events) in the square brackets[6] where there is no occurrence of P_3 in the interval. In order to invalidate an occurrence of the pattern, an instance of P_3 must happen in the interval formed by the end time of the first delimiting event and the start time of the second delimiting event. In this example delimiting events are just two instances of the same event, i.e., P_1. Different treatments of negation are also possible, however we adopt one from [AdCh06].

- P_3 FINISHES P_2 is detected when an instance of P_3 ends at the same time as an instance of P_2 but starts later.

- P_2 MEETS P_3 happens when the interval of an occurrence of P_2 ends exactly when the interval of an occurrence of P_3 starts.

It is worth noting that the defined pattern language captures the set of all possible thirteen relations on two temporal intervals as defined in Allen's interval algebra [Alle83]. The set can also be used for rich temporal reasoning.

In this example, event patterns are considered under the *unrestricted policy*. In EP, consumption policies deal with an issue of *selecting* particular events occurrences when there are more than one event instance applicable and *consuming* events after they have been used in patterns. We have discussed consumption policies in Section 5.1, and will further discuss implementation of different consumption policies in ETALIS Language for Events in Section 7.4.

---

[6]Note that in the above example for DURING we used different parenthesis to denote an interval. This is so only because of the specific case in that example. We could have a derived event, defined on the same interval (instead of 0 SEQ 6), in which case we would not have used parenthesis at all. On the other hand, for the NOT operator we always use square brackets to denote an interval.

6.3 Declarative Semantics of the Language

We define the declarative formal semantics of ELE in a model-theoretic way (see Subsection 3.2.2). We first explain what an *interpretation* is. Then a model will be defined as a special kind of interpretation – one that makes the set of ELE rules (an event program) true.

The interpretation of constant symbols, function symbols, and predicates in an ELE rule base is similar to one defined for a definite program (see Definition 3.2) with the following two differences. First, a predicate symbol p is called a static predicate p^s in ELE. Second, we assume a fixed interpretation of the occurring function symbols, i.e., for every function symbol f of arity n, we presume a predefined function $f^* : Con^n \to Con$. That is, in our setting, functions are treated as built-in utilities (see Subsection 3.2.1 for discussion on built-in predicates).

As usual, a *variable assignment* is a mapping $\mu : Var \to Con$ assigning a value to every variable. We let μ^* denote the canonical extension of μ to terms:

$$\mu^* : \begin{cases} c \mapsto c & \text{if } c \in \mathbf{C}, \\ v \mapsto \mu(v) & \text{if } v \in Var, \\ f(t_1,\ldots,t_n) \mapsto f^*(\mu^*(t_1),\ldots,\mu^*(t_n)) & \text{for } f \in \mathbf{F}_n, \\ \mathrm{p}(t_1,\ldots,t_n) \mapsto \begin{cases} true & \text{if } \mathscr{R}^s \models p(\mu^*(t_1),\ldots,\mu^*(t_n)), \\ false & \text{otherwise.} \end{cases} \end{cases}$$

Thereby, $\mathscr{R}^s \models p(\mu^*(t_1),\ldots,\mu^*(t_n))$ is defined by the standard least Herbrand model semantics.

In addition to $\mathscr{R}$, we fix an *event stream*, which is a mapping $\varepsilon : Ground^e \to 2^{\mathbb{Q}^+}$ from event ground predicates into sets of nonnegative rational numbers. It indicates what elementary events occur at which time instants.

Definition 6.2 *An* interpretation $\mathscr{I} : Ground^e \to 2^{\mathbb{Q}^+ \times \mathbb{Q}^+}$ *is defined as a mapping from the event ground atoms to sets of pairs of nonnegative rationals, such that* $q_1 \leq q_2$ *for every* $\langle q_1, q_2 \rangle \in \mathscr{I}(g)$ *for all* $g \in Ground^e$. ◇

In the following, we define a model for a rule set $\mathscr{R}$ as an interpretation which makes every rule in $\mathscr{R}$ true.

Definition 6.3 *Given an event stream* ε, *an interpretation* $\mathscr{I}$ *is called a model for a rule set* $\mathscr{R}$ – *written as* $\mathscr{I} \models_\varepsilon \mathscr{R}$ – *if the following conditions are satisfied:*

1. $\langle q, q \rangle \in \mathscr{I}(g)$ *for every* $q \in \mathbb{Q}^+$ *and* $g \in Ground^e$ *with* $q \in \varepsilon(g)$

2. *for every rule atom* $\leftarrow$ *pattern and every variable assignment* μ *we have* $\mathscr{I}_\mu(atom) \subseteq \mathscr{I}_\mu(pattern)$ *where* $\mathscr{I}_\mu$ *is inductively defined as displayed in Figure 6.3.* ◇

pattern	$\mathscr{I}_\mu(\text{pattern})$
$\text{p}^e(t_1,\ldots,t_n)$	$\mathscr{I}(\text{p}^e(\mu^*(t_1),\ldots,\mu^*(t_n)))$
P WHERE t	$\mathscr{I}_\mu(P)$ if $\mu^*(t) = true$
	$\emptyset$ otherwise.
q	$\{\langle q,q\rangle\}$ for all $q\in\mathbb{Q}^+$
$(P).q$	$\mathscr{I}_\mu(P)\cap\{\langle q_1,q_2\rangle \mid q_2-q_1\leq q\}$
$P1$ SEQ $P2$	$\{\langle q_1,q_4\rangle \mid \langle q_1,q_2\rangle\in\mathscr{I}_\mu(P1)$ and $\langle q_3,q_4\rangle\in\mathscr{I}_\mu(P2)$ and $q_2<q_3\}$
$P1$ AND $P2$	$\{\langle\min(q_1,q_3),\max(q_2,q_4)\rangle \mid \langle q_1,q_2\rangle\in\mathscr{I}_\mu(P1)$ and $\langle q_3,q_4\rangle\in\mathscr{I}_\mu(P2)\}$
$P1$ PAR $P2$	$\{\langle\min(q_1,q_3),\max(q_2,q_4)\rangle \mid \langle q_1,q_2\rangle\in\mathscr{I}_\mu(P1)$
	and $\langle q_3,q_4\rangle\in\mathscr{I}_\mu(P2)$ and $\max(q_1,q_3)<\min(q_2,q_4)\}$
$P1$ OR $P2$	$\mathscr{I}_\mu(P1)\cup\mathscr{I}_\mu(P2)$
$P1$ EQUALS $P2$	$\mathscr{I}_\mu(P1)\cap\mathscr{I}_\mu(P2)$
$P1$ MEETS $P2$	$\{\langle q_1,q_3\rangle \mid \langle q_1,q_2\rangle\in\mathscr{I}_\mu(P1)$ and $\langle q_2,q_3\rangle\in\mathscr{I}_\mu(P2)\}$
$P1$ DURING $P2$	$\{\langle q_3,q_4\rangle \mid \langle q_1,q_2\rangle\in\mathscr{I}_\mu(P1)$ and $\langle q_3,q_4\rangle\in\mathscr{I}_\mu(P2)$ and $q_3<q_1<q_2<q_4\}$
$P1$ STARTS $P2$	$\{\langle q_1,q_3\rangle \mid \langle q_1,q_2\rangle\in\mathscr{I}_\mu(P1)$ and $\langle q_1,q_3\rangle\in\mathscr{I}_\mu(P2)$ and $q_2<q_3\}$
$P1$ FINISHES $P2$	$\{\langle q_1,q_3\rangle \mid \langle q_2,q_3\rangle\in\mathscr{I}_\mu(P1)$ and $\langle q_1,q_3\rangle\in\mathscr{I}_\mu(P2)$ and $q_1<q_2\}$
NOT$(P1).[P2,P3]$	$\mathscr{I}_\mu(P2$ SEQ $P3) \setminus \mathscr{I}_\mu(P2$ SEQ $P1$ SEQ $P3)$

Figure 6.3: Definition of extensional interpretation of event patterns. We use $P(x)$ for patterns, $q_{(x)}$ for rational numbers, $t_{(x)}$ for terms and PR for event predicates.

For an interpretation $\mathscr{I}$ and some $q \in \mathbb{Q}^+$, we let $\mathscr{I}|_q$ denote the interpretation defined by $\mathscr{I}|_q(g) = \mathscr{I}(g) \cap \{\langle q1,q2\rangle \mid q2-q1 \leq q\}$. Given interpretations $\mathscr{I}$ and $\mathscr{J}$, we say that $\mathscr{I}$ is *preferred* to $\mathscr{J}$ if $\mathscr{I}|_q \subset \mathscr{J}|_q$ for some $q \in \mathbb{Q}^+$. A model $\mathscr{I}$ is called *minimal* if there is no other model preferred to $\mathscr{I}$. Obviously, for every event stream ε and rule base $\mathscr{R}$ there is a unique minimal model $\mathscr{I}^{\varepsilon,\mathscr{R}}$. Essentially, this model can be obtained by starting from ε and applying the rules in ascending order with respect to the duration of the event generated by the rule.

Theorem 1 *For every event stream ε and rule base $\mathscr{R}$ there is a unique minimal model $\mathscr{I}^{\varepsilon,\mathscr{R}}$.*

Proof 1 *For every rational number q with $q \in \mathbb{Q}_\varepsilon = \bigcup_{g\in Ground^e} \varepsilon(g)$, we define an interpretation $\mathscr{I}_q$ by bottom-up saturation of ε_q where $\varepsilon_q(g) = \varepsilon(g) \cap \{\langle q_1,q_2\rangle \mid q_2 \leq q\}$ under the rules of $\mathscr{R}$ where the NOT subexpressions are evaluated against $\bigcup_{q'\in\mathbb{Q}_\varepsilon, q'<q} \mathscr{I}_{q'}$. The minimal model can then be defined by $\mathscr{I}^{\varepsilon,\mathscr{R}} := \bigcup_{q\in\mathbb{Q}_\varepsilon} \mathscr{I}_q$. Minimality is a straightforward consequence of the fact that derived intervals always contain the intervals associated to the premise atoms due to the definition of the semantics of patterns (cf. Figure 6.3).*

Finally, given an atom a and two rational numbers q_1, q_2, we say that the event $a^{[q_1,q_2]}$ is a *consequence* of the event stream ε and the rule base $\mathscr{R}$ (written $\varepsilon, \mathscr{R} \models a^{[q_1,q_2]}$), if $\langle q_1,q_2\rangle \in \mathscr{I}_\mu^{\varepsilon,\mathscr{R}}(a)$ for some variable assignment μ.

It is obvious that the behaviour of the event stream ε beyond the time point q_2 is irrelevant for determining whether $\varepsilon, \mathscr{R} \models a^{[q_1,q_2]}$. More formally, for any two event streams ε_1 and ε_2 with $\varepsilon_1(g) \cap \{\langle q,q' \rangle \mid q' \leq q_2\} = \varepsilon_2(g) \cap \{\langle q,q' \rangle \mid q' \leq q_2\}$ we have that $\varepsilon_1, \mathscr{R} \models a^{[q_1,q_2]}$ exactly if $\varepsilon_2, \mathscr{R} \models a^{[q_1,q_2]}$. This justifies to take the perspective of ε being only partially known (and continuously unveiled along a time line) while the task is to detect event-consequences as soon as possible.

6.3.1 Complexity Properties

The theoretical properties of the presented formalism heavily depend on the conditions put on the formalism's signature. On the negative side, without further restrictions, the formalism turns out to be ExpTime-complete as a straightforward consequence from according results in [DEGV01].

On the other side, the formalism turns not only decidable but even tractable if both **C** and the arity of functions and predicates is bounded:

Theorem 2 *Given natural numbers k,m, the problem of detecting complex events in an event stream ε with an ETALIS rule base $\mathscr{R}$ which satisfies $|\mathbf{C}| \leq k$ and $\mathbf{F}_n = \mathbf{P}_n^s = \mathbf{P}_n^e = \emptyset$ for all $n \geq m$ is* PTIME*-complete w.r.t. $|\mathscr{R}| + |\varepsilon|$.*

Proof 2 PTIME*-hardness directly follows from the fact that the formalism subsumes function-free Horn logic which is known to be hard for* PTIME*, see e.g. [DEGV01].*

For containment in PTIME*, recall that in our formalism, function symbols have a fixed interpretation. Hence, given an ETALIS rule base $\mathscr{R}$ with finite **C**, we can transform it into an equivalent function-free rule base $\mathscr{R}'$: we eliminate every n-ary function symbol* f *by introducing an auxiliary $n+1$-ary predicate* p_f *and "materializing" the function by adding ground atoms* $p_f(c_1,\ldots,c_n, f^*(c_1,\ldots,c_n))$*. This can be done in polynomial time, given the above mentioned arity bound. Naturally, also the size of $\mathscr{R}'$ is polynomial compared to the size of $\mathscr{R}$.*

Next, observe that under the above circumstances, the least Herbrand model of $\mathscr{R}^{s'}$ (which is then arity-bounded and function-free) can be computed in polynomial time (as there are only polynomially many ground atoms). Finally, note that the number of time points occurring in an event stream ε is linearly bounded by $|\varepsilon|$, whence there are only polynomially many relevant "interval-endowed ground predicates" $a^{[q_1,q_2]}$ possibly entailed by ε and $\mathscr{R}^{e'}$. Finally these entailments can be checked in polynomial time in a forward-chaining manner against the respective (polynomial) grounding of $\mathscr{R}^{e'}$. This concludes the proof.

6.4 Examples

It is worthwhile to briefly consider the modelling capabilities of the pattern language, introduced in Section 6.2 and Section 6.3 . To do so, let us show few examples related to real time observations and measurements of environmental phenomena (e.g., weather observations of temperature, relative humidity, wind speed and direction, precipitation and so forth).

For instance, one might be interested in defining an event that detects increase in wind speed, defined as two successive reports related to the same location. The following pattern specifies the speed increase of at least 10%:

windSpeedIncrease($Loc, WSpd_2$) ←
  wind($Loc, WSpd_1$) SEQ wind($Loc, WSpd_2$) WHERE $WSpd_2 > WSpd_1 \cdot 1.1$.

Let us now define an event denoting duration of a fire at certain location:

activeFire(Loc) ←
  NOT(fireLocalized(Loc))[fireReported(Loc), fireLocalized(Loc)].

We can also combine windSpeedIncrease event (shown above) to form a new complex event, fireAlarm:

fireAlarm(Loc) ←
  NOT(fireLocalized($Loc, WSpd$)).
  [fireReported(Loc), windSpeedIncrease($Loc, WSpd$))].

Similarly, we might be interested in detecting the heat index, i.e., an index that combines air temperature and relative humidity in an attempt to determine the human-perceived equivalent temperature (how hot it feels):

heatIndex($Loc, Index(Tmp, Hum)$) ←
  (temperature(Loc, Tmp) AND humidity(Loc, Hum)).30*min*

For the definition of the function *Index*, see Wikipedia[7]. Note that we have also defined a time frame of 30 minutes in which temperature and humidity readings are expected from respective sensors. This event rule also shows, how event information (about an index or other data) can be "passed" on to the defined complex events by using variables.

Let us further mention few examples from a financial domain. For example, one might be interested in defining an event matching stock market working days:

workingDay() ←
  NOT(marketCloses())[marketOpens(), marketCloses()].

Moreover, we might be interested in detecting the event of two bankruptcies happening on the same market working day:

dieTogether(X, Y) ←
  (bankrupt(X) SEQ bankrupt(Y)) DURING workingDay().

Note how variables may be employed to conditionally group events into complex ones if they refer to the same entity:

---

[7]The heat index: http://en.wikipedia.org/wiki/Heat_index

6.4. Examples

indirectlyAcquires$(X,Y) \leftarrow$ buys(Z,Y) AND buys(X,Z)

Even more elaborate constraints can be put on the applicability of a pattern by endowing it with a boolean type term as filter[8]. Thus, we can detect a stock prize increase of at least 50% in a time frame of 7 days.

remarkableIncrease$(X) \leftarrow$
$\bigl($price(X,Y_1) SEQ price$(X,Y_2)\bigr)$.7 WHERE $Y_2 > Y_1 \cdot 1.5$

We will gradually introduce more complex event rules in the remaining parts of this work.

6.4.1 An Example Application

It is worthwhile to demonstrate an example EP application with background knowledge processing. We consider a sensor-based traffic management system. The system monitors continuously generated traffic events, and diagnoses areas with slow traffic (bottleneck areas).

For example, a bottleneck area is detected when two events, denoting slow traffic in the same area, subsequently occur within 30 minutes. Rule (6.1) detects such a situation.

bottleneckArea$(Area) \leftarrow$
$\bigl($trafficEvent(Rd, S_1, N_1, W_1) SEQ
trafficEvent$(Rd, S_2, N_2, W_2)\bigr)$.30*min*
WHERE {
slowTraffic(Rd, S_1),
slowTraffic(Rd, S_2),
areaCheck$(Area, N_1, W_1)$,
areaCheck$(Area, N_2, W_2)$}. (6.1)

A trafficEvent carries information about a public road (Rd) for which the event is relevant, current traffic speed (S_i), and geographic location coordinates (N_i, W_i) of its source sensor. Apart from the temporal condition – denoted with SEQ operator and the 30-minute time window – traffic events need to satisfy other conditions too. First, they need to be considered for the same road (i.e., the two traffic events are joined on the same attribute, Rd). Second, they need to denote slow traffic and belong to the same area (see WHERE clause in rule (6.1)). We develop a simple KB – written as Prolog-style rules[9] (6.3)-(6.4) – to enable evaluation of these conditions. Further on, let us define speed thresholds for particular roads, e.g., traffic under 40 kph is considered as slow on the road rd_1 (see facts (6.2)).

---

[8]Note that also comparison operators like $=, <$ and $>$ can be seen as boolean-typed binary functions and, hence, fit well into the framework.
[9]Note that we use $\leftarrow$ for defining ELE pattern rules, and : − for defining static (Prolog) rules.

$$\begin{array}{l}\texttt{threshold}(rd_1, 40).\\ \texttt{threshold}(rd_2, 30).\\ \texttt{threshold}(rd_3, 50).\\ ....\end{array} \quad (6.2)$$

Rule (6.3) gets information about speed from two traffic events (S_1, S_2), and evaluates to true if the speed is below the threshold for a road *Rd*.

$$\texttt{slowTraffic}(Rd, S) : -\texttt{threshold}(Rd, X), S < X. \quad (6.3)$$

For simplicity reasons we define traffic areas as rectangles specified as four point coordinates[10].

$$\begin{array}{l}\texttt{area}(a_1, 4042, 4045, 7358, 7361).\\ \texttt{area}(a_2, 4045, 4048, 7361, 7363).\\ \texttt{area}(a_3, 4048, 4051, 7363, 7365).\\ ....\end{array} \quad (6.4)$$

For given coordinates of an event sensor, rule (6.5) retrieves a traffic area. Additionally, the second event needs to come from the same area. To enforce this condition, traffic events are joined by the same *Area* attribute, see rule 6.1.

$$\begin{array}{l}\texttt{areaCheck}(Area, N, W) : -\\ \quad \texttt{area}(Area, X_1, X_2, Y_1, Y_2),\\ \quad X_1 < N, N < X_2, Y_1 < W, W < Y_2!.\end{array} \quad (6.5)$$

Now, when a trafficEvent occurs – followed by another occurrence of the same event – ETALIS will check the time window constraint. If the constraint is satisfied, ETALIS will check whether the traffic is slow (by evaluating rule (6.3)), and whether both events come from the same area (rule (6.5)), in which case a bottleneckArea event is triggered.

In this simple example, we have demonstrated how to combine EP capabilities with evaluation of a background knowledge, thereby providing an effective (real time) situation assessment. Note that rules enable a flexible situation assessment even if facts about current speed limits change dynamically (e.g., due to changes in weather conditions). The example also demonstrates *temporal* and *spatial* processing over continuously arriving events.

---

[10] Other shapes can be represented by rules too.

7

Operational Semantics of the Language

Having presented syntax and declarative semantics of event patterns in Chapter 6, next we turn to the execution model of ELE. We explain how complex events can be effectively detected at run-time, following the semantics of the language. We start this section with the implementation of sequence. This operator as well as conjunction, disjunction, negation and parallel operator have been introduced in [AFSS09, AFRS$^+$10, AFRS$^+$11b, ARFS12a]. We will continue this chapter by presenting iterative rules, aggregation patterns and sliding windows introduced in [ARFS11a]. Finally at the end, we will turn to some practical considerations such as consumption of events.

7.1 Overview

We propose a novel EP approach in which complex events are *deduced* or derived from simpler events. Complex events are defined as *deductive rules*, and events are represented as *facts*. Every time an atomic event (relevant with respect to the set of monitored complex events) occurs, the system updates its knowledgebase, i.e., it adds a respective fact to the internal state of complex events. Essentially, this internal state encodes what atomic events have already happened and what are still missing for the completion of a certain complex event. Complex events are detected as soon as the last event required for their detection has occurred. Descriptions telling which occurrence of an event furthers the detection of complex events – including the relationships between complex events, events they consist of, or additional domain knowledge – are given by deductive rules and facts. Consequently, detection of complex events then amounts to an *inferencing* problem.

Our approach is established on *goal-directed, event-driven* rules, and decomposition of complex event patterns into *two-input intermediate events* (i.e., *goals*). Goals are automatically asserted by rules as relevant events occur. They can persist over a period of time "waiting" to support detection of a more complex goal. This process of asserting more and more complex goals shows the progress towards detection of a complex event.

In the remaining part of this chapter we give more details about a *goal-directed, event-driven* mechanism with respect to event pattern operators of ELE. In our approach goals are crucial for computation of complex events. They show the current state of progress toward matching an event pattern. Moreover they allow for detection of the state of any complex event, at any time. Therefore goals can enable *reasoning* over events (e.g., correlating complex events to each other, establishing more complex constraints between them etc.). They can persist over a period of time. It is worth mentioning that we also use rules to delete goals. Once a goal is "consumed", it is removed from the database[1]. In this way goals are kept persisted as long as (but not longer) they are needed.

7.2 Execution Model for ETALIS

7.2.1 Sequence

Let us consider a sequence of events represented by rule (7.1), i.e., an event e is detected when an event a[2] is followed by an occurrence of b, and finally by c. We can always represent the above pattern as e ← ((a SEQ b) SEQ c). In general, rules (7.2) represent two equivalent rules[3].

$$e \leftarrow a \text{ SEQ } b \text{ SEQ } c. \tag{7.1}$$

$$\begin{aligned} &e \leftarrow p \text{ BIN } r \text{ BIN } s \ldots \text{ BIN } t. \\ &e \leftarrow (((p \text{ BIN } r) \text{ BIN } s) \ldots \text{ BIN } t). \end{aligned} \tag{7.2}$$

We refer to this kind of "events coupling" as *binarization* of events. Effectively, in binarization we introduce *two-input* intermediate events (ie). For example, now we can rewrite rule (7.1) as ie ← a SEQ b, and the e ← ie SEQ c. Every monitored event – including atomic, complex and intermediate events – will be assigned with one or more *logic rules*, fired whenever that event occurs. Using the binarization, it is more convenient to construct *event-driven* rules for three reasons. First, it is easier to implement an event operator when events are considered on a "two by two" basis. Second, the binarization increases the possibility for *sharing* among events and intermediate events, when the

---

[1] Removal of "consumed" goals can be omitted if events are required in a log for further processing or analysing.

[2] More precisely, by "an event a" is meant an *instance* of the event a.

[3] If no parentheses are given, we assume all operators to be left-associative. While in some cases, like SEQ sequences, this is irrelevant, other operators such as PAR are not associative, whence the precedence matters.

7.2. Execution Model for ETALIS

granularity of intermediate patterns is reduced. Third, the binarization eases the *management* of rules. As we will see later in this section, each new use of an event (in a pattern) amounts to appending one or more rules to an existing rule set. However it is important that for the management of rules, we do not need to *modify* existing rules when adding new ones[4].

Here we presented a left-associative binarization (events and goals are coupled from left to right). The left-associative binarization is a good choice when the rightmost event(s) in a pattern rule have a higher occurrence rate than the others (e.g., event c occurs more frequently than event b, and further event a in rule (7.1)), since in that situation event $triple(\tau_3, T_5, T_6)$ is joined later. It is also possible to do such a coupling from right to left. The right-associative coupling is beneficial when the leftmost event(s) have a higher rate of occurrence(s). Other combinations are possible, too. See for example bushy plan and inner plan in [MeMa09]. These, and similar plans and cost optimizations as proposed in [MeMa09] are applicable in our framework. They are, however, out of scope of this work and will be addressed in future.

In the following, we give more details about assigning rules to each monitored event. We also provide an algorithm (using a Prolog-like syntax) for detecting a sequence of events. Note that events in rule (7.1) and rule (7.2) are represented as propositions (e.g., a, b, c). In general, an event a has a timestamp $[T_1, T_2]$ where T_1, T_2 are represented as nonnegative rational numbers $q \in \mathbb{Q}^+$. An event also carries other data parameters $X_1, X_2, ..., X_n$, hence it is represented by: $a^{[T_1, T_2]}(X_1, X_2, ..., X_n)$ (see Section 6.2 for details). However, for the sake of readability we will use a shorter notation: $a(T_1, T_2)$.

Algorithm 1 accepts as input a rule referring to a binary sequence ie ← a SEQ b, and produces event-driven backward chaining (EDBC) rules. These are executable rules in ETALIS. In the remaining part of this section we will explain EDBC rules in details (for each operator in ELE). Let us start with EDBC rules for the sequence pattern.

The binarization step must precede the rule transformation presented by Algorithm 1. Rules, produced by this algorithm, belong to one of two different classes of rules. We refer to the first class as *goal inserting rules*. The second class corresponds to *checking rules*. For example, rule (7.3) belongs to the first class as it inserts goal(b(_,_), a(T_1, T_2), ie(_,_)). The rule will fire when an event a occurs, and the meaning of the goal it inserts is as follows: "an event a has occurred at $[T_1, T_2]$, and we are waiting for a b event to happen in order to detect an ie event". The goal does not carry information about times for events b and ie, as we do not know when they will occur. In general, the *second* event in a goal always denotes the event that has just occurred. The role of the *first* event is to specify what we are waiting for to detect an event that is on the *third* position.

Rule (7.4) belongs to the second class, referred to as a *checking rule*. It checks whether certain prerequisite goals already exist in the database, in which case it triggers the more complex event. For example, rule (7.4) will fire whenever a b event occurs. The

---
[4]This holds even if patterns with negated events are added.

Algorithm 1 Sequence.
Input: event binary goal ie ← a SEQ b.
Output: event-driven backward chaining rules for SEQ operator.
Each event binary goal ie ← a SEQ b is converted into: {
   $a(T_1,T_2)$: − for_each(a,1,$[T_1,T_2]$).
   $a(1,T_1,T_2)$: − assert(goal(b(_,_),a(T_1,T_2),ie(_,_))).
   $b(T_3,T_4)$: − for_each(b,1,$[T_3,T_4]$).
   $b(1,T_3,T_4)$: − goal(b(T_3,T_4),a(T_1,T_2),ie),$T_2 < T_3$,
               retract(goal(b(T_3,T_4),a(T_1,T_2),ie(_,_))),ie(T_1,T_4).
}

rule checks whether goal(b(_,_),a(T_1,T_2),ie(_,_)) already exists (i.e., a has previously happened), in which case the rule triggers ie by calling an ie(T_1,T_4) event. The time occurrence of the ie event (i.e., T_1,T_4) is defined based on the occurrence of constituting events (i.e., a(T_1,T_2), and b(T_3,T_4), see Section 6.3 for details about semantics of SEQ operator). Calling ie(T_1,T_4), this event is effectively propagated either upward (if it is an intermediate event) or triggered as a finished complex event.

We see that our *backward* chaining rules compute goals in a *forward* chaining manner (as specified by a requirement in Section 5.4). The goals are crucial for computation of complex events. They show the current state of progress toward matching an event pattern. Moreover, they allow for determining the "completion state" of any complex event, at any time. For instance, we can query the current state and get information how much of a certain pattern is currently fulfilled (e.g., what is the current status of a certain pattern, or notify me if the pattern is 90% completed). Further, goals can enable *reasoning* over events (e.g., answering which event occurred before some, another event, although we do not know a priori what are explicit relationships between these two; correlating complex events to each other; establishing more complex constraints between them and so forth, see Section 8.4).

Goals can persist over a period of time. It is worth noting that *checking rules* can also delete goals. Once a goal is "consumed", it is removed from the database[5]. In this way, goals are kept persistent as long as (but not longer) than needed. In Section 7.4, we will return to different policies for removing goals from the database.

$$a(1,T_1,T_2) : - \text{assert}(\text{goal}(b(\_,\_),a(T_1,T_2),ie(\_,\_))). \quad (7.3)$$

$$b(1,T_3,T_4) : - \text{goal}(b(T_3,T_4),a(T_1,T_2),ie), T_2 < T_3,$$
$$\text{retract}(\text{goal}(b(T_3,T_4),a(T_1,T_2),ie(\_,\_))), \quad (7.4)$$
$$ie(T_1,T_4).$$

$$\text{for\_each}(Pred,N,L) : -$$
$$((FullPred = ..[Pred,N,L]), \text{event\_trigger}(FullPred), \quad (7.5)$$
$$(N_1 \, is \, N+1), \text{for\_each}(Pred,N_1,L)) \lor \text{true}.$$

---
[5]Removal of "consumed" goals is typically needed for space reasons but might be omitted if events are required in a log for further processing or analyzing.

7.2. Execution Model for ETALIS

Finally, in Algorithm 1 there exist more rules than the two mentioned types (i.e., rules inserting goals and checking rules). We see that for each different event type (i.e., a and b in our case) we have one rule with a `for_each` predicate. It is defined by rule (7.5). Effectively, it implements a loop, which for any occurrence of an event goes through each rule specified for that event (predicate) and fires it. For example, when a occurs, the first rule in the set of rules from Algorithm 1 will fire. This first rule will then loop, invoking all other rules specified for a (those having a in the rule head). In our case, there is only one such a rule, namely rule (7.3). However, in general, there may be as many of these rules as usages of a particular event in an event program. Let us observe a situation in which we want to extend our event pattern set with an additional pattern that contains the event a (i.e., additional usage of a). In this case, the rule set representing a set of event patterns needs to be updated with new rules. This can be done even at runtime. Let us assume the additional pattern to be monitored is $ie_j \leftarrow$ k SEQ a. Then the only change we need to make is to add one rule to insert a goal and one checking rule (in the existing rule set). The change is realised as an update to rules produced by Algorithm 1 by adding the following two rules below[6].

$a(2, T_1, T_2) : -$ `assert(goal(b(_,_),a(`T_1, T_2`),ie(_,_)))`.
$a(3, T_1, T_2) : -$ `goal(a(_,_),k(`T_3, T_4`),ie`$_j$`(_,_]))`, $T_4 < T_1$,
        `retract(goal(a(_,_),k(`T_3, T_4`),ie`$_j$`(_,_)))`,ie$_j(T_3, T_2)$.

Event rules with WHERE clause are handled in a similar manner as rules without it. Consider rule (7.6) where q is a static predicate. After the binarization, the rule will be rewritten as ie $\leftarrow$ a SEQ b, and e $\leftarrow$ ie SEQ q.

$$e \leftarrow a \text{ SEQ } b \text{ WHERE } q \qquad (7.6)$$

Occurrence of sequence of events a and b will trigger an ie event. The ie event in turn will trigger e $\leftarrow$ ie SEQ q. If the static predicate, q, evaluates to true, then the rule will call the e event. Calling e, this event is effectively propagated either upward (if it is an intermediate event) or triggered as a complex event.

Note that the static predicate, q, is evaluated after detection of a sequence of events a and b. Sometimes it is possible to evaluate a static predicate before the event part is detected (since it represents the static or slowly evolving knowledge). If it evaluates to false, we do not need to pursue further detection of the pattern. This optimisation is, however, the subject of our future work.

So far, we have described in detail a mechanism for EP with EDBC rules. We have also described the transformation of event pattern rules into rules for real time events detection using the *sequence* operator. In general, for a given set of rules (defining complex patterns) there will be as many transformed rules as there are usages of distinct atomic events. Some rules however may be *shared* among different patterns. As said, the binarization breaks up patterns into binary sub-patterns (intermediate events). If two or more

---
[6]Note that an *id* of rules is incremented for each next rule being added (i.e., 2,3...)

patterns share the same sub-patterns, they will also share the same set of EDBC rules. That is, during the transformation, only one set of EDBC rules will be produced for a distinct event binary goal (no matter how many times the goal is used in the whole event program). In large programs (e.g., where event patterns are built incrementally, i.e., one pattern upon another one) such a sharing may improve the overall system performance as the execution of redundant rules is avoided.

The complete transformation in Algorithm 1 is proportional to the number and length of user defined event pattern rules, hence such a transformation is linear, and moreover is performed at design time.

Conceptually, our backward chaining rules for the sequence operator look very similar to rules for other operators. In the remaining part of this section we show the algorithms for other event operators, and briefly describe them.

7.2.2 Conjunction

Conjunction is another typical operator in EP. An event pattern based on conjunction occurs when all events which comprise that conjunction occur. Unlike the sequence operator, here the constitutive events can happen at times with no particular order between them. For example, ie ← a AND b defines an ie event as conjunction of events a and b.

Algorithm 2 Conjunction.

Input: event binary goal ie ← a AND b.
Output: event-driven backward chaining rules for AND operator.
Each event binary goal ie ← a AND b is converted into: {
  $a(T_1, T_2) :-$ for_each$(a, 1, [T_1, T_2])$.
  $a(1, T_3, T_4) :-$ goal$(a(\_,\_), b(T_1, T_2), ie(\_,\_))$,
          retract(goal$(a(\_,\_), b(T_1, T_2), ie(\_,\_)))$,
          $T_5 = \min\{T_1, T_3\}, T_6 = \max\{T_2, T_4\}, ie(T_5, T_6)$.
  $a(2, T_3, T_4) :- \neg($goal$(a(\_,\_), b(T_1, T_2), ie(\_,\_)))$,
          assert(goal$(b(\_,\_), a(T_3, T_4), ie(\_,\_)))$.
  $b(T_1, T_2) :-$ for_each$(b, 1, [T_1, T_2])$.
  $b(1, T_3, T_4) :-$ goal$(b(\_,\_), a(T_1, T_2), ie(\_,\_))$,
          retract(goal$(b(\_,\_), a(T_1, T_2), ie(\_,\_)))$,
          $T_5 = \min\{T_1, T_3\}, T_6 = \max\{T_2, T_4\}, ie(T_5, T_6)$.
  $b(2, T_3, T_4) :- \neg($goal$(b(\_,\_), a(T_1, T_2), ie(\_,\_)))$,
          assert(goal$(a(\_,\_), b(T_3, T_4), ie(\_,\_)))$.
}

Algorithm 2 shows the output of a transformation of *conjunction* event patterns into EDBC rules (for conjunction). The procedure for dividing complex event rules into *binary event goals* is the same as in Algorithm 1. However, rules for *inserting* and *checking* goals are different. Both classes of rules are specific to conjunction. We have a pair of these rules created for both, event a as well as for event b. Whenever a occurs (denoted

7.2. Execution Model for ETALIS

as some interval (T_1, T_2)) the algorithm checks whether an instance of b has already happened (see rule (7.7) from Algorithm 2). An instance of b has already happened if the current database state contains goal(a(_,_),b(T_1,T_2),ie(_,_)). In this case the event ie(T_5, T_6) is triggered (i.e., a call for ie(T_5, T_6) is issued). Otherwise, a goal which states that an instance of a has occurred, is inserted (i.e., assert(goal(b(_,_),a(T_1, T_2),ie(_, _))) is executed by rule (7.8)). Now if an instance of b happens later (at some (T_3, T_4)), rule (7.9) will succeed (if a has previously happened). Otherwise rule (7.10) will insert goal(a(_, _),b(T_1, T_2),ie(_, _)).

$$a(1,T_3,T_4) :- \text{goal}(a(\_,\_),b(T_1,T_2),\text{ie}(\_,\_)),$$
$$\text{retract}(\text{goal}(a(\_,\_),b(T_1,T_2),\text{ie}(\_,\_))), \quad (7.7)$$
$$T_5 = \min\{T_1,T_3\}, T_6 = \max\{T_2,T_4\}, \text{ie}(T_5,T_6).$$

$$a(2,T_3,T_4) :- \neg(\text{goal}(a(\_,\_),b(T_1,T_2),\text{ie}(\_,\_))),$$
$$\text{assert}(\text{goal}(b(\_,\_),a(T_3,T_4),\text{ie}(\_,\_))). \quad (7.8)$$

$$b(1,T_3,T_4) :- \text{goal}(b(\_,\_),a(T_1,T_2),\text{ie}(\_,\_)),$$
$$\text{retract}(\text{goal}(b(\_,\_),a(T_1,T_2),\text{ie}(\_,\_))), \quad (7.9)$$
$$T_5 = \min\{T_1,T_3\}, T_6 = \max\{T_2,T_4\}, \text{ie}(T_5,T_6).$$

$$b(2,T_3,T_4) :- \neg(\text{goal}(b(\_,\_),a(T_1,T_2),\text{ie}(\_,\_))),$$
$$\text{assert}(\text{goal}(a(\_,\_),b(T_3,T_4),\text{ie}(\_,\_))). \quad (7.10)$$

In Section 6.3 we have presented a *declarative* semantics of ELE. We provide an implementation of the language in Prolog, and since Prolog is not purely declarative, we need to take care when using non-declarative features of Prolog[7]. Hence in the following we discuss whether the operational semantics - as presented so far in this section – corresponds to the declarative semantics of the language.

$$c \leftarrow a \ op_1 \ b.$$
$$d \leftarrow b \ op_2 \ c. \quad (7.11)$$

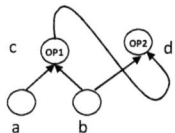

Figure 7.1: Example program

Consider an example program defined by rules (7.11) and its corresponding graphical representation shown in Figure 7.1. Note that event b is used twice in rules (7.11), hence

---
[7]This remark applies, in general, when a declarative formalism is to be implemented with other non-declarative languages (e.g., procedural languages such as Java, C, C++, etc.)

we have two edges in Figure 7.1. For each edge of b we will have one EDBC rule (e.g., if op_i is SEQ where i can be either 1 or 2) or two EDBC rules (e.g., if op_i is AND), see Algorithm 1 and Algorithm 2, respectively. To ensure the declarative property of the language, the order in which rules of these two edges are executed needs to be irrelevant. That is, if ETALIS system evaluates rule(s) from the first edge followed by evaluation of rule(s) from the second edge, we need to obtain the same results as if the order was the opposite. If this holds for every binary pair of events connected by any event operator in a program, then we can be sure that the operational semantics preserve correctness of the execution, regardless of the order in which rules are selected for the execution.

Let us assume that both op_1 and op_2 in rules (7.11) is replaced by SEQ operator, and that event a happened followed by event b. In this situation we expect to derive event c only. Event d will not be triggered as event c did not strictly happened after event b. That is, T_2 of event b is not strictly smaller than T_1 of event c (essentially they are equal), see Algorithm 1. Consequentially, event d will not be detected regardless of the order in which rules for two b edges are evaluated.

Let us assume that op_2 in rules (7.11) is replaced by AND operator, and again, event a happened followed by event b. In this situation we expect to derive both, event c and event d. When event b occurs, the system can first evaluate rule for the SEQ edge (op_1), and then rules for the AND edge (op_2), or vice versa. For both cases we expect event d to be triggered.

Suppose the SEQ edge of event b is evaluated first. The system will detect event c. This event will be used to start detection of the conjunction (defined by the second rule in rules (7.11)). Effectively, event b will trigger rule (7.9) and rule (7.10) in Algorithm 2^8. Rule (7.9) will fail, and rule (7.10) will succeed by inserting goal (b (_,_), c (T_3, T_4), d (_,_)). Next, when rules of the AND edge of event b are evaluated, rule (7.7) and rule (7.8) will fire[9]. Finally, rule (7.7) will succeed by triggering event d. We see that successful evaluation of rule (7.10), followed by successful evaluation of rule (7.7), leads to detection of event d.

Now suppose that the AND edge of event b is evaluated first. In this situation, rule (7.8) will be successfully evaluated followed by an evaluation of rule (7.9). As a result, the detection will take place in the reverse order, but it will be still possible to detect event d.

While Algorithm 1 enables detection of events in one direction, Algorithm 2 enables the detection in both directions. Therefore we use a modification of Algorithm 2 to handle other operators too (e.g., PAR , MEETS , FINISHES etc.), i.e., whenever binary events may come in both orders.

---

[8] Note that in the rule heads we now have event c.
[9] Note that in the rule heads we now have event b.

7.2.3 Concurrency

A concurrent or parallel composition of two events (ie ← a PAR b) is detected when events a and b both occur, and their intervals overlap (i.e., we also say they happen *synchronously*).

Algorithm 3 shows what is an output of automated transformation of a *concurrent* event pattern into rules which serve a *data-driven backward chaining* event computation. The procedure for dividing complex event rules into *binary event goals* is the same (as already described), and takes place prior to the transformation. Rules for *inserting* and *checking* goals are similar to those in Algorithm 2. The only change in Algorithm 2 is a *sufficient* condition, ensuring the interval overlap (i.e., $T_3 < T_2$).

Algorithm 3 Concurrency.

Input: event binary goal ie ← a PAR b.
Output: event-driven backward chaining rules for PAR operator.
Each event binary goal ie ← a PAR b is converted into: {
   a(T_1, T_2) :− for_each(a, 1, $[T_1, T_2]$).
   a$(1, T_3, T_4)$:− goal(a(_,_),b(T_1,T_2),ie(_,_)), $T_3 < T_2$,
               retract(goal(a(_,_),b(T_1,T_2),ie(_,_))),
               $T_5 = \min\{T_1, T_3\}, T_6 = \max\{T_2, T_4\}$, ie$(T_5, T_6)$.
   a$(2, T_3, T_4)$:− ¬(goal(a(_,_),b(T_1,T_2),ie(_,_))), $T_3 < T_2$,
               assert(goal(b(_,_),a(T_3,T_4),ie(_,_))).
   b(T_1, T_2) :− for_each(b, 1, $[T_1, T_2]$).
   b$(1, T_3, T_4)$:− goal(b(_,_),a(T_1,T_2),ie(_,_)), $T_3 < T_2$,
               retract(goal(b(_,_),a(T_1,T_2),ie(_,_))),
               $T_5 = \min\{T_1, T_3\}, T_6 = \max\{T_2, T_4\}$, ie$(T_5, T_6)$.
   b$(2, T_3, T_4)$:− ¬(goal(b(_,_),a(T_1,T_2),ie(_,_))), $T_3 < T_2$,
               assert(goal(a(_,_),b(T_3,T_4),ie(_,_))).
}

7.2.4 Disjunction

An algorithm for detecting *disjunction* (OR) of events is trivial. The disjunction operator divides rule into separate disjuncts, where each disjunct triggers the parent (complex) event. That is, a disjunction after binarization looks as rule (7.12), and is converted to separate disjuncts (7.13).

$$e \leftarrow a \text{ OR } b. \qquad (7.12)$$

$$\begin{aligned} e &\leftarrow a. \\ e &\leftarrow b. \end{aligned} \qquad (7.13)$$

7.2.5 Negation

Negation in EP is typically understood as *absence* of an event that is negated. In order to create a time interval in which we are interested to detect absence of an event, we define a negated event in the scope of other complex events. Algorithm 4 describes how to handle negation in the scope of a sequence. It is also possible to detect negation in an arbitrarily defined time interval.

Algorithm 4 Negation.
Input: event pattern ie ← NOT(c).[a,b].
Output: event-driven backward chaining rules for negation.
Each event binary goal ie ← NOT(c).[a,b] is converted into: {
  $a(T_1, T_2) :- $ for_each$(a, 1, [T_1, T_2])$.
  $a(1, T_1, T_2) :- $ assert(goal$(b(_,_), a(T_1, T_2), $ ie$(\_,\_)))$).
  $b(T_1, T_2) :- $ for_each$(b, 1, [T_1, T_2])$.
  $b(1, T_5, T_6) :- $ goal$(b(_,_), a(T_1, T_2), $ ie$(\_,\_))$,
          $\neg($goal$(\_, c(T_3, T_4), \_)), T_2 < T_5, T_2 < T_3, T_4 < T_5$,
          retract(goal$(b(_,_), a(T_1, T_2), $ ie$(\_,\_))),$ ie$(T_1, T_6)))$.
  $c(T_1, T_2) :- $ for_each$(c, 1, [T_1, T_2])$.
  $c(1, T_1, T_2) :- $ assert(goal$(\_, c(T_1, T_2), \_))$.}
}

Rules for detection of negation are similar to rules from Algorithm 1. We need to detect a sequence (i.e., a SEQ b), and additionally to check whether an occurrence of c happened in-between the event a and b. That is why a rule $b(1, T_5, T_6)$ needs to check whether $\neg($goal$(\_, c(T_3, T_4), \_))$ (with certain time condition) is true. If yes, this means that event c has not happened during a detected sequence (i.e., $a(T_1, T_2)$ SEQ $b(T_5, T_6)$), and ie(T_1, T_6) will be triggered. It is worth noting that a non-occurrence of c is monitored from the time when event a has been detected until the beginning of an interval which event b is detected on.

7.2.6 Interval-Based Operations

In the following part of this section we provide brief descriptions for the remaining relations between two intervals. Each relation is easily checkable with one rule.

7.2.6.1 Duration

An event happens during (i.e., DURING) another event if the interval of the first is contained in the interval of the second. Rule (7.14) takes two intervals as parameters[10]. First, it checks whether all parameters are actually defined as intervals (see rule (7.15)). Then

---
[10]Symbol '@' is used in Prolog built-in predicates ($>, <, \geq$ etc.) to compare terms alphabetically or numerically. When this symbol is omitted, terms are compared arithmetically.

7.2. Execution Model for ETALIS

it compares whether the start of the second interval (TI_2_S) is less than the start of the first interval (TI_1_S). Additionally it checks whether the end of the first interval (TI_1_E) is less than the end of the second interval (TI_2_E).

$$\begin{aligned}
\text{duration}(TI_1, TI_2) : -\ &TI_1 = [TI_1\_S, TI_1\_E],\\
&\text{validTimeInterval}(TI_1),\\
&TI_2 = [TI_2\_S, TI_2\_E],\\
&\text{validTimeInterval}(TI_2),\\
&TI_2\_S@ < TI_1\_S, TI_1\_E@ < TI_2\_E.
\end{aligned} \quad (7.14)$$

$$\text{validTimeInterval}(TI) : -\ TI = [TI\_S, TI\_E], TI\_S@ < TI\_E. \quad (7.15)$$

7.2.6.2 Start

We say that an event starts (i.e., STARTS) another if an instance of the first event starts at the same time as an instance of the second event, but ends earlier. Therefore rule (7.16) checks whether the start of both intervals are equal and whether the end of the first event is smaller than the end of the second one.

$$\begin{aligned}
\text{starts}(TI_1, TI_2) : -\ &TI_1 = [TI_1\_S, TI_1\_E],\\
&\text{validTimeInterval}(TI_1),\\
&TI_2 = [TI_2\_S, TI_2\_E],\\
&\text{validTimeInterval}(TI_2),\\
&TI_1\_S = TI_2\_S, TI_1\_E@ < TI_2\_E.
\end{aligned} \quad (7.16)$$

7.2.6.3 Equal

Two events are equal (i.e., EQUALS) if they happen right at the same time. Rule (7.17) implements this relation.

$$\begin{aligned}
\text{equals}(TI_1, TI_2) : -\ &TI_1 = [TI_1\_S, TI_1\_E],\\
&\text{validTimeInterval}(TI_1),\\
&TI_2 = [TI_2\_S, TI_2\_E],\\
&\text{validTimeInterval}(TI_2),\\
&TI_1\_S = TI_2\_S, TI_1\_E = TI_2\_E.
\end{aligned} \quad (7.17)$$

7.2.6.4 Finish

One event finishes (i.e., FINISHES) another one if an occurrence of the first ends at the same time as an occurrence of the second event, but starts later. Rule (7.18) check this condition.

$$\begin{aligned}
\texttt{finishes}(TI_1, TI_2) :- \; & TI_1 = [TI_1\_S, TI_1\_E], \\
& \texttt{validTimeInterval}(TI_1), \\
& TI_2 = [TI_2\_S, TI_2\_E], \\
& \texttt{validTimeInterval}(TI_2), \\
& TI_2\_S@ < TI_1\_S, TI_1\_E = TI_2\_E.
\end{aligned} \qquad (7.18)$$

7.2.6.5 Meet

Two events meet (i.e., MEETS) each other when the interval of the first ends exactly when the interval of the second event starts. Hence, the condition $TI_1\_E = TI_2\_S$ in rule (7.19) is sufficient to detect this relation.

$$\begin{aligned}
\texttt{meets}(TI_1, TI_2) :- \; & TI_1 = [TI_1\_S, TI_1\_E], \\
& \texttt{validTimeInterval}(TI_1), \\
& TI_2 = [TI_2\_S, TI_2\_E], \\
& \texttt{validTimeInterval}(TI_2), \\
& TI_1\_E = TI_2\_S.
\end{aligned} \qquad (7.19)$$

7.3 Iterative and Aggregative Patterns

In this section, we show how unbound *iterations* of events – possibly in combination with *aggregate* functions – can be expressed within our defined formalism. We have introduced iterative and aggregative patterns against event streams in [ARFS11a].

7.3.1 From Event Rules to Event Iterative Rules

Many of formalisms, concerned with EP, feature operators indicating that an event may be iterated arbitrarily often. Mostly, the notation of these operators is borrowed from regular expressions in automata theory: the *Kleene star* (·*) matches zero or more occurrences whereas the *Kleene plus* (·+) indicates one or more occurrences.

For example, the pattern expression a SEQ b^+ SEQ c would match any of the event sequences *abc*, *abbc*, *abbbc* etc. It is easy to see that – given our semantics – this pattern expression is equivalent to the pattern a SEQ b SEQ c (as essentially, it allows for "skipping" occurring events)[11]. Likewise, all patterns in which this kind of Kleene iteration occurs can be transformed into non-iterative ones.

However, frequently iterative patterns are used in combination with *aggregate functions*, i.e., a value is accumulated over a sequence of events. Mostly, EP formalisms define

---

[11]Note that due to the chosen semantics, this encoding would also match sequences like *acbbc* or *abbacbc*. However, if wanted, these can be excluded by using the slightly more complex pattern $(a$ SEQ b SEQ $c)$ EQUALS NOT$(a$ OR $c).[a,c]$.

7.3. Iterative and Aggregative Patterns

new language primitives to accommodate this feature. Within ELE, this situation can be handled via recursive event rules.

As an example, assume `tempIncrease` event should be triggered whenever the temperature rises over a previous maximum, and further `tempAlarm` event is triggered if the maximum gets over 100 degrees Fahrenheit. For this, we have to iterate whenever there is a new maximum temperature indicated by the atomic `temp` events. This can be realized by the below set of rules.

$$\begin{aligned} \texttt{tempIncrease}(T) &\leftarrow \texttt{temp}(T). \\ \texttt{tempIncrease}(T_2) &\leftarrow \texttt{tempIncrease}(T_1) \text{ SEQ } \texttt{temp}(T_2) \\ &\quad \text{WHERE } T_2 > T_1. \\ \texttt{tempAlarm}(T) &\leftarrow \texttt{tempIncrease}(T) \text{ WHERE } T > 100. \end{aligned} \quad (7.20)$$

In the same vein, every aggregative pattern can be expressed by sets of recursive rules, where we introduce auxiliary events that carry the intermediate results of the aggregation as arguments.

As a further remark, note that for a given natural number n, the n-fold sequential execution of an event a (a pattern usually written as a^n) can be recognized by iteration(a,n) defined as follows:

$$\begin{aligned} \texttt{iteration}(a,1) &\leftarrow a. \\ \texttt{iteration}(a,k+1) &\leftarrow a \text{ SEQ } \texttt{iteration}(a,k). \end{aligned}$$

This allows us to express patterns where events are repeated many times in a compact way.

A common scenario in EP is to detect patterns on moving *length-based windows*. Such a pattern is detected when certain events are repeated as many times as the window length is. A sliding window moves on each new event to detect a new complex event (defined by the length of a window). The following rules implement such a pattern in ETALIS for the length equal to n (n is typically predefined):

$$\begin{aligned} \texttt{iteration}(a,1) &\leftarrow a. \\ \texttt{iteration}(a,k+1) &\leftarrow \text{NOT}(a).[a, \texttt{iteration}(a,k)]. \\ e &\leftarrow \texttt{iteration}(a,n). \end{aligned}$$

For instance, for $n=5$, the event e will be triggered every time when the system encounters five occurrences of the a event.

7.3.1.1 An Example Application with Iterative Rules

The following example demonstrates the usage of ELE by defining a common financial pattern called the "tick-shape" pattern [DGLO[+]09]. Let's consider a simple day trader pattern that looks for a peak followed by a continuous fall in price of stocks, followed by a rise in price. We are interested in a raise only if (and as soon as) it grows higher than the beginning price. The "tick-shape" pattern is monitored for each company symbol over online stock events:

$$\begin{aligned}
&\text{down}(I,P1,P2) \leftarrow \text{NOT}(\text{stock}(I,P)).[\text{stock}(I,P1),\text{stock}(I,P2)] \\
&\qquad \text{WHERE } P1 < P2. \\
&\text{down}(I,P1,P3) \leftarrow \text{NOT}(\text{stock}(I,P)).[\text{down}(I,P1,P2),\text{stock}(I,P3)] \\
&\qquad \text{WHERE } P2 > P3. \\
&\text{up}(I,P1) \leftarrow \text{stock}(I,P1). \\
&\text{up}(I,P2) \leftarrow \text{NOT}(\text{stock}(I,P)).[\text{up}(I,P1),\text{stock}(I,P2)] \\
&\qquad \text{WHERE } P1 < P2. \\
&\text{tickShape}(I) \leftarrow \text{down}(I,P1,P2) \text{ MEETS} \\
&\qquad \text{NOT}(\text{stock}(I,P)).[\text{up}(I,P3),\text{stock}(I,P4)] \\
&\qquad \text{WHERE } P3 < P1 \wedge P4 > P1.
\end{aligned} \qquad (7.21)$$

In this example, we first start detecting a short increase (in order to detect the peak) and subsequent fall in price using down$(I,P1,P2)$ iterative rules. Thereby, I takes the identifier of the monitored company, $P1$ the price at the peak directly preceding the decrease and $P2$ the price at the end of the interval. The usage of the NOT pattern ensures that no stock events in between are left out and hence, the decrease in price is monotone. Similarly we can detect a rise in price, defined by up$(I,P1)$ (where $P1$ assumes the price at the end of the interval). Finally, tickShape(I) will be triggered when a down event meets an up event which ends at a prize value below the preceding peak, and the next incoming stock event for I reports a prize above that peak value.

7.3.2 Implementation of Aggregative Patterns

In ETALIS Language for Events, *aggregate* functions are handled by utilizing *iterative* rules. The language offers a common set of aggregates: sum(Var) (sums the values of Var for all selected events), count (counts the number of solutions for all selected events from an unbound stream), avg (computes average, and is implemented as combination of sum and count), max(Var) (computes the maximum value of Var for all selected events from an unbound stream), and min(Var) (computes the minimum value of Var for all selected events)[12].

The aggregate functions are computed incrementally, adhering to an event at a time processing (see Section 5.6). The aggregate functions are computed incrementally, by starting with an initial value for the increment, and iterating the aggregate function over events. However, window size and the sliding window require us to use efficient data

---
[12]Custom aggregate functions (using different built-in operators) can also be implemented with no further restrictions.

7.3. Iterative and Aggregative Patterns

structures and algorithms in logic programming (e.g., in Prolog) to obtain fast implementations.

For any aggregate function we implement the following two rules.

$$
\begin{aligned}
&\texttt{iteration}(StartCntr = 0, StartVal) \leftarrow \texttt{start\_event}(StartVal). \\
&\texttt{iteration}(OldCntr + 1, NewVal) \leftarrow \\
&\quad \texttt{iteration}(OldCntr, OldVal) \text{ SEQ } \texttt{a}(AggArg) \\
&\quad \text{WHERE } \{\texttt{assert}(AggArg), \\
&\quad\quad \texttt{window}(WndwSize, OldCntr, OldVal, AggArg, NewVal)\}.
\end{aligned}
\tag{7.22}
$$

The first rule starts the iteration process (when `start_event` occurs with its initial value (*StartVal*) and possible condition on that value (see the first rule). The second rule defines the iteration itself, i.e., whenever an event participating in the iteration occurs (event a), it will trigger the rule and generate a new `iteration` event.

In each iteration it is possible to calculate certain operations (an aggregate function). To achieve this, the iterative rule contains the static part (the WHERE clause) for two reasons: to save data from the seen events as history relevant with respect to the aggregation function (see `assert`(*AggArg*)), and to compute the sliding window incrementally (i.e., to delete events that expired from the sliding window and calculate the aggregate function on the rest, see the `window` expression).

The functionality of `assert` predicate is simply to add data on which aggregation is applied (i.e., an aggregation argument *AggArg*) to database. Sliding `window` functionality is also simple, and it is realised by rule (7.23).

$$
\begin{aligned}
&\texttt{window}(WndwSize, OldCntr, OldVal, AggArg, NewVal) : - \\
&OldCntr + 1 >= WindowSize - > \\
&\texttt{retract}(LastItem), \\
&\texttt{spec\_aggregate}(OldValue, AggArg, NewValue); \\
&\texttt{spec\_aggregate}(OldValue, AggArg, NewValue).
\end{aligned}
\tag{7.23}
$$

In Prolog an "if-then-else" statement, e.g., if *condition* then do_it_1 else do_it_2, is expressed as the following statement: $condition- > do\_it_1$; do_it_2. We use the "if-then-else" statement in rule (7.23) to check whether the current counter value (i.e., the incremented old counter, $OldCntr + 1$) exceeds the window size in which case we `retract` the last item from the window and compute a specific aggregate function (by `spec_aggregate`). Recall that the new data element (*AggArg*) was previously added by the iteration rule (`assert`(*AggArg*)). If the counter does not exceed the window's value, we simply compute a specific aggregate function (see the last line in rule (7.23)).

Based on these iterative pattern and sliding window rules we can implement other various aggregation functions. The iterative rules (7.24) implement the sum aggregate function on certain values from selected events.

As we already explained, the iteration begins when start_event occurs and sets the *StartVal*. The iteration is further continued whenever event a occurs. Note that events start_event and a can be of the same type. We can additionally have a WHERE clause to set filter conditions for both *StartVal* and *AggArg*. We omit filters here to keep the pattern rules simple, however it is clear that neither every start_event must start the iteration nor that every a must be accepted in an ongoing iteration. The assert predicate adds new data (*AggArg*) to the current sum, and the window rule deducts the expired (last) value from the window in order to produce *NewSum*.

Note that the same rules can be used to compute the moving average (avg) (hence we omit to repeat them here). As we have the current sum and the counter value, we can simply add $AvgVal = NewSum/(OldCntr + 1)$ in the WHERE clause of the second rule.

$$\begin{aligned}&\text{sum}(StartCntr = 0, StartVal) \leftarrow \texttt{start\_event}(StartVal).\\&\text{sum}(OldCntr+1, NewSum) \leftarrow \\&\quad \text{sum}(OldCntr+1, OldSum) \text{ SEQ } \texttt{a}(AggArg)\\&\quad \text{WHERE } \{\texttt{assert}(AggArg),\\&\quad\quad \texttt{window}(WndwSize, OldCntr,\\&\quad\quad\quad OldSum + AggArg, AggArg, NewSum)\}.\end{aligned}$$ (7.24)

$$\begin{aligned}&\texttt{window}(WndwSize, OldCntr, CurrSum, NewSum) : -\\&\quad OldCntr + 1 >= WindowSize - >\\&\quad \texttt{retract}(LastItem),\\&\quad NewSum = CurrSum - LastItem;\\&\quad NewSum = CurrSum - LastItem.\end{aligned}$$

In general, the iterative rules give us possibility to realize essentially any aggregate functions on event streams, no matter whether events are *atomic* or *complex* (note that there is no assumption whether event a is atomic or complex). We can also have *multiple* aggregations, computed on a single iterative pattern (when they are supposed to be calculated on the same event stream). For instance, the same iterative rules can be used to compute the average and the standard deviation. This feature can potentially save computation resources and increase the overall performance. Finally, it is worth noting that we are not constrained to compute the Kleene plus closure only on *sequences* of events (as it is common in other approaches [ADGI08, MeMa09]). With no restriction, instead of SEQ we can also put other event operators such as AND or PAR .

The following iterative pattern computes the *maximum* over a sliding window of events.

7.3. Iterative and Aggregative Patterns

$$\max(StartCntr = 0, StartVal) \leftarrow \texttt{start\_event}(StartVal).$$
$$\max(OldCntr + 1, NewMax) \leftarrow$$
$$\quad \max(OldCntr + 1, OldMax) \text{ SEQ } \texttt{a}(AggArg)$$
$$\quad \text{WHERE } \{\texttt{assert}(AggArg),$$
$$\quad \quad \texttt{window}(WndwSize, OldCntr, NewMax)\}.$$
$$(7.25)$$

$$\texttt{window}(WndwSize, OldCntr, NewMax) : -$$
$$\quad OldCntr + 1 >= WindowSize - >$$
$$\quad \texttt{retract}(LastItem), get(NewMax);$$
$$\quad get(NewMax).$$

The rules are very similar to rules for other aggregation functions (e.g., see rules (7.25)). However there is one difference in implementation of the window rule. The history of events necessary for computing aggregations on sliding windows can be kept in the memory using different data structures. Essentially we need a *queue* where the latest event (or its aggregation value) is inserted into the queue and the oldest event from the window is removed. For example, we implemented efficiently the sum and the average aggregates using two data structures: *stacks* and *difference lists*. Stacks can be easily implemented in Prolog using *assert* and *retract* commands, and difference list are convenient as the cost for deleting the oldest element that expired from the window is O(1).

Queues with difference lists are however not good enough for computing aggregations such as the *maximum* and the *minimum*. For these functions, searching the maximum (or the minimum) in a sliding window, when the current maximum (minimum) is deleted, requires a price of O(Window) (to find the new maximum or the minimum). Still to provide an efficient implementation we use balanced binary search trees. We know what is the event that will be deleted from the history queue. We keep a red-black (RB) balanced tree to be indexed on the aggregate argument, so that we can do cleanup of overdue events efficiently. In each node, we keep a counter to know how many times an event with the aforementioned key came. At each time the maximum (minimum) is the rightmost (leftmost) leaf. Additionally we can also keep the timestamp of events. This allows us also to prune events (data) based on the *time* with respect to the sliding window. With the balanced tree this search is reduced to O(logN). For instance, for a window of 1000 events, the price of 1000 operations is reduced to at most 10 at each step ($2^{10} = 1024$).

Pruning events based on their timestamps is the basis for *time-based* sliding windows. So far we have discussed *count-based* sliding windows (i.e., the pruning is based on the number of events in the window). For event patterns with time-based sliding windows, we do not need the window rule (e.g., rule (7.23)). Instead, we use only iterative patterns with a garbage collector (set to prune events out of the specified sliding window). Events are stored internally in order as they come (we index them on the timestamp information $[T_2, T_1]$). This eases the process of pruning expired events using our memory management techniques, presented in Section 10.3.

The *count* aggregation is typically used on time-based sliding windows, see pattern (7.26). Whenever a relevant event occurs (e.g., event *a*), its timestamp will be asserted by the *getCount* predicate and the current counter number will be returned. Additionally we set a garbage collector to incrementally remove outdated timestamps, so that *getCount* always returns the correct result. In the same vein, we have realized other aggregate functions with the time-based sliding windows (i.e., sum, avg, max, min).

$$\begin{aligned}&\texttt{iteration}(StartCntr = 0, StartVal) \leftarrow \texttt{start\_event}(StartVal).\\&\texttt{iteration}(NewCntr) \leftarrow \\&\quad\texttt{iteration}(OldCntr) \text{ SEQ } \texttt{a}(AggArg)\\&\quad\text{WHERE } \{NewCntr = \texttt{getCount}([T_2, T_1]), \texttt{window}(3min)\}.\end{aligned} \quad (7.26)$$

7.4 Consumption Policies

When detecting a complex event, there may be several event occurrences (of the same type), that could be used to form that complex event. *Consumption policies* (or event contexts) deal with the issue of selecting particular occurrence(s), which will be used in the detection of a complex event. For example, consider again rule (7.1) from Subsection 7.2.1 – which we rewrite for convenience as rule (7.27) below – and a sequence of atomic events that happened in the following order: a(1), a(2), a(3), b(4), b(5), c(6) where an event attribute denotes a time point when an event instance has occurred.

$$e \leftarrow \texttt{a} \text{ SEQ } \texttt{b} \text{ SEQ } \texttt{c}. \quad (7.27)$$

We expect that, when an event of type b occurs, an intermediate event ie must be triggered. However, the question is, which occurrence of a will be selected to build that event, a(1), a(2) or a(3) (the same question applies for event b)?

According to the semantics of ELE, presented in Section 6.3, all instances of a's will be selected. Such a policy is known as *unrestricted* policy [ChMi94, YoBa05]. Note that if we define a policy which selects only a(1), or only a(3), the policy could damage the declarative property of the language. This might happen as different policies may cause different orders in which event rules are evaluated (see discussion on consumption policies in Section 5.1). On the other hand, consumption policies are useful and well adopted in EP. Therefore, we present how common consumption policies can be implemented in ELE. However note that this section should be treated as an extension of the language – related to practical considerations of ELE – rather than an integral part of the language itself.

In the remaining part of this section we illustrate three widely used consumption policies: *recent*, *chronological*, and *unrestricted* policy [ChMi94, YoBa05], and show how they can be easily implemented by rules in our framework. Other, custom-based, polices could be realised in a similar manner. For instance, in [ADGI08] there have been defined:

7.4. Consumption Policies

strict contiguity, *partition contiguity*, *skip till next match*, and *skip till any match*. These policies are defined in order to extract valid events from unbound stream of events according to certain contiguity requirements. Further discussion related to these policies is out of scope of this work. However, it is worth noting that, due to the fact that our formalism is based on event at a time processing (see Section 5.6), an implementation of these, and various other policies in our formalism is possible too.

7.4.1 Consumption Policies Defined on Time Points

In the above example, we assumed that the stream of events a(1), a(2), a(3), b(4), b(5), c(6) contains only atomic events.

Recent Policy. With this policy, the most recent event of its type is considered to construct complex events. In our example, when a(2) occurs it will replace a(1). Similarly, when a(3) occurs it will replace a(2). This means that when b(4) occurs, it will be matched with a(3) to compose ie(3,4). It is said that the matched events are *consumed* as these particular event instances will not be available for the considered rule after the matching. To trigger another ie event (by the same rule) we need another pair of "fresh" instances of a and b.

The recent policy could be modified still to keep replaced events (instead of deleting them). For example, after detection of the ie(3,4) event, the a(2) event would be still available to rule (7.27). This means when b(5) occurs, the pair, a(2) and b(5), will be selected to form ie(2,5). The ie(2,5) event replaces the less recent occurrence, ie(3,4)[13]. Finally, when event c(6) occurs, event e(2,6) will be triggered.

The recent policy can be easily implemented in our framework. Let us consider Algorithm 1, particularly the rule which inserts a goal (in our example, this will be goal(b,a,ie)). Whenever an instance of a occurs, there will be a new goal inserted with a corresponding timestamp. For instance, for a(1), the goal(b(_),a(1),ie(_,_)) is added; for a(2), the goal(b(_),a(2),ie(_,_)) will be asserted, and so forth). If we insert these goals into the database using the last in first out (LIFO) structure, we obtain the *recent policy*. In our prototype implementation, this is done with a rule of the following form:

$$\text{assert}(\text{goal}(X)) \colon -\text{asserta}(\text{goal}(X)). \tag{7.28}$$

asserta is a standard Prolog built-in that adds a term to the *beginning* of the database. Whenever a goal is inserted to the database, it is put on the top of a relation. Hence whenever we read a goal, the one inserted last will be returned.

Chronological Policy. This policy "consumes" events in chronological order. In our example, this means that when b(4) occurs it will match to a(1) (although a(2) and a(3)

---
[13]The less recent occurrence of two intervals is judged based on the intervals' end (T_2). In the following section this issue is discussed in more details.

happened in the meantime). Looking chronologically, a(1) happened first and hence is one to be selected. After a(1) any other instance of a is ignored till the next b happens.

Similarly – as for the recent policy – we may want to keep other instance of a. For example, in our case a(1) and b(4) will form ie(1,4), and further a(2) followed by b(5) will trigger ie(2,5). When c(6) happens, it will trigger e(1,6).

It is straightforward to implement the chronological policy too. Now, the goals in Algorithm 1 are inserted in the first in first out (FIFO) mode. Equivalently, we use the following rule to realize the chronological policy:

$$\text{assert}(\text{goal}(X)) := \text{assertz}(\text{goal}(X)). \tag{7.29}$$

assertz is a standard Prolog built-in that adds a term to the *end* of the database. Whenever a goal is inserted to the database, it is put at the end of a relation. Consequently, whenever we read a goal, the first inserted goal will be returned first.

Unrestricted Policy. In this policy, all occurrences are valid. Consequently, no event is consumed (and no event is deleted unless it expires e.g., from a time window), which makes this policy not suitable in many practical cases. Going back to our example, this implies that we detect the following instances of ie: ie(1,4), ie(2,4), ie(3,4), ie(1,5), ie(2,5), ie(3,5). The event e will be triggered just as many times, that is: e(1,6), e(2,6), e(3,6)...

We obtain the unrestricted policy simply by not using the construct for deleting goals (i.e., retract) from the database. If we replace the rule for b(1) in Algorithm 1 with rule (7.30), even consumed goals will not be deleted from the database[14]. Hence they will be available for future compositions.

$$b(1, T_3, T_4) := \text{goal}(b(T_3, T_4), a(T_1, T_2), ie), T_2 < T_3, ie(T_1, T_4). \tag{7.30}$$

Consumption policies are an important part of an EP framework. We notice that different policies change the semantics of event operators. For example, with the same operator we have detected different complex events (the recent policy detects e(2,6), while the chronological policy detects e(1,6)).

7.4.2 Consumption Policies Defined on Time Intervals

So far we have discussed consumption policies assuming that atomic events (in an input stream) are considered. As atomic events happen in time points, it is possible to establish a *total order* of their occurrences. Consequently it is easy, for example, to answer which event instance (out of two) happened more recently. When we deal with complex events

---

[14]Note that they can still be deleted if a time window is defined, and it expires

7.4. Consumption Policies

($T_1 \neq T_2$), a total order is not always possible. This subsection provides possible options in defining consumption policies in such a case.

Recent Policy. Let us consider the following sequence of input events: a(1,30), a(15,30), b(35,50). In our example rule (7.27) (from Section 7.4), the question now is which instance of event a is more *recent*, a(1,30) or a(15,30)? In our opinion, this question depends on a particular application domain. There are three possible options. First, an event detected on a *longer event duration* is selected to be the recent one (i.e., a(1,30)). This option is suitable when aggregation functions (for example, sum, average and so forth) are applied along time windows. Hence, events detected on longer durations possibly reflect more accurate results. The second option is to choose an event with a *shorter duration* (i.e., a(15,30)). This preference is suitable when indeed more recent events are desired. For example, we are interested in data (carried by events) that are as up to date as possible. Finally, the third possibility is to pick up an event instance based on *data value selection* i.e., non-temporal properties. For instance, events ending at the same time, a(1,30,$X, Vol = 1000$) and a(15,30,$X, Vol = 10000$), are selected based on an attribute value (e.g., greater volume *Vol*).

We implement these three cases with rules (7.31)-(7.33). When an a occurs, there is a policy check performed. In rule (7.31), for two events with the same ending (i.e., a(T_1, T_3) and a(T_2, T_3)) we make sure that one with a longer path ($T_1 < T_2$) is selected. In rule (7.32), we replace goals if the time condition is opposite ($T_1 > T_2$). Finally, in data value (or attribute value) selection, we distinguish based on a chosen attribute (e.g., $Vol_1 > Vol_2$).

$$\begin{aligned}&\texttt{event\_trigger(a}(T_1,T_3,Vol_1)):- \\ &\quad \texttt{goal(\_,a}(T_2,T_3,\_,\_),\_), T_1 < T_2, \\ &\quad \texttt{retract(goal(\_,a}(T_2,T_3,\_,\_),\_)), \\ &\quad \texttt{assert(goal(\_,a}(T_1,T_3,Vol_1),\_)).\end{aligned} \quad (7.31)$$

$$\begin{aligned}&\texttt{event\_trigger(a}(T_1,T_3,Vol_1)):- \\ &\quad \texttt{goal(\_,a}(T_2,T_3,\_,\_),\_), T_1 > T_2, \\ &\quad \texttt{retract(goal(\_,a}(T_2,T_3,\_,\_),\_)), \\ &\quad \texttt{assert(goal(\_,a}(T_1,T_3,Vol_1),\_)).\end{aligned} \quad (7.32)$$

$$\begin{aligned}&\texttt{event\_trigger(a}(T_1,T_3,Vol_1)):- \\ &\quad \texttt{goal(\_,a}(T_2,T_3,Vol_2,\_),\_), Vol_1 > Vol_2, \\ &\quad \texttt{retract(goal(\_,a}(T_2,T_3,Vol_2),\_)), \\ &\quad \texttt{assert(goal(\_,a}(T_1,T_3,Vol_1),\_)).\end{aligned} \quad (7.33)$$

Policy rules (7.31)-(7.33) are fired before inserting a new goal. It is worth noting that such an update of a goal is performed incrementally. We pay an additional price for forcing a particular consumption policy. However, the policy rules (7.31)-(7.33) are rather simple rules. In return, they ensure that no more than one goal with the same timestamp (with respect to a certain policy) is kept in memory during the processing. Therefore the policy rules enable a better *memory management* in our framework.

Chronological Policy. The main principle in the implementation of this policy is the same as in the recent policy. The only difference is that now we consider the same start and the different ending in multiple event occurrences $(a(T_1,T_2),a(T_1,T_3))$. To implement this policy, rule (7.31) will now contain the time condition from rule (7.32), and vice versa. Rule (7.33) remains unchanged, as well as *unrestricted policy* (which is the same as for the case with atomic events, see Subsection 7.4.1).

8

The Event Processing Network in ETALIS

Event-driven systems are conceptually based on the notion of an Event Processing Network (EPN). EPN consist of event producers, consumers, Event Processing Agents (EPAs), and channels. There exist several types of EPAs where each type fulfils a certain functionality of EP. Purpose of an EPN is to orchestrate EPAs in order to achieve a high-level functionality required by an event-driven system. We have introduced the concept of an EPN in Section 2.3. For more details about this topic, the interested reader is referred to [EtNi10, ChSc10].

As presented in Figure 2.1 (in Chapter 2), a typical EPN is not monolithic. Instead it is composed of a number of EPAs. We assume that an instance of a running ETALIS implements an agent. EPAs do the actual processing of events in the network, hence in the remaining part of this section we focus on specification of different EPAs in ELE. We show how to implement common EPAs in ELE, including filtering, pattern detection, projection, translation, enrichment, splitting, aggregation, and composition. Moreover we present EPAs that – apart from events – deal with knowledge processing tasks too.

In this section we do not provide additional constructs of the language. Instead, we show how common EPAs operations can be implemented with the existing expressive power of the language.

8.1 Filtering

We start describing different agents in an EPN by a *filtering* EPA. A filtering EPA is used to extract relevant events with respect to an EP application, and hence to increase the overall performance of an EPN.

A filter operation is specified by a filter expression. ETALIS supports two types of filters: an *event type* filter and an *event content* filter.

8.1.1 Event Type Filter

This type of a filter filters out events based on event types. We may have a filter expression that filters out event instances of certain event types. In ETALIS, this type of a filter is implemented by default, since it is built-in in its underlying execution model (see Chapter 7). Namely, user defined pattern rules are transformed into EDBC rules. To trigger an EDBC rule, an event must unify with the rule head. Events that unify with no rule head are ignored. Hence, ETALIS does event type filtering automatically (i.e., only event types – that are used in specification of an event program (or an agent) – are processed, thereby ignoring events of other event types.

8.1.2 Event Content Filter

In general, a filter expression of a content filter can be a function computed from terms of an event instance. In ETALIS, a content filter expression is typically specified in the WHERE clause (see Section 6.2). For example, rule (8.1) filters out sensor events with values for X greater than 10, or values for Y less than or equal to 20. It is said that an event passes a filter if an expression in the WHERE clause evaluates to *true*. Since ETALIS has been implemented in Prolog, it supports all comparison Prolog operations in a filter expression (e.g., greater than, less than, equal, not equal, greater than or equal to and so forth), arithmetic operations (addition, subtraction, multiplication, division and modulo), and logic connectives (conjunction, disjunction and negation)[1].

Apart from the WHERE clause, the content filtering may additionally be achieved in the following way. Rule (8.1) filters out a sensor reading about 'wind'. There may exist other types of sensor reading too, e.g., 'temperature', 'air pressure' and so forth. Since in LP a goal variable may be a priori bound to a certain value, this feature enables ETALIS to filter the content of events with no additional implementation effort.

$$\text{windReading}(X,Y) \leftarrow \text{sensor}('wind',X,Y) \\ \text{WHERE } \{X > 10, Y \leq 20\}. \tag{8.1}$$

---

[1] Essentially ETALIS implementation accepts any valid Prolog expression in the WHERE clause, including features that are beyond ELE.

It is worth mentioning that ETALIS supports *dynamic filtering*, i.e., filtering with a changing filter expression. In general, rules in ETALIS may dynamically be changed (added and removed). This feature enables us to change a filtering expression too. Suppose a merchant service accept payments for goods with floating prices. Depending on supply and demand in the market, the merchant service may lower or increase thresholds for bid prices. Dynamic filtering enables to automatically change a filter expression based on an external decision component.

Finally, note that in this presentation of the filtering EPA we did not specify whether an EPA operats on atomic or complex events. In ETALIS, there is no conceptual difference in applying an EPA operation to either of them. This observation applies to filtering, as well as to remaining EPAs presented in this section.

8.2 Pattern Detection

In ETALIS, *pattern detection* (or *pattern matching*) relates to the process of matching events – represented as ground atoms – according to predefined patterns. Patterns are expressed as bodies of ELE rules. As soon as a rule body gets satisfied by occurring events, a complex event – specified by the rule head – is inferred. We have already presented the pattern detection capabilities of ELE in Chapter 6. Essentially, the language supports patterns built by using sequence, conjunction, disjunction, negation, concurrency, Allen's interval-based relations [Alle83], time window-based patterns and iterative and aggregative patterns (see Section 7.3). Also in the remaining parts of this work, we will demonstrate a number of pattern matching examples, most notably in Chapter 12 and Chapter 13. Therefore in this subsection we skip further discussion on this topic.

8.3 Transformation

In Section 2.3 we have seen what kind of transformations may be applied to events. In this section we will show how each of these transformations may be realised in ETALIS.

8.3.1 Projection

The *project* EPA projects out certain terms carried by an input event, similarly as a relation in relational algebra is projected on certain attributes.

The following rule demonstrates how certain terms (event data) are projected out. We consider stock events as provided by Google Finance service[2]. Suppose a project agent, containing rule (8.2), receives stock events and produces currentPrice events. A stock event includes information about a company ID, a stock exchange name, currency

---
[2]http://www.google.com/finance

in which prices are given, the current price, the price change, and the percentage of the price change, respectively. The projected event, in turn, contains only information on the company ID, and the price.

$$\texttt{stock}(CompanyID, Price) \leftarrow \\ \texttt{stock}(CompanyID, Exchange, Currency, Price, Change, PercChg). \quad (8.2)$$

In practise, we usually write a single rule to combine two or more operations. For instance, projection rule (8.2) could be accompanied with a filter expression, or we could detect a pattern combining two or more events, and then to project out certain terms in the derived event. This observation holds for other EPAs too. Our intention in this chapter is, however, to focus on implementation of each EPA operation. Throughout this work we will see many event pattern rules that combine more than one operation.

8.3.2 Translation

The *translate* EPA translates an input event into an output event according to a translation function. Suppose that `stock` events have prices in US Dollars (USD), and a stock trading application deals with prices in Euros (EUR). Given the currency ratio between EUR and USD, rule (8.3) translates prices carried by events. Additionally, it assigns *Currency* type with a new constant 'EUR' (instead of 'USD').

$$\texttt{stock}(CompanyID, Exchange,'EUR', Price_2, Change, PercChg) \leftarrow \\ \texttt{stock}(CompanyID, Exchange,'USD', Price_1, Change, PercChg) \quad (8.3) \\ \text{WHERE } Price_2 \text{ is } (Price_1 * 1.45).$$

Various other arithmetic and string operations may be employed as translation functions, too.

8.3.3 Enrichment

The *enrich* EPA can copy, modify, or insert new terms into the input event. New terms are usually taken from a global state element.

In various EP applications it is common that few agents access global state data, represented as static or slowly changing data or knowledge. In ETALIS, global state data can be captured either in a database or in an ontology. This data may be used to *enrich* an event with additional information. For instance – whenever a `sensor` event occurs – a `temperature` event is triggered. The `temperature` event consists of the initial event data – a sensor `Id`, and the current reading value X – *enriched* by additional information. The additional information is taken from a database relation *sensor_info*, and can be pulled by a sensor store `Id`. The `sensor_info` relation contains information about sensors, including the sensor location (*Loc*), measurement unit for each sensor (*MUnit*, e.g., either expressed in Fahrenheit or Celsius), and the sensor precision (*MPrec*, e.g., error rate below 5% or below 1%).

$$\text{temperature}(Id, X, Loc, MUnit, MPrec) \leftarrow \text{sensor}(Id,'temp', X) \\ \text{WHERE sensor\_info}(Id, Loc, MUnit, MPrec). \quad (8.4)$$

In the rule pattern above, the relation *store_info* contains *explicit* data. With no restriction, it could also contain a changing (updatable) data; or *implicit* knowledge derived by rules, possibly spanning over multiple relations or involving *recursions*, and so forth.

8.3.4 Splitting

The *split* EPA performs the same operation as the translation EPA, except that it can emit more than one output event. Each output event may have its own translation function associated with it. The following rules implement a *split* EPA with a translation function similar to example rule (8.3). When the agent receives a stock event, there will be three copies of the output event created, each produced by applying a certain translation function (e.g., the currency conversion).

$$\begin{aligned}
\text{stock}(Id,'EUR',Price) &\leftarrow \text{stock}(Id,'USD',Price) \\
&\text{WHERE } Price_2 \text{ is } (Price_1 * 0.73039). \\
\text{stock}(Id,'CNY',Price) &\leftarrow \text{stock}(Id,'USD',Price) \\
&\text{WHERE } Price_2 \text{ is } (Price_1 * 6.38296). \\
\text{stock}(Id,'CHF',Price) &\leftarrow \text{stock}(Id,'USD',Price) \\
&\text{WHERE } Price_2 \text{ is } (Price_1 * 0.89208).
\end{aligned} \quad (8.5)$$

The *split* EPA is also used in situations where a certain event needs to be multiplied and distributed to interested parties. For example, consider an automated stock brokerage system that sells stocks to its clients. Data about clients are stored in a client relation (8.7). In particular, the client relation contains a client id (*Cid*), a stock id (*Id*) which the client is interested to buy, and the amount of wanted stocks (*Amt*). Different brokerage agents process stocks for different clients. Hence when a stock is reported to the system, the event is multiplied as many times as there are clients interested in that stock. That is, the stock *Id* is matched with *Id* of the client relation. For instance, for an occurrence of a stock(*goog*, 515) event, two copies of the stock event would be created, namely stock(*kavx*, *goog*, 515, 3815) and stock(*kcqt*, *goog*, 515, 1815).

To iterate over a static relation and avoid writing multiple rules (as in example rules (8.5)), we have implemented an EVENT_MULTIPLY predicate that serves as a macro for the multiply operation[3], see rule (8.6).

$$\text{stock}(Cid, Id, Price, Amt) \leftarrow \text{stock}(Id, Price) \\ \text{EVENT\_MULTIPLY client}(Cid, Id, Amt). \quad (8.6)$$

---
[3]Implementation details can be found at http://code.google.com/p/etalis/

$$\text{client}(kavx, goog, 3815)$$
$$\text{client}(kblu, msft, 2995) \quad\quad (8.7)$$
$$\text{client}(kcqt, goog, 1815)$$

8.3.5 Aggregation

The *aggregate* EPA takes multiple events as input and produces a single derived event by applying an aggregation function over input events. Aggregation is a stateful operation since output of this operation can contain information derived form more than one input event. That is, the results of applying an aggregation to an event needs to be saved for events that are yet to come. Hence to implement an aggregation EPA we utilise *iterative* rules. In each iteration an aggregation function is applied to an event that has just received, and a derived event – which keeps the current state of the aggregation function – is triggered.

We have already discussed iterative rules and aggregations in Section 7.3. In particular, we have shown how a common set of aggregates, such as sum, count, average, maximum, and minimum are computed. Other domain-dependant aggregate functions, using different built-in operators, can also be implemented with no restrictions. In Section 13.2 we will show few such examples. Hence, similarly as for the pattern detection EPA, we will skip further discussion about the aggregate EPA here.

8.3.6 Composition

A *compose agent* joins events[4] form one stream against events from the other one, similarly as two relations are joined in databases. Joining events need to meet a *match condition* (e.g., the same value of the join attribute).

Let us borrow an example from [EtNi10] to demonstrate use of composition of events. Suppose that a highway authority wishes to measure the speed of vehicles travelling over a particular section of highway. It installs a camera at either end, one to produce an arrival event whenever a vehicle enters the section, and the other to produce a departure event when a vehicle leaves, and then has to match the arrival event for a particular vehicle with the departure event for the same vehicle so that it can see how long the vehicle has spent in the section of the road.

The following rule represents a join event obtained as a match of an arrival event with a departure event for the same vehicle *Id*. We notice that composition of events in ELE can be obtained as a simple sequence of events, since in LP join is achieved through the unification of terms on common variables. Further on, recall that each event in ELE is defined on an interval $[T_1, T_2]$. By the definition of the SEQ operator, the join event will

---
[4]more precisely, by events we mean event instances.

be defined on an interval giving exactly the duration that a vehicle has spent travelling over a particular section of highway.

In other examples, the order of joining events may be irrelevant, in which case SEQ can be replaced by AND.

$$\text{join}(Id) \leftarrow \text{arrival}(Id) \text{ SEQ departure}(Id). \quad (8.8)$$

Note that, in general case, arrival and departure events come from two different streams. The current implementation of ETALIS – presented in Chapter 12 – is however limited to a single thread. To support multi-threading we use Java threads that may concurrently feed an ETALIS agent with events from multiple event providers. Currently, it is programmer's responsibility to implement how events from multiple providers are multiplexed into a stream. This limitation of ETALIS is a topic of our future work.

A compose agent may also join an event stream with a static relation (or a database relation) as shown in rule 8.9.

$$c(Id) \leftarrow \text{departure}(Id) \text{ WHERE arrival}(Id). \quad (8.9)$$

Suppose there exist more arrival events to be matched with one departure event. In this case, a static relation containing arrival events would serve as a buffer. The size of the buffer may be defined as a (count or time) window. For example, while new arrival events could be asserted on the fly as aggregation values were asserted in rule 7.22, a rule similar to rule 7.23 (without spec_aggregate) could be used to maintain the buffer size.

8.4 Knowledge-Based Event Processing Agents

So far, we have described how common agents in EP can be implemented in our framework. In this section, we explore an additional feature, namely the knowledge processing and reasoning capability. This feature is enabled by the logic nature of our approach.

8.4.1 Event Processing with Transitive Closure Rules

To give the reader a feeling how *deductive* rules can be used in combination with the rest of the ETALIS framework, we present an illustrative example with transitive closure.

Let us observe a common situation in aviation, related to detection of *clear air turbulence* (cat) on jet streams. Jet streams are important for aviation, as flight time can be dramatically affected by either flying with the flow or against the flow of a jet stream. Clear air turbulence, a potential hazard to the safety of aircraft passengers, is often found in a jet stream's vicinity. In the following example, we define a JetStreamWarning event as a dangerous situation whenever a clear air turbulence (denoted as a cat event) is followed by an airplane position event.

$$\text{jetStreamWarning}(Loc_1, Loc_2) \leftarrow$$
$$\big(\text{cat}(Loc_1) \text{ AND } \text{airplane}(Loc_2)\big).5hours \qquad (8.10)$$
$$\text{WHERE jetLink}(Loc_2, Loc_1).$$

$$\text{jetLink}(X,Y) :- \text{linked}(X,Y).$$
$$\text{jetLink}(X,Z) :- \text{linked}(X,Y), \text{jetLink}(Y,Z). \qquad (8.11)$$

$$\text{linked}(1,2).$$
$$\text{linked}(2,3).$$
$$\text{linked}(3,4). \qquad (8.12)$$
$$\ldots$$

To make sure that the cat affects the observed jet stream, we deploy transitive closure rules (8.11). The rules span over a set of facts (8.12), defining the jet stream as a set of connected points. Since both, the cat and the airplane events change their positions, the rules check whether they belong to the same jet stream. Note that the check is useful for an airplane only if position of a detected cat is in the front of the current position of the airplane.

Transitive closure rules (8.11) are deductive rules[5], and together with the linked relation (8.12), they enable us to perform on the fly *reasoning* (i.e., to examine whether a new clear air turbulence is dangerous with respect to an observed jet stream or not).

According to the US National Business Aviation Association[6] (NBAA) air routes are *dynamic*. This means that they can be modified as needed in order to take advantage of favorable winds that change on a daily basis. Hence a solution based only on querying of jet stream static points would not be optimal. Concluding this example, we note that since facts (8.12) are dynamic, an occurrence of a new cat is not known in advance, and the airplane position is changing too. Hence our approach to combine EP with deductive reasoning is an appropriate approach for on the fly jet stream monitoring.

8.4.2 Rule-Based Event Classification

As a next example we demonstrate the use of background rules for events *classification* – viewed as a sort of rule-based filtering operation (see Subsection 8.1.1).

Let us consider again the heat index – similar to the heat index rule from Section 6.4 – that is an index which combines air temperature and relative humidity in an attempt to determine the human perceived equivalent temperature (how hot it feels).

---

[5]The example could be extended to deal with cat areas (instead of cat points). Also, by introducing an id to a jet stream, we could monitor more than one jet stream at the same time.
[6]NBAA: http://www.nbaa.org/ops/airspace/issues/wind-routes/

8.4. Knowledge-Based Event Processing Agents

In particular, we are interested to automatically generate *shade values* of the heat index. For instance, whenever there is a new sensor reading event (heatIndex), we want the system to generate a human readable note (e.g., caution, danger etc.). Additionally, the system needs to generate an area for which the note applies to. Rule (8.13) defines such a pattern.

$$\begin{aligned}&\texttt{heatIndexEffect}(\textit{Note}, \textit{Area}) \leftarrow \\ &\quad \texttt{heatIndex}(\textit{Loc}, \textit{Index}) \\ &\quad \text{WHERE } \{\texttt{shadeValuesRule}(\textit{Index}, \textit{Note}), \texttt{areaRule}(\textit{Loc}, \textit{Area})\}.\end{aligned} \quad (8.13)$$

Example rules (8.14) – written in Prolog syntax – serve to filter out the heat *Index* values smaller than 80, and classify the remaining ones into four categories: *'Caution'* (between 80 and 90); *'ExtremeCaution'* (between 90 and 105); *'Danger'* (between 105 and 130); and *'ExtremeDanger'* for values greater than or equal to 130.

Note that in [EtNi10] this functionality is known as filtering with *context partitions*, as the heat Index event carry index values which belong to a fixed number of context partitions (shaded values).

$$\begin{aligned}&\texttt{shadeValuesRule}(\textit{Index},'\textit{Caution}') : - \\ &\quad 80 =< \textit{Index}, \textit{Index} < 90, !. \\ &\texttt{shadeValuesRule}(\textit{Index},'\textit{ExtremeCaution}') : - \\ &\quad 90 =< \textit{Index}, \textit{Index} < 105, !. \\ &\texttt{shadeValuesRule}(\textit{Index},'\textit{Danger}') : - \\ &\quad 105 =< \textit{Index}, \textit{Index} < 130, !. \\ &\texttt{shadeValuesRule}(\textit{Index},'\textit{ExtremeDanger}') : - \\ &\quad 130 =< \textit{Index}, !.\end{aligned} \quad (8.14)$$

Further on, background knowledge specified by rules (8.15) can be used to focus on certain monitoring areas, and to classify GPS coordinates (X,Y) according to areas they belong to (e.g., $'Area'_1, ..., 'Area'_n$). Hence rules (8.15) may also be seen as a mechanism to filter out incoming events based on city areas they come from. In [EtNi10], this features is also known as filtering with a *spatial context*.

$$\begin{aligned}&\texttt{areaRule}(\texttt{loc}('N', X,'W', Y),'\textit{Area}'_1) : - \\ &\quad 4042 < X, X < 4049, 7358 < Y, Y < 7370, !. \\ &\quad .... \\ &\texttt{areaRule}(\texttt{loc}('N', X,'W', Y),'\textit{Area}'_n) : - \\ &\quad 4034 < X, X < 4040, 7368 < Y, Y < 7399, !.\end{aligned} \quad (8.15)$$

Table 8.1: Namespace abbreviations.

Prefix	URI	Description
wt	http://knoesis.wright.edu/ssw/page/ont/weather.owl#	Weather ontology
xsd	http://www.w3.org/2001/XMLSchema#	XML Schema Vocabulary
rdf	http://www.w3.org/1999/02/22-rdf-syntax-ns#	RDF Vocabulary
rdfs	http://www.w3.org/2000/01/rdf-schema#	RDF Schema Vocabulary

8.4.3 Event Processing with Reasoning About Subclass Relationships

In the following we show yet another use of deductive reasoning in conjunction with EP. Background knowledge is represent as an ontology, where terms carried by events are defined as concepts (classes) in an ontology.

Assume we need to detect a complex event, `enhancedFire`, which arises when in the area of an active fire there is an additional `weatherObservation`. Some weather observations have significant influence on actions taken with respect to an ongoing wildfire. For example, strong wind may be particularly dangerous for an active fire area. The following pattern specifies such a situation.

$$\begin{aligned}&\texttt{enhancedFire}(Loc) \leftarrow \\ &\quad \bigl(\texttt{activeFire}(Loc)\ \text{AND} \\ &\quad \texttt{weatherObservation}(Loc, Observ)\bigr).3hours \\ &\quad \text{WHERE}\ \bigl(\texttt{rdfs}:\texttt{subClassOf}(Observ, {'}\texttt{wt}:\texttt{WindObservation}{'}\bigr).\end{aligned} \qquad (8.16)$$

Let us now define background knowledge about weather observations. We use the Resource Description Framework (RDF) [KlCa04] as a common format for expressing graph-structured data. RDF Schema (RDFS) [BrGM04] adds additional expressivity in order to support the design of simple vocabularies, also encoded in RDF. Table 8.1 provides a list of namespace definitions used in the remaining part of this subsection.

We can define *windObservation* as a subclass of *weatherObservation*[7], and further to define *diablo* and *sundowner* as two kinds of *windObservation*.

```
wt:windObservation    rdfs:subClassOf    wt:weatherObservation .
wt:diablo             rdfs:subClassOf    wt:windObservation .
wt:sundowner          rdfs:subClassOf    wt:windObservation .
```

We assume that there exist various types of weather observations defined in the background knowledgebase. For example, `observ_1` is a specific type of `wt:diablo`, and in general there exist more than one instance for each type.

---

[7] According to Weather Ontology from [PSHS10], *weatherObservation* is a subclass of *Observation*, and there exist various types of *weatherObservation* such as *pressureObservation*, *TemperatureObservation*, *radiationObservation*, and *windObservation*.

8.4. Knowledge-Based Event Processing Agents

```
observ_1
  rdf:type          wt:diablo ;
  wt:speed          "60"^^xsd:int ;
  wt:temperature    "30"^^xsd:int ;
  wt:region         "California"^^xsd:string .

observ_2
  rdf:type          wt:sundowner ;
  wt:speed          "40"^^xsd:int ;
  wt:temperature    "100"^^xsd:int ;
  wt:region         "California"^^xsd:string .
```

Finally, let us use a subclass relation rule (deductive rule), stating that a is an instance of Y if X is subclass of Y and a is an instance of X (see rule (8.17)).

$$\mathtt{rdf:type}(a,Y) := \mathtt{rdfs:subClassOf}(X,Y), \mathtt{rdf:type}(a,X). \qquad (8.17)$$

Now, if events `activeFire` and `weatherObservation` both occur within 3 hours, the system needs to check the type of `weatherObservation`. `enhancedFire` pattern will be matched if `weatherObservation` is of type wind. Let us assume that `weatherObservation` carries `observ_1`. Retrieving the RDF description for `observ_1`, the system has information that `observ_1` is of type `wt:diablo`. Then by using rule (8.17), the system will *deduce* that `wt:diablo` is a *windObservation* and it will finally trigger the `enhancedFire` complex event.

Moreover, the complex event will be also detected if `weatherObservation` was detected having `observ_2` as a type (since `observ_2` is of type `wt:sundowner`, and the latest is a `windObservation`).

In this example we have arguably demonstrated the power of our formalism which combines EP and deductive reasoning. In order to detect complex situations, events need to satisfy *temporal* constellations (e.g., both events need to happen within three hours), as well as *semantic* relations (e.g., data carried by events need to satisfy, for example, class/subclass or other domain specific relations).

Part III

ETALIS Extensions

9

Retraction in Event Processing

In this chapter we address the problem of *retraction* in Event Processing (EP) as presented in [ARFS11b]. Events are often assumed to be *immutable* and therefore always *correct*. Retraction in EP deals with the circumstance that certain events may be revoked. This necessitates to reconsider complex events which might have been computed based on the original, flawy history as soon as part of that history is corrected.

9.1 Problem Statement for Event Retraction

EP systems such as [ADGI08, ArBW06, KrSe09, CCDF$^+$03] detect complex events based on reported atomic events. Once a complex event has been detected, typically there is no chance to *revise* this event later. Events are assumed to be immutable and therefore always correct. In practice, there is a number of reasons requiring *retractions* of derived events. For example, an event was reported by mistake, but did not happen in reality (and the mistake was realized later), or an event happened, but it was not reported (due to failure of either a sensor, or failure of an event transmission system). Also very often streaming data sources contend with noise (e.g., financial data feeds, Web streaming data, updates etc.) resulting in erroneous inputs and therefore, erroneous EP results. As recognised in [RMCZ06] few event stream sources issue *revision tuples* (retraction events) that amend previously issued events. An EP system should therefore be capable to take these retractions into account and produce correct revision outputs.

As mentioned in Section 4.3, there exist approaches that deal with retraction in EP [BGAH07, RMCZ06, MaCh08]). These approaches are based on *buffering* and *synchro-*

nization points (punctuations). That is, if retraction is needed (e.g., due to corrections of event timestamps, out of order events etc.), an input stream is buffered in between synchronization points so that certain events get *reordered*. Buffering essentially *blocks* the stream, and as such in our opinion, it is not an optimal technique for EP.

We propose an approach which is not based on buffering and reordering. It can be highly undesirable to block the processing until all the early events have *provably* arrived or until they are *reordered*. Instead, our approach is based on keeping partial results (we refer to them as *goals*). Retraction by its nature requires certain data to be saved for possible corrections. However in our approach, the increase of available memory automatically enables delivery of more *accurate* results (with respect to retractions). More memory means that more partial results can be kept longer, and hence their retractions are possible for a longer time.

On the other hand, by increasing available memory in existing approaches [BGAH07, RMCZ06, MaCh08]) the same effect does not happen in the same way. Correction of results, in presence of retractions, are handled in a batch mode (using synchronization points). That is, synchronization points are triggered from time to time, and results are possible corrected in between two synchronization points. A correction that is older than a previous synchronization point is not possible. Hence accuracy of the results, in the first place, depends on synchronization points and their frequency (not on memory). Additionally, retractions based on synchronization points make the overall processing more complex, since these points must involve additional semantics about the nature of event streams (e.g., synchronization points confirm that a certain value or timestamp of an event will no longer appear in the future streams [DMRH04], which is hard to be determined in general case).

9.1.1 A Motivating Example: Processing Events with Transactions

In many applications, transactions can be understood as actions that interfere with events. Figure 9.1 depicts the typical interplay of events and transactions. First, transactions can be seen as *sources* of events, generated during the execution of transactions. These events (denoted as *Tr. Events*) are subject to further processing. They are used in transaction *monitoring* and *auditing* systems, or in provisioning of statistical and accounting reports, key performance indicators (KPI) and so forth. They can also be combined with events from multiple external event sources (denoted as *In Events*) to form more complex events. Complex events represent meaningful situations relevant for a particular business, and hence help in making decisions under time constraints. These events (denoted as *Out Events 1*) may also be used outside an EP system. Finally, (complex) events may also flow from the EP system back to the *Transaction Processor* (e.g., to trigger or synchronize other transactions, see Figure 9.1). We refer to these events as *Out Events 2*.

The notion of *transactions* started from the world of databases, and was later adopted also in logic programming (LP) [ApBW88], concurrent programming [DoFl06] and so on. All-or-nothing transactions provide guarantees that each work-unit (i.e., a part of a

9.1. Problem Statement for Event Retraction

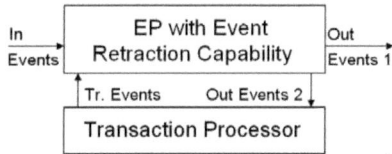

Figure 9.1: Conceptual interaction of events and transactions

transaction) must either be completed in its entirety or has no effect whatsoever. If a transaction fails, the state before the transaction started needs to be restored.

9.1.1.1 Event Retraction with External Complex Events

As already said, events may be triggered in the scope of a transaction in order to provide real time monitoring of the progress of certain parts of a long running transaction, or to be logged and later used by an auditing system. However if a transaction fails, all events occurring in the scope of that transaction need to be revised. The Transaction Processor may initiate the retraction of all atomic events triggered in the course of this failed transaction. However these events, in meantime, could have been used in the detection of other complex events. Moreover they might have already left the EP system (see *Out Events 1* in Figure 9.1). In order to have a means to revise certain decisions (made upon complex events), the system needs to trigger a revised event for each retracted complex event. In Figure 9.1, we refer to such an event processor as *EP with Event Retraction Capability*.

9.1.1.2 Event Retraction and Compensations

Transaction executions must be isolated from each other. When accessing data, a transaction with a commit/rollback mechanism blocks other transactions that access the same data (during the entire execution). When transactions are long-lived, it is unreasonable to prevent access to uncommitted data by forcing other transactions to wait until the updating transaction commits, since the delay caused by this is unacceptable. Transaction systems that allow concurrent data access (for efficiency reasons, in particular in long-lived transactions (LLT)) exploit *compensating transactions* [GMSa87]. Compensating transactions are intended to handle situations where it is required to undo either committed or uncommitted transactions that affect other transactions, without resorting to cascading aborts. The compensating transaction of a transaction T undoes, from a semantic point of view, any of the actions performed by T.

If a failed transaction was triggered by a complex event, then a corresponding compensation transaction may also be triggered by an event. If an EP system has a capability to handle retraction, the compensation can be triggered by the revised version of the event that triggered the failed transaction. Such an automated event-driven mechanism for triggering transactions and their compensations is essential, first for enabling real time transaction processing (especially for LLT), second it ensures correctness of the interplay of complex events and transactions from the semantic point of view.

9.1.1.3 Summary of the Problem

With this conceptual settings in place, we define event retraction as follows: Event retraction is seen as a problem where events – used in detection of other complex events – are *retracted*, hence the goal is to find consequences of retracted events. That is, event retraction deals with discovering what other complex events need also to be retracted (due to retraction of more simple events).

While we consider the event retraction problem in a transaction processing environment, the problem is relevant wherever event retraction of events is carried out. It typically occurs when EP is intervened with transaction processing. However neither the problem statement nor the solution presented in this work are limited only to event retraction with transactions.

9.2 ETALIS Formalism for Event Retraction

We define the declarative formal semantics of the ETALIS Language for Events (ELE) – where occurring events may be revoked – in a model-theoretic way. It is an extension to the ETALIS formalism defined in Chapter 6.

Recall the definition of a variable assignment μ, its extension μ^*, and the set of rules $\mathscr{R}$ from Section 6.3. In addition to them, we define an *event stream* $\mathscr{S} = (\mathbb{E}, \text{ev}, \text{occ}, \text{rev})$. Thereby, $\mathbb{E}$ is a set of events, $\text{ev}: \mathbb{E} \to \textit{Ground}$ a function assigning a ground atom (specifying the event type and possibly additional information) to every event and $\text{occ}, \text{rev}: \mathbb{E} \twoheadrightarrow \mathbb{Q}^+$ partial functions assigning to events time points at which they occur or are revoked, respectively. As a side condition, we presume that for all $e \in \mathbb{E}$ with $\text{rev}(e)$ defined, $\text{occ}(e)$ is defined as well and $\text{occ}(e) < \text{rev}(e)$, i.e., an event can only be revoked after it has occurred[1]. Moreover, we require the event stream to be free of accumulation points, i.e., for every $q \in \mathbb{Q}^+$, the set $\{q' \in \mathbb{Q}^+ \mid q' < q \text{ and } q' = \text{occ}(e) \text{ for some } e \in \mathbb{E}\}$ is finite.

Given an event stream $\mathscr{S} = (\mathbb{E}, \text{ev}, \text{occ}, \text{rev})$ and a time "viewpoint" $v \in \mathbb{Q}^+$, we now define the auxiliary function $\varepsilon_v : \textit{Ground} \to 2^{\mathbb{Q}^+}$ from ground atoms into sets of nonnegative rational numbers by

$$\varepsilon_v(at) := \text{occ}\big(\text{ev}^{-1}(at) \cap \big(\text{occ}^{-1}([0,v]) \setminus \text{rev}^{-1}([0,v])\big)\big)$$

It thereby indicates at what time instants what event types occur according to all the (occurrence and revocation) information obtained up to the time viewpoint v.

---
[1] Note also that we focus on retraction of *events*. Retraction (revision) of background knowledge is out of scope.

9.2. ETALIS Formalism for Event Retraction

Now, we define an interpretation $\mathscr{I}: Ground \to 2^{\mathbb{Q}^+ \times \mathbb{Q}^+}$ as a mapping from the ground atoms to sets of pairs of nonnegative rationals, such that $q_1 \leq q_2$ for every $\langle q_1, q_2 \rangle \in \mathscr{I}(g)$ for all $g \in Ground$.

Given an event stream $\mathscr{S}$ and a viewpoint $v \in \mathbb{Q}^+$, we call an interpretation $\mathscr{I}$ *model* for a rule set $\mathscr{R}$ – written as $\mathscr{I} \models_\mathscr{S}^v \mathscr{R}$ – if the following conditions are satisfied:

C1 $\langle q, q \rangle \in \mathscr{I}(g)$ for every $g \in Ground$ and $q \in \varepsilon_v(g)$.

C2 for every rule $atom \leftarrow pattern$ and every variable assignment μ we have $\mathscr{I}_\mu(atom) \subseteq \mathscr{I}_\mu(pattern)$ where $\mathscr{I}_\mu$ is inductively defined as displayed in Figure 6.3 in Section 6.3.

Given an interpretation $\mathscr{I}$ and some $q \in \mathbb{Q}^+$, we let $\mathscr{I}|_q$ denote the interpretation defined via $\mathscr{I}|_q(g) = \mathscr{I}(g) \cap \{\langle q_1, q_2 \rangle \mid q_2 - q_1 \leq q\}$.

Given two interpretations $\mathscr{I}$ and $\mathscr{J}$, we say that $\mathscr{I}$ is *preferred* to $\mathscr{J}$ if there exists a $q \in \mathbb{Q}^+$ with $\mathscr{I}|_q \subset \mathscr{J}|_q$.

A model $\mathscr{I}$ is called *minimal* if there is no other model preferred to $\mathscr{I}$. It is easy to show that for every event stream $\mathscr{S}$, viewpoint $v \in \mathbb{Q}^+$, and rule base $\mathscr{R}$ there is a unique minimal model $\mathscr{I}^{\mathscr{S},v,\mathscr{R}}$.

Finally, given an atom a and two rational numbers q_1, q_2, we say that the event $a^{[q_1,q_2]}$ is a *consequence* of the event stream ε and the rule base $\mathscr{R}$ at the viewpoint v (written $\mathscr{S}, v, \mathscr{R} \models a^{[q_1,q_2]}$), if $\langle q_1, q_2 \rangle \in \mathscr{I}_\mu^{\mathscr{S},v,\mathscr{R}}(a)$ for some variable assignment μ.

Clearly, the problem of deciding $\mathscr{S}, v, \mathscr{R} \models a^{[q_1,q_2]}$ is time polynomial with respect to the combined size of $\mathscr{R}$ and $\mathscr{S}$, given bounded arity of the used predicates and polynomial computation time for the built-in functions. This result is a straightforward consequence from the fact that there are only polynomially many $a^{[q_1,q_2]}$ to be considered and their validity can be computed in a bottom-up way with increasing interval length. The computational overhead introduced by event revision is not measurable in terms of worst-case complexity which is PTime with and without the revision component.

In the sequel, we will see how this declarative, time-dependent semantics is realized incrementally, as v proceeds, i.e., the "computed semantics" at some time viewpoint v is revised to obtain the semantics at some latter stage, instead of computing everything from scratch. However before we turn to that task, let us illustrate one concrete example with *event retraction* and ETALIS rules.

9.2.1 Event Retraction Example

An automated stock brokerage system sells stocks to its clients. The system emits an event described by `availableStock` to a client every time when the respective stocks become available. The event contains information about the company's stock *ID*, the current price *Pri*, and the available amount of stocks *Amt*. A client (identified by *CID*) may now signal the request to buy the offered stocks by sending an event `trChecked` back to the system, stating the wanted amount Amt_1 of stocks. Event `availableStock` followed by event `trChecked` will trigger a complex event `buyStocks` according to the following rule:

$$\text{buyStocks}(CID,ID,Pri,Amt_1) \leftarrow \text{availableStock}(ID,Pri,Amt) \text{ SEQ}$$
$$\text{trChecked}(CID,ID,Pri,Amt_1) \text{ WHERE } Amt_1 \leq Amt.$$

Upon detection, event `buyStocks` will trigger two transactions: the first transaction transfers money from the client's account to the broker's account, the second transaction maintains the balance of available stocks (by subtracting Amt_1 from Amt). The maintenance is necessary as available stocks are also offered to other interested clients. Since the stock trading is carried out in real time, it is important that execution in the stock brokerage system is automated and that the transaction of one client does not block executions of other clients (as long as $Amt > 0$). Now, suppose that event `balanceChange` is triggered whenever the balance of available stocks changes from Amt_2 to Amt_3 by customer identified as CID (i.e., whenever the second transaction completes). For example, these events may be used for transaction execution monitoring, statistical analysis etc. Let us furthermore assume that the following pattern is used to detect stock trades of suspiciously large volume, which may hint at a potential fraud.

$$\text{bigTrade}(CID,ID,Amt_1) \leftarrow \text{buyStocks}(CID,ID,Pri,Amt_1) \text{ SEQ}$$
$$\text{balanceChange}(CID,Amt_2,Amt_3) \text{ WHERE } (Amt_2 - Amt_3) > 10000.$$

Many transactions concurrently change the balance, and after each change, event `balanceChange` is triggered. Now let us suppose that an event `bigTrade` has been detected, and a fraud investigation was initiated. Just a second afterwards, the money transfer transaction fails (due to insufficient account balance of a customer). In this situation, the amount of available stocks will be restored by executing a compensation transaction. Moreover, the corresponding `balanceChange` event needs to be retracted. Finally, the `bigTrade` complex event needs to be revoked too, leading to the cancelation of the fraud investigation.

The automated stock brokerage system operates with flexible policies, allowing customers to cancel their transaction within certain time (and making stocks available to other customers). The system also operates with many customers concurrently. If after detection of event `bigTrade`, a customer cancels her transaction (by *retracting* event `trChecked`) the atomic event `buyStocks` will be revoked too, which in turn will necessitate the retraction of event `bigTrade`.

This small example arguably demonstrates usefulness of the introduced formalism in practise.

9.3 Operational Semantics for Retractable Event Processing

In the following, we give more details about an operational semantics for retractable EP. It is a continuation of the operational semantics for ELE as presented in Chapter 7.

9.3.1 Sequence

Algorithm 5 accepts as input a rule referring to a binary sequence $ie_1 \leftarrow$ a SEQ b, and produces executable rules for the sequence pattern. A detected sequence can also be *retracted* if either the a event or the b event is retracted. Retraction events of a and b are denoted as rev_a and rev_b, respectively. If a retraction occurs, it is further propagated amongst other patterns (built upon the ie_1 event).

Algorithm 5 Sequence with retraction.

Input: event binary goal $ie_1 \leftarrow$ a SEQ b.
Output: event-driven backward chaining rules for SEQ operator including retraction.
Each event binary goal $ie_1 \leftarrow$ a SEQ b is converted into: {

$\quad$ a$(ID, [T_1, T_2])$:− for_each(a,1,$ID, [T_1, T_2]$).
$\quad$ a$(1, ID, [T_1, T_2])$:− assert(goal(b(_,[_,_]),a$(ID,[T_1,T_2])$,
$\qquad\qquad\qquad\qquad$ ie_1(_,[_,_]))).
$\quad$ rev_a$(ID, [T_3, T_4])$:− for_each(rev_a,1,$ID, [T_3, T_4]$).
$\quad$ rev_a$(1, ID, [T_3, T_4])$:− goal(b(_,[_,_]),a$(ID,[T_1,T_2])$,
$\qquad\qquad\qquad\qquad$ ie_1(_,[_,_])),retract(goal(b(_,[_,_]),
$\qquad\qquad\qquad\qquad$ a$(ID,[T_1,T_2])$)).
$\quad$ rev_a$(2, ID, [T_3, T_4])$:− ($ie_1(ID, [T_1, T_2])$,
$\qquad\qquad\qquad\qquad$ retract($ie_1(ID, [T_1, T_2])$),rev_$ie_1(ID, [T_1, T_2])$);
$\qquad\qquad\qquad\qquad$ true.
$\quad$ b$(ID, [T_3, T_4])$:− for_each(b,1,$ID, [T_3, T_4]$).
$\quad$ b$(1, ID, [T_3, T_4])$:− goal(b(_,[_,_]),a$(ID,[T_1,T_2])$,
$\qquad\qquad\qquad\qquad$ ie_1(_,[_,_])),$T_2 < T_3$,$ie_1(ID, [T_1, T_4])$.
$\quad$ rev_b$(ID, [T_5, T_6])$:− for_each(rev_b,1,$ID, [T_5, T_6]$).
$\quad$ rev_b$(1, ID, [T_5, T_6])$:− ($ie_1(ID, [T_1, T_4])$,
$\qquad\qquad\qquad\qquad$ retract($ie_1(ID, [T_1, T_4])$),rev_$ie_1(ID, [T_1, T_4])$);
$\qquad\qquad\qquad\qquad$ true.
$\quad$ $ie_1(ID, [T_1, T_4])$:− for_each(ie_1,1,$ID, [T_1, T_4]$).
$\quad$ $ie_1(1, ID, [T_1, T_4])$:− assert($ie_1(ID, [T_1, T_4])$).
}

The binarization step must precede the rule transformation. We first consider rules that handle sequence without event retraction. We will recall some explanations related to EDBC rules from Section 7.2 to keep this section more comprehensive and easier to follow. These rules in Algorithm 5 do not have prefix *rev_ev_name* (e.g., rev_a$(1,ID,[T_3,T_4])$), and belong to one of two different classes of rules. We refer to the first class as to *goal inserting rules*. The second class corresponds to *checking rules*. For example, the second rule in Algorithm 5 (i.e., with a$(1,ID,[T_1,T_2])$ in the rule head) belongs to the first class of rules, as it inserts *goal*(b(_,_) ,a(T_1,T_2), ie_1(_,_)):

$\text{a}(1, \mathit{ID}, [T_1, T_2]) : -\texttt{assert}\,(\texttt{goal}(\text{b}(\_,[\_,\_]), \text{a}(\mathit{ID}, [T_1, T_2]), \text{ie}_1(\_,[\_,\_])))$.

This rule will fire when an event of type a occurs, and the meaning of the inserted goal is as follows: "an event a has occurred at $[T_1, T_2]$,[2] and we are waiting for event b to happen in order to detect event ie_1." Obviously, the goal does not carry information about times for b and ie_1, as we don't know when they will occur. In general, the *second* event in a goal always denotes the event that has just occurred. The role of the *first* argument is to specify what we are waiting for, to detect an event that is on the *third* position.

The rule with $\text{b}(1, \mathit{ID}, [T_3, T_4])$ in the rule head (see Algorithm 5) belongs to the second class (i.e., *checking rule*):

$\text{b}(1, \mathit{ID}, [T_3, T_4]) : -\text{ie}_1(\_,[\_,\_])), T_2 < T_3, \text{ie}_1(\mathit{ID}, [T_1, T_4])$.

This rule checks whether certain prerequisite goals already have been asserted, in which case it triggers the more complex event. In this example, the rule will fire whenever event b occurs. The rule checks whether $goal(\text{b}(\_,[\_,\_])$, a $(\mathit{ID}, [T_1, T_2])$, ie_1 $(\_,[\_,\_]))$ already exists (i.e., a has previously happened), in which case the rule triggers ie_1, by calling $\text{ie}_1(\mathit{ID}, [T_1, T_4])$. After detection of event ie_1, $goal(\,\text{b}(\_,[\_,\_])$, a $(\mathit{ID}, [T_1, T_2])$, ie_1 $(\_,[\_,\_]))$ could be removed from the database to free up memory (as it is "consumed"). However this is not the case, as the goal still may be useful if the retraction of event a takes place (see below the case when event rev_a happens).

The time occurrence of ie_1 (i.e., $[T_1, T_4]$) is defined based on the occurrence of constituting events (i.e., $\text{a}(\mathit{ID}, [T_1, T_2])$, and $\text{b}(\mathit{ID}, [T_3, T_4])$, see Section 6.3). By calling ie_1 $(\mathit{ID}, [T_1, T_4])$, this event will be inserted as a fact (see Algorithm 5). If later the retraction process takes place, this fact will serve as a proof that event ie_1 occurred and hence may be retracted. If event ie_1 is further used in composition of other complex events, there will exist another rule with ie_1 in the rule head (apart from the current rules). The purpose of those rules would be to propagate the occurrence of event ie_1 upward (since it is an intermediate event).

Let us now explain how Algorithm 5 handles *event retraction* in a sequence of two events. If once detected, event ie_1 may be retracted by an occurrence of either event rev_a or rev_b. That is why there are two sets of *retraction* rules: rev_a and rev_b, see Algorithm 5. Additionally, events rev_a and rev_b may retract other detected events, if they were used in their detections and their *ID*s match. The identification (ID) is used to make a distinction between possible retractions of instances of the same event types.

If an event rev_a happens, rules $\text{rev\_a}(1, \mathit{ID}, [T_3, T_4])$ and $\text{rev\_a}(2, \mathit{ID}, [T_3, T_4])$ aim to nullify a prior occurrence of an event a. In particular, if an event a has happened, a goal $goal(\text{b}(\_,[\_,\_]), \text{a}(\mathit{ID}, [T_1, T_2]), \text{ie}_1(\_,[\_,\_]))$ will be inserted into the database. Therefore the subsequent occurrence of rev_a needs to delete that goal. The following rule does that.

---

[2] Apart from the timestamp, an event may carry other data parameters. They are omitted here for the sake of readability.

9.3. Operational Semantics for Retractable Event Processing

rev_a(1,*ID*,[T_3,T_4]) : − goal(b(_,[_,_]),a(*ID*,[T_1,T_2]),ie$_1$(_,[_,_])),
  retract(goal(b(_,[_,_]),a(*ID*,[T_1,T_2])))*.*

If the following sequence of events occurs: a, rev_a, b, then event ie$_1$ will not be detected (as rev_a would nullify the occurrence of a). If event rev_a happens after event b, event ie$_1$ will need to be retracted (as it has already been detected). The following rule is used in the latter scenario.

rev_a(2,*ID*,[T_3,T_4]) : − ie_1(*ID*,[T_1,T_2]),retract(*ie*_1(*ID*,[T_1,T_2])),
  (rev_ie$_1$(*ID*,[T_1,T_2]);true)*.*

If an event rev_b happens, the revision is possible only after an occurrence of an event b. In this situation we have only one possibility, i.e., to retract a derived event ie_1 and nullify its occurrence (by issuing an event rev_ie$_1$). The following rules fulfils that functionality.

rev_b(1,*ID*,[T_5,T_6]) : − (ie$_1$(*ID*,[T_1,T_4]),
  retract(ie$_1$(*ID*,[T_1,T_4])),rev_ie$_1$(*ID*,[T_1,T_4]));
  true*.*

In the previously described algorithm, we need to save event rev_ie$_1$ in order to enable possible revisions (see the last rule in Algorithm 5). It means that revision is enabled under the assumption that certain intermediate (or derived) events are kept in memory. Depending on the memory size and the input event throughput, this data is sooner or later scheduled for garbage collection.

Second, we assumed that all events in a binarized pattern have the same *ID* (i.e., ie$_1$(*ID*) ← a(*ID*) BIN b(*ID*)). It is worth noting that some intermediate or complex events may be composed of events with different *ID*s. In such cases, an additional *ID* may be added, e.g., ie$_1$(ID_1,ID_2). ID_1 will then denote an *ID* of the left-hand-side event (a(ID_1)), and ID_2 will denote an *ID* of the right-hand-side event (b(ID_2)). Checking these *ID*s, when certain events are retracted, allows us still to use the presented algorithm for event retraction with no further restrictions.

Rules produced by the transformation in Algorithm 5 are executable rules (Prolog rules). With no restriction these rules may be accompanied by other Prolog rules, used for example to express background or domain *knowledge* (see examples from Section 8.4).

9.3.2 Conjunction

Let us consider conjunction operator (AND) with possible events retractions. Algorithm 6 transforms a user defined pattern rule into executable rules for conjunction. If necessary, the transformation also handles retraction. The retraction occurs if either of the two events, in a conjunction, is retracted.

Let us again assume that retraction of event a is represented by triggering another event rev_a, and retraction of event b with event rev_b.

Algorithm 6 Conjunction with retraction.
Input: event binary goal $ie_1 \leftarrow a$ AND b.
Output: event-driven backward chaining rules for AND operator including retraction.
Each event binary goal $ie_1 \leftarrow a$ AND b is converted into: {
$\quad\quad$ a$(ID, [T_1, T_2])$: $-$ for_each(a, 1, $[T_1, T_2]$).
$\quad\quad$ a$(1, ID, [T_3, T_4])$: $-$ goal(a(_, [_,_]), b$(ID, [T_1, T_2])$,
$\quad\quad\quad\quad\quad\quad\quad\quad$ ie$_1$(_, [_,_])),
$\quad\quad\quad\quad\quad\quad\quad\quad$ $T_5 = \min\{T_1, T_3\}, T_6 = \max\{T_2, T_4\}$, ie$_1(ID, [T_5, T_6])$.
$\quad\quad$ a$(2, ID, [T_1, T_2])$: $-$ $\neg$(goal(a(_, [_,_]), b(_, $[T_1, T_2]$),
$\quad\quad\quad\quad\quad\quad\quad\quad$ ie$_1$(_, [_,_]))),
$\quad\quad\quad\quad\quad\quad\quad\quad$ assert(goal(b(_, [_,_]), a$(ID, [T_1, T_2])$,
$\quad\quad\quad\quad\quad\quad\quad\quad$ ie$_1$(_, [_,_]))).
$\quad$ rev_a$(ID, [T_3, T_4])$: $-$ for_each(rev_a, 1, $ID, [T_3, T_4]$).
$\quad$ rev_a$(1, ID, [T_3, T_4])$: $-$ goal(b(_, [_,_]), a$(ID, [T_1, T_2])$,
$\quad\quad\quad\quad\quad\quad\quad\quad$ ie$_1$(_, [_,_])),
$\quad\quad\quad\quad\quad\quad\quad\quad$ retract(goal(b(_, [_,_]), a$(ID, [T_1, T_2])$,
$\quad\quad\quad\quad\quad\quad\quad\quad$ ie$_1$(_, [_,_]))).
$\quad$ rev_a$(1, ID, [T_3, T_4])$: $-$ (ie$_1(ID, [T_1, T_2])$,
$\quad\quad\quad\quad\quad\quad\quad\quad$ retract(ie$_1(ID, [T_1, T_2])$), rev_ie$_1(ID, [T_1, T_2])$);
$\quad\quad\quad\quad\quad\quad\quad\quad$ true.
$\quad\quad$ b$(ID, [T_3, T_4])$: $-$ for_each(b, 1, $[T_3, T_4]$).
$\quad\quad$ b$(1, ID, [T_3, T_4])$: $-$ goal(b(_, [_,_]), a$(ID, [T_1, T_2])$,
$\quad\quad\quad\quad\quad\quad\quad\quad$ ie$_1$(_, [_,_])),
$\quad\quad\quad\quad\quad\quad\quad\quad$ $T_5 = \min\{T_1, T_3\}, T_6 = \max\{T_2, T_4\}$, ie$_1(ID, [T_5, T_6])$.
$\quad\quad$ b$(2, ID, [T_1, T_2])$: $-$ $\neg$(goal(b(_, [_,_]), a(_, $[T_1, T_2]$),
$\quad\quad\quad\quad\quad\quad\quad\quad$ ie$_1$(_, [_,_]))),
$\quad\quad\quad\quad\quad\quad\quad\quad$ assert(goal(a(_, [_,_]), b$(ID, [T_1, T_2])$,
$\quad\quad\quad\quad\quad\quad\quad\quad$ ie$_1$(_, [_,_]))).
$\quad$ rev_b$(ID, [T_1, T_2])$: $-$ for_each(rev_b, 1, $ID, [T_1, T_2]$).
$\quad$ rev_b$(1, ID, [T_1, T_2])$: $-$ goal(a(_, [_,_]), b$(ID, [T_3, T_4])$,
$\quad\quad\quad\quad\quad\quad\quad\quad$ ie$_1$(_, [_,_])),
$\quad\quad\quad\quad\quad\quad\quad\quad$ retract(goal(a(_, [_,_]), b$(ID, [T_3, T_4])$,
$\quad\quad\quad\quad\quad\quad\quad\quad$ ie$_1$(_, [_,_]))).
$\quad$ rev_b$(2, ID, [T_1, T_2])$: $-$ (ie$_1(ID, [T_3, T_4])$, retract(ie$_1(ID, [T_3, T_4])$),
$\quad\quad\quad\quad\quad\quad\quad\quad$ rev_ie$_1(ID, [T_3, T_4])$); true.
$\quad\quad$ ie$_1(ID, [T_1, T_4])$: $-$ for_each(ie$_1$, 1, $ID, [T_1, T_4]$).
$\quad\quad$ ie$_1(1, ID, [T_1, T_4])$: $-$ assert(ie$_1(ID, [T_1, T_4])$).
}

9.3. Operational Semantics for Retractable Event Processing

If event a happened, rules with a in the rule head will either trigger ie_1, or will insert a goal waiting for b (see Algorithm 6). We have the first case if event b previously happened (i.e., goal(a(_,[_,_]),b($ID,[T_1,T_2]$),ie_1(_,[_,_])) exists). The second possibility is just to insert goal(b(_,[_,_]),a($ID,[T_1,T_2]$),ie_1(_,[_,_]))).

On the other hand, rules with rev_a in the rule head nullify the occurrence of either event a or event ie_1 (if any of them happened). The consequence of a prior occurrence of event a may be nullified by deleting goal(b(_,[_,_]),a ($ID,[T_1,T_2]$), ie_1 (_,[_,_])):

rev_a($1,ID,[T_3,T_4]$) : −
   goal(b(_,[_,_]),a($ID,[T_1,T_2]$),ie_1(_,[_,_])),
   retract(goal(b(_,[_,_]),a($ID,[T_1,T_2]$)))).

If both events, a and b, happened prior to event rev_a; the following rule will retract event ie_1.

rev_a($1,ID,[T_3,T_4]$) : −ie_1($ID,[T_1,T_2]$),
   retract(ie_1($ID,[T_1,T_2]$)),(rev_ie_1($ID,[T_1,T_2]$);true).

Analogue to this reasoning, Algorithm 6 handles event rev_b. There exist two nullifications that event rev_b needs to perform (if it happens). First, if event b has already occurred, it needs to delete a goal that proves that occurrence. The following rule checks whether $goal(a$(_,[_,_])$,b(ID,[T_3,T_4]),ie_1$(_,[_,_])) exists in memory; and if yes, it will delete the goal.

rev_b($1,ID,[T_1,T_2]$) : −
   goal(a(_,[_,_]),b($ID,[T_3,T_4]$),ie_1(_,[_,_])),
   retract(goal(a(_,[_,_]),b($ID,[T_3,T_4]$),ie_1(_,[_,_])))).

The second task of rev_b is to check whether event ie_1 has been detected. If yes, its occurrence needs to be retracted and event rev_ie_1 is triggered. This event is propagated further in case event ie_1 was used in detection of other (more) complex events. The propagated event will continue to nullify consequences of the previously detected event ie_1. If event ie_1 was not detected by the time of event rev_b, the second rule succeeds by doing nothing (i.e., it is *true*), see the following rule for rev_b.

rev_b($2,ID,[T_1,T_2]$) : −
   ie_1($ID,[T_3,T_4]$),retract(ie_1($ID,[T_3,T_4]$)),
   (rev_ie_1($ID,[T_3,T_4]$);true).

Algorithm 5 and Algorithm 6 represent modified versions of Algorithm 1 and Algorithm 2, respectively, where modifications are use to address possible events retractions. In analogy to them, other ELE operators – defined in Section 6.3 and Chapter 7 – can be constructed in similar fashion and are hence omitted here.

9.3.3 Time-Life Window for Event Retractions

Retractions of events need to be limited to certain time intervals. This requirement is needed since retraction requires an event history to be kept, and due to the limited memory resources, that cannot last forever.

For various application domains, the time interval in which retractions are possible need to be defined in accordance to that domain. For instance, in the domain of transaction executions we may define that event retraction is possible within a time interval in which a transaction has started and has either been committed or aborted, i.e., we use the transaction life time as a time frame in which event retraction is possible. The argumentation for this assumption lies in the fact that all events triggered in the scope of a transaction are considered valid (otherwise the transaction would have failed). On the other hand, if a transaction fails, generated events are false and hence need to be retracted.

Regardless of the definition of a time-life window for a particular domain, we need a memory management technique to remove an unnecessary event history from memory. We have developed few strategies for this purpose, and they will be presented in the following chapter.

10

Processing Out-of-Order Events

EP deals the task of processing streams of events with the goal of detecting event patterns of interest. Many today's EP systems [ADGI08, Alve09, CKAK94, WuDR06, CCDF$^+$03] typically assume the *total order* of streaming events. In practice, real time processing often faces delays caused by network latencies, sensor and machine failures and so forth. These reasons – in turn – may cause some events to be delayed. Delayed events are known as *out-of-order* events since they get reported to an EP system later than their timestamps suggest. By handling out-of-order events an EP system needs to keep certain events longer than they are normally needed (in order to handle *late* events). Therefore, an effective removal of overdue events is needed. In this chapter we discuss out-of-order EP, as well as an implementation of a general low-level garbage collector [FoAR11].

10.1 Overview of Out-of-Order Event Processing

In most cases EP systems typically assume that events are *totally ordered*, i.e., the order in which events are received by the system is the same as their timestamp order. This assumption is called *total order assumption* [LLDR$^+$07]. In reality events may arrive *out-of-order* due to network latencies, different sources and even machine failures. Many EP and experimental systems [ADGI08, Alve09, CKAK94, WuDR06, CCDF$^+$03] cannot handle out-of-order events properly. They process events at the time when they come. Hence, a late event will have a larger timestamp than the events which have already arrived earlier. As a consequence, systems not considering out-of-order arrival will disregard the timestamp and may either detect incorrect complex events or fail to detect some valid patterns that occurred [LLDR+07]. To solve this problem, other systems [LLDR+07, BGAH07, BFSF08] propose to use *buffers* to keep the event history for a certain time window. If out-of-order events occur, they will be *reordered* in the buffer so that the event stream afterwards can be treated (and processed) as an in-order stream. While this approach works in general, it causes a certain *delay* in EP. However, the main requirement of EP systems is to process data (events) under *time* constraints. This implies that keeping the whole or parts of the unnecessary history of events is undesired or even unacceptable. Such approaches are rather close to database processing.

In the remaining part of this chapter we present a solution for out-of-order EP which does not additionally *delay* detection of complex events. A complex event is split up into a set of *binary goals*, i.e., each goal represents a subpattern of two events. Goals are chained so that in order to fulfil a goal, previous goals in the chain need to be already fulfilled. A complex event is detected when the top goal is achieved. Hence our approach is compliant with the other parts of the ETALIS framework presented in this work. That is, it is based on *deductive rules* which are extended to handle both, in-order and out-of-order events [FoAR11].

In in-order EP, chained goals are getting *incrementally* fulfilled as relevant events occur. To handle *out-of-order* events, we add (additional) out-of-order goals. These goals enable detection of subpatterns in reverse direction. For instance, if an ordinary goal enables detection of a subpattern "an event a followed by an event b", a corresponding out-of-order goal will enable detection of "an event b followed by an event a" if the timestamp of the event a suggests that it happened before the event b. Similarly, as a complex event can be represented by a set of ordinary (two event) goals, it can be also represented as a set of out-of-order goals.

10.1.1 Motivating Example

We present the following use-case scenario to motivate and exemplify the rationale for out-of-order EP.

A large hedge fund consists of multiple independent but closely cooperating agents and branches. Its main fund is trading stock instruments and is international in scope. Its investment strategy employs EP and automated mathematical models to analyse and execute trades purely electronically. The hedge fund uses EP-based models to predict price changes in stocks. These models are based on analysing event streams as they are gathered, then looking for movements to make predictions. One such program might monitor stocks of two companies (e.g., Google Inc. and Microsoft Corporation, denoted with symbols "G" and "M", respectively). Suppose an event rule detects complex event ce_1 when there is increase in Google stock price for more than 20%, see rule (10.1). Likewise, complex event ce_2 detects the increase in Microsoft stocks of the same percentage, see rule (10.2). Event ce_3 is represented by rule (10.3) and triggered when both, ce_1 and ce_2 occur.

10.1. Overview of Out-of-Order Event Processing

To allow more expressive event patterns – which go beyond of the state of the art [ADGI08, LLDR+07, BGAH07, BFSF08] – we integrate *temporal* knowledge (events) with *static* or *updatable* knowledge (e.g., background knowledge related to liquidity of the company). The latter knowledge may be represented as a set of *facts* and *rules*, and can be *reasoned* about when certain events occur. For example, rule (10.4) checks a special condition proving that company C is *transactional* and *not banned* from trading. Such a company can be determined by additional rules (defining what is a transactional company that is not banned for trading) which we omit to keep the example simple and focused. We see that these rules are *domain specific* knowledge as they, for example, specify stock trade *policies* specific for certain hedge fonds. We also see that we do not talk only about detection of complex events (e.g., an event a is followed by event b in last 10 seconds), but rather about detection of *real time situations*, e.g., stocks of company A increased by 15% in the period when stocks of its competitor decreased for 20% and/or are banned from trading. What is a competitor to certain company, and when is a company banned from trading is specified as domain knowledge. Further, it is worth noting that the liquidity of the company may *change* in time. Therefore, to detect this situation, rule (10.4) (as well as other policy rules) need to be evaluated every time when complex events ce_1, ce_2 and ce_3 occur. Hence to detect real time situations of interest we combine EP with an on-line evaluation of background knowledge. Detection of a real time situation can be useful for triggering external actions, e.g., whenever complex event ce_3 is detected buy "G" stocks, see rule (10.6).

$$ce_1 \leftarrow \big(\texttt{stock}(Agent1,'G',Pr1,Vol1) \text{ SEQ} \\ \texttt{stock}(Agent2,'G',Pr2,Vol2)\big) \\ \text{WHERE } (Pr1 < 1.20 * Pr2, verify\_company\_cat("G"')). \tag{10.1}$$

$$ce_2 \leftarrow \big(\texttt{stock}(Agent1,'M',Pr1,Vol1) \text{ SEQ} \\ \texttt{stock}(Agent2,'M',Pr2,Vol2)\big) \\ \text{WHERE } (Pr1 < 1.20 * Pr2, verify\_company\_cat("G"')). \tag{10.2}$$

$$ce_3 \leftarrow ce_1 \text{ AND } ce_2. \tag{10.3}$$

$$verify\_company\_cat(C) : - \\ \texttt{category}(C, transactional), not\ prohibited(C). \tag{10.4}$$

$$ce_3 : - \\ trigger\_external\_action(buy\_stock("G"', 100)). \tag{10.5}$$

$$ce_3 : -trigger\_external\_action(buy\_stock("G"', 100)). \tag{10.6}$$

One significant problem of the model is that stock events (multiplexed from all their traders, agents, sources and observers) may arrive in an *out-of-order* fashion. This happens due to different latencies in the network connections for the different sources, or due

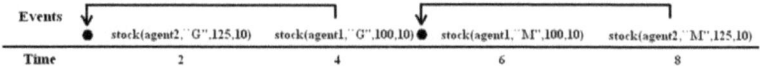

Figure 10.1: Received vs. real order of events

to different system clocks under which events have been generated. As a consequence, out-of-order events may cause an EP system to detect *unintended* complex events or to *miss* to detect certain complex events, which in turn may produce unintended predictions of stock changes.

Consider an example event stream from Figure 10.1. The figure shows four events in the order they have arrived. The time scale shows that the first event occurred at a time point $t_1=2$, the second one at $t_2=4$ and so on. We see that stock($agent1,"G",100,10$) has arrived after stock($agent2,"G",125,10$), however the arrow over the event, indicates its correct position on the time scale. Therefore, this event is said to have arrived out-of-order. The dot in the figure shows the correct position of the event (i.e., if it was an "in-order" event). Similarly stock($agent2,"M",125,10$) is also an out-of-order event, and should have been reported before stock($agent1,"M",100,10$).

When the given event stream is used for detection of complex event patterns, defined by rules (10.1)-(10.3), issues described in the following two subsections arise.

10.1.1.1 Missed Complex Events due to Out-of-Order Events

We see that a sequence stock ($agent1,"G",100,10$), stock ($agent2,"G",125,10$) should be detected as a valid pattern. However, with the execution model presented in Subsection 7.2.1 this will not be possible. The problem is that when stock ($agent2, "G", 125,10$) arrives, the system checks whether some stock ($agent1,"G", 100,10$) has previously happened. Since there was no goal inserted by any occurrence of stock ($agent1,"G", 100,10$) (at the time of the check), stock ($agent2,"G", 125,10$) will simply be discarded. At the moment when the event stock ($agent1,"G", 100,10$) is received, the event stock ($agent2,"G", 125,10$) is gone. Thus the sequence stock ($agent1,"G", 100,10$) SEQ stock ($agent2,"G",125,10$) is missed.

10.1.1.2 False Positive Complex Events due to Out-of-Order Events

Evaluating rule (10.2) for the given stream of events, the pattern stock($agent1,"M", 100,10$) SEQ stock ($agent2,"M", 125,10$) for ce_2 is detected. However these pattern represents an incorrect sequence. It should not have been detected if the out-of-order event had been processed correctly.

10.1.1.3 Summary of the Problem with Out-of-Order Events

The problem of out-of-order EP has two obvious solutions: one is to implement a multiplexer with a delay period (i.e., delay propagation of events for a few seconds, while events are received and ordered in the proper order of their creation date); the other one is to change the event composition algorithm so to accept out-of-order events in the same way as in-order events. The first solutions has the main disadvantage that it has to *delay* processing (while an important requirement for EP systems is efficiency in response time) and it needs to store events (which breaks another important requirement of EP, i.e., to process events as they come and to store as little of the history data as possible). EP deals with huge amounts of events (e.g., tens of thousands per second and more), so a delaying mechanism is not optimal. While related work [LLDR+07, BGAH07, BFSF08] so far has relayed on that line of research, in this work we propose a solution founded on the second approach.

The problem of processing of out-of-order events is strongly connected to another important issue. Namely by handling out-of-order events an EP processor needs to keep certain events longer than they are usually needed (in order to handle late events). Therefore, an effective *garbage collection* of overdue events (from the temporary history of events) is needed. This work also provides the design and implementation of a general low-level garbage collector for events, integrated with an out-of-order event processor.

10.2 Out-of-Order Event Processing

In this section we present a solution for handling out-of-order events. To explain how our approach handles late events let us consider again a sequence of two events: ie ← a SEQ b (i.e., we assume that the binarization procedure has been applied, see Chapter 7). The solution modifies the initial algorithm for sequence (see Algorithm 1) by adding two additional rules. A rule that generates a goal (i.e., a$(1, T_1, T_2)$) is accompanied by a checking rule (i.e., a$(2, T_1, T_2)$), and vice versa, the checking rule b$(1, T_3, T_4)$ is now added (a rule that generates a goal, b$(2, T_3, T_4)$). Therefore we process the sequence in both directions: an in-order direction (as in Algorithm 1); and an out-of-order direction (with newly added rules in Algorithm 7).

Rules a$(1, T_1, T_2)$ and a$(2, T_1, T_2)$ will be evaluated when an event a(T_1, T_2) occurs (i.e., at $[T_1, T_2]$). Rule a$(1, T_1, T_2)$ will insert a goal goal(b(_,_),a(T_1,T_2),ie(_,_)) into the database. Additionally rule a$(2, T_1, T_2)$ will check whether the event *a* is an out-of-order event, in which case the system will also trigger an event ie. The event *a* is an out-of-order event if a goal goal_out(a(_,_),b(T_3,T_4),ie(_,_)) exists in the database, and $T_2 < T_3$. The latter condition says that although the event a(T_1, T_2) just happened (at some $[T_1, T_2]$), there is an event b(T_3, T_4) that has already happened such that its timestamp is bigger that the *a*'s timestamp[1]. This suggests that event *a* is an out-of-order event, and an event ie(T_1, T_4) should be indeed triggered.

---
[1] We assume that events cannot happen before their timestamp suggests.

Algorithm 7 Sequence with out-of-order events.
Input: event binary goal ie ← a SEQ b.
Output: event-driven backward chaining rules for SEQ operator including out-of-order events.
Each event binary goal ie ← a SEQ b is converted into: {
   $a(T_1, T_2)$:− for_each(a,1,$[T_1, T_2]$).
   $a(1, T_1, T_2)$:− assert(goal(b(_,_),a(T_1, T_2),ie(_,_))).
   $a(2, T_1, T_2)$:− goal_out(a(_,_),b(T_3, T_4),ie(_,_)),$T_2 < T_3$,
      retract(goal_out(a(_,_),b(T_3, T_4),ie(_,_))),ie(T_1, T_4).
   $b(T_3, T_4)$:− for_each(b,1,$[T_3, T_4]$).
   $b(1, T_3, T_4)$:− goal(b(T_3, T_4),a(T_1, T_2),ie),$T_2 < T_3$,
      retract(goal(b(T_3, T_4),a(T_1, T_2),ie(_,_))),ie(T_1, T_4).
   $b(2, T_3, T_4)$:− assert(goal_out(a(_,_),b(T_3, T_4),ie(_,_))).
}

Rules – that will fire when an event b(T_3, T_4) occurs at some $[T_3, T_4]$ – work similarly as those for a(T_1, T_2). Rule b(1,T_3, T_4) will check whether an event a(T_1, T_2) has already happened (i.e., goal(b(_,_),a(T_1, T_2),ie(_,_)) exists in the database), and if yes, it will trigger an event ie(T_1, T_4). That is an in-order case of processing events a and b. Additionally rule b(2,T_3, T_4) will insert a goal goal_out(a(_,_),b(T_3, T_4),ie(_,_)), which will be used by a(2,T_1, T_2) if an out-of-order event *a* occurs.

Effectively, the price paid for handling out-of-order events is mainly reflected throughout insertion of out-of-order goals (e.g., goal_out(a(_,_),b(T_3, T_4),ie(_,_)) and the fact that they need to be cleared up after certain time (to free up the memory). Therefore, in the next section we discuss a solution for the garbage collection of outdated out-of-order goals. But first, let us consider again the issue with out-of-order processing from Subsubsection 10.1.1.1. When the stock ($agent2,"G",125,10$) event arrives with the $[T_3, T_4]$ timestamp, a goal goal_out (a(_,_), stock($T_3, T_4, agent2,"G",$
125,10), ie (_,_)) will be asserted by the rule denoted as b (2,T_3, T_4) in Algorithm 7. Now, when the stock ($agent2,"G",100,10$) event arrives with the $[T_1, T_2]$ timestamp, the complex event ce$_1$ will be triggered by the checking rule (which is denoted as a (2,T_1, T_2) in Algorithm 7). This rule will fire the ce$_1$ event since the check for goal_out (a(_,_), stock ($T_3, T_4, agent2,"G",125,10$), ie(_,_)) evaluates to *true*, and $T_2 < T_3$ is satisfied (as depicted by the left backward arrow in Figure 10.1). Regardless from the fact that the stock ($agent2,"G",125,10$) event arrived at $t = 4$, i.e., later than the stock ($agent1,"G",100,10$) event (which arrived at $t = 2$), Algorithm 7 still detects the ce$_1$ event with a correct timestamp.

Finally, let us go back to the issue with out-of-order processing from
Subsubsection 10.1.1.2. When the stock ($agent1,"M",100,10$) event arrives with the $[T_1, T_2]$ timestamp, followed by the stock ($agent2,"M",125,10$) event with the $[T_3, T_4]$ timestamp, the complex event ce$_2$ will not be triggered by the checking rule (denoted as b(1,T_3, T_4) in Algorithm 7). The rule does not fire the ce$_2$ event since $T_2 < T_3$ is not satisfied (as depicted by the right backward arrow in Figure 10.1). Regardless from the fact that the stock ($agent1,"M",100,10$) event arrived before the stock

10.3. Memory Management

($agent1, "G", 100, 10$) event – hence satisfying the sequence condition – and the price condition in the WHERE clause was satisfied too, Algorithm 7 will not wrongly detect the ce_2 event.

We stop here with the further presentation of algorithms for out-of-order processing. Analogue to Algorithm 7, other ELE operators as defined in Section 6.3 and processed by Algorithm 2 and Algorithm 4 can be easily constructed to handle out-of-order events in similar fashion. We have, however, implemented all operators and evaluated them in Chapter 13.

It is worth noting that event retraction (Chapter 9) can be combined with out-of-order EP. Presence of *negation* can cause situations in which a complex event is detected, and then needs to be revised due to an out-of-order event. For example, a complex event is detected if occurrence of an event a is followed by an event b with no c in between. If an EP system detects that complex event and encounters a lately arrived c afterwards – which was proved to happen in between a and b – it needs to threat c as an out-of-order event, and hence to retract the detected complex event.

10.3 Memory Management

To deal with out-of-order events safely, no data can ever be purged from memory since EP assumes processing of infinite streams of data [LLDR$^+$07]. However, this requirement is an exaggeration and is impracticable due to overuse of memory. In practise, network latencies can be approximated, and data at some point must be deleted from memory. In Algorithm 7, occurrences of each event are recorded by inserting a goal in memory. Some of these goals are removed at the time they are "consumed" (when building more complex events), while the others can be pruned using a time window[2].

It is common in EP to define event patterns based on time windows. Therefore, we have developed time-based garbage collection strategies. The time-based garbage collection is the natural approach for EP to release the memory necessary for the execution of events.

We have implemented the time guarantees for out-of-order, as well as for in-order event detection. The following strategies have been developed: pushed constraints; general garbage collection; and event-pattern garbage collection.

The common way to deal with garbage collection of overdue events is to define a time window for the event pattern, and check this constraint during the composition of the complex event. For instance, an event binary goal:

$$ruleId([ooo\_window(10)])rule: \ e_i \leftarrow a \ \text{SEQ} \ b \ \text{SEQ} \ c.$$

---

[2]When specified time elapses, goals from unfulfilled patterns can be deleted.

specifies that the length of a time window for out-of-order events is 10 seconds (i.e., *ooo_window*(10)). This means, the system guarantees that out-of-order events will be processed correctly if their delay is smaller than the specified window is[3].

10.3.1 Pushed Constraints

Our first implementation of a garbage collector modifies the binarization – by pushing the constraints for time guarantees into binary events – and modifies Algorithm 7 by checking the constraints before triggering composed events (see Algorithm 8). Pushing the constraints during binarization ensures that time guarantees are checked at each step, so unnecessary intermediary sub-complex events are not generated if the time guarantees are not satisfied.

Algorithm 8 Sequence with constraint checks.
Input: event binary goal *RuleLabelConditions* ie ← a SEQ b.
Output: event-driven backward chaining rules for SEQ operator including out-of-order events and constraint checks.
Each event binary goal ie ← a SEQ b is converted into: {
 $a(T_1, T_2)$: − for_each(a,1,$[T_1, T_2]$).
 $a(1, T_1, T_2)$: − assert(goal(b(_,_),a(T_1,T_2),ie(_,_))).
 $a(2, T_1, T_2)$: − goal_out(a(_,_),b(T_3,T_4),ie(_,_)),$T_2 < T_3$,
    check_constraints(*RuleLabelConditions*)
    retract(goal_out(a(_,_),b(T_3,T_4),ie(_,_))),ie(T_1,T_4).
 $b(T_3, T_4)$: − for_each(b,1,$[T_3, T_4]$).
 $b(1, T_3, T_4)$: − goal(b(T_3,T_4),a(T_1,T_2),ie),$T_2 < T_3$,
    check_constraints(*RuleLabelConditions*)
    retract(goal(b(T_3,T_4),a(T_1,T_2),ie(_,_))),ie(T_1,T_4).
 $b(2, T_3, T_4)$: − assert(goal_out(a(_,_),b(T_3,T_4),ie(_,_))).
}

One advantage of this approach is that any constraints can be verified, not only for out-of-order event detection. Such constraints are common in EP, e.g., the event detection started after or before a certain time. Moreover, this approach is declarative, i.e., new constraints can be defined for any rule and the handling of the constraints is defined by writing a user defined *check_constraint* rule for that constraint type. However, the approach also has important disadvantages. First, ETALIS enables sharing of common formulas during binarization (i.e., shared intermediate complex events are computed only once and shared in multiple event formulas). Pushing the constraints and labels for each rule makes sharing not possible anymore. However, a bigger disadvantage is the fact that the time guarantee is checked for each detected event. An efficient solution would clear events when they are overdue, i.e., not every time an event is detected. For instance, if the system detects 100,000 events in two seconds and the time window is set to 2 seconds,

---
[3]The labelling of rules and lists of properties for rules is a common practice in defeasible logic programming where rules can override, oppose, cancel or mutex other rules. We found convenient to use the same labelling notation for out-of-order events too.

then the system is expected to clean the overdue events only once (after two seconds), i.e., without performing 100,000 checks.

10.3.2 General and Pattern-Based Garbage Collection

We prune expired goals periodically using alarm predicates (triggers generated periodically by the system). The general approach for garbage collection (GC) is utilized to reduce an event path on which out-of-order events are processed. Essentially it enables an out-of-order event to be late for a fixed window of time with respect to the system clock, denoted by *SystemClock*. The GC window W specifies the maximum time range between the first and last event for any pattern detection (i.e., infinitely long complex patterns are of no interest). Every event $e_i(T_1, T_2)$ should be kept in memory at least the time defined by W, and all events are allowed to be purged if $SystemClock > [T_1 + W]$. GC is applied for all intermediate goals, not only for out-of-order EP.

We use the following rule to sketch the pruning of unnecessary goals. This sort of garbage collector is triggered by the system generated events (defined by the system time *SystemClock* and the GC window W).

$$\begin{aligned}
&\texttt{garbageCollector}(\textit{SystemClock}) \leftarrow \\
&\quad \textit{findAll}(\textit{goal}(\_, X([T_1, T_2], W), \_)\ \text{SEQ}\ \textit{SystemClock} > [T_1 + W], \\
&\quad \texttt{goal}(\_, X([T_1, T_2]), \_, L)), \\
&\quad \texttt{for\_each}(\textit{member}(\textit{goal}(\_, X([T_1, T_2]), \_, L)))(\\
&\quad \texttt{del}(\textit{goal}(\_, X([T_1, T_2]), \_))) \\
&\quad \text{and}\ \textit{alarm}(\textit{garbageCollector}(\textit{SystemClock} + W), W).
\end{aligned}$$

The general garbage collection works well when there is a single garbage collection window W for the whole system (e.g., the network delay is the same for all sources).

The window essentially specifies what is a guaranteed "minimum" time, ensured by the system, that out-of-order events will be processed correctly: if the GC via alarms is set to W time window, the presented procedure correctly handles out-of-order events within that window.

Let us consider now a case when different elements in the system have *different delays* and time guarantees, i.e., there exist different garbage collection times for different patterns. In this case, the garbage collection alarms are defined at the level of *each rule*. The procedure starts GC alarms for each rule separately, looking for intermediate goals for those rules checking the condition $SystemClock > [T_1 + Window(e_i)]$.

Similarly to the pushed constraints case, rules are defined with properties, and the binarization pushes the rule properties to sub-components. However, alarm events for garbage collection are scheduled to happen in $Window(e_i)$ time. The scheduling of alarms is done right after the compilation of pattern rules in an event program. The approach is conservative: if one writes patterns without a garbage collection window, no alarm is generated. However, we also permit dynamic properties by inserting/deleting properties on the fly *ins/del*(*property*(*RuleId*, *PropertyName*, *PropertyValue*)). In this case, the GC is started *automatically* during the execution (depending on the situation). This means that if the system currently has more available memory it can extend the window time W (which guarantees correct out-of-order EP); and opposite, if the system is currently short with memory (due to other tasks), it can temporarily shorten the window. In this respect, our approach offers possibility for both, the *time-based* as well as the *memory-based* GC and out-of-order processing.

11
EP-SPARQL: Extending ETALIS for the Semantic Web

Streams of events appear increasingly today in various Web applications such as blogs, feeds, social networks, sensor data streams, geospatial information, on-line financial data and so forth. Event Processing (EP) is concerned with timely detection of compound events within streams of simple events. State of the art EP provides on the fly analysis of event streams, but cannot combine streams with *background knowledge* and cannot perform *reasoning* tasks. On the other hand, semantic tools can effectively handle background knowledge and perform reasoning thereon, but cannot deal with rapidly changing data provided by event streams.

To bridge the gap, we propose Event Processing SPARQL (EP-SPARQL) [AFRS11a] as a new language for complex events and Stream Reasoning. We provide syntax and formal semantics of the language and devise an effective execution model for the proposed formalism. The execution model is grounded on the operational semantics of the ETALIS Language for Events (ELE). Therefore EP-SPARQL can be seen as an extension of ELE, in particular tailored for event-driven and Semantic Web applications.

11.1 Introduction

In the recent decade, information representation on the Web has undergone a shift from static or quasi-static to dynamic. The average size of singular information items has become smaller (compare, e.g. blogs with tweets) and their mutual temporal relatedness gained in importance. In many domains the view on information has changed from a bag-of-knowledge to a stream-like, event-based perspective.

Current EP systems provide on the fly analysis of data streams enabling real time decisions and actions, but fall short of combining streams with higher-level knowledge representation and reasoning necessary for handling background knowledge describing the *context* or *domain* in which streaming data are interpreted. After all, both *semantic* as well as *temporal* relationships are needed for an appropriate description of complex events. The work on ELE – presented in Chapter 6 – was motivated to address this issue. Standard Semantic Web technologies allow for handling background knowledge in the form of *ontologies* representing time-invariant or slowly evolving knowledge. Since we see more and more knowledge publicly available through Semantic Web initiatives (e.g., Linked Data), we were motivated to extend ELE – as a general language for EP – towards a more Semantic Web oriented language for EP.

World Wide Web Consortium[1] (W3C) – the main international standards organization for the Web, including the Semantic Web – has standardised the Resource Description Framework (RDF) [KlCa04, HiKR09] as a general method for modelling of factual data and the exchange of this data on the Web. The RDF data model is based upon the idea of making statements about information in the Web. Statements are represented in the form of subject-predicate-object expressions known as *triples*.

Information – represented as RDF triples – can further be structured by using RDF Schema (RDFS) vocabularies. RDFS [BrGM04] is a knowledge representation language which provides basic elements for the description of ontologies. The vocabulary of RDF consists of classes, properties and few utility constructs, allowing conceptual modelling similar to entity-relationship or class diagrams.

SPARQL Protocol and RDF Query Language (SPARQL) is a language for querying RDF data [PrSe08, HiKR09]. SPARQL is also a W3C standard. The language allows for a query to consist of triple patterns, conjunctions, disjunctions, optional patterns and various extensions[2]. To some extent, SPARQL queries are syntactically similar to SQL queries (i.e., SELECET - FROM - WHERE clauses). For a thorough introduction to RDF, RDFS, SPARQL see, e.g. [HiKR09].

The goal of this work is to provide a framework for EP in the realm of the Semantic Web. We will use RDF and RDFS to describe static or slowly evolving knowledgebase (KB), and provide a SPARQL-like language which operates on streaming triples. As such, the language can be used for *Event Processing* and *Stream Reasoning* exceeding the state of the art in both EP and the Semantic Web. We believe that such a framework is needed in order to address *dynamic aspects* in streaming knowledge, and move towards the *real time Semantic Web*. Our contribution in this chapter involves:

---

[1] World Wide Web Consortium: http://www.w3.org/
[2] http://www.w3.org/wiki/SPARQL/Extensions

- **EP-SPARQL: A language for Event Processing and Stream Reasoning.** We provide the syntax and a formal semantics of a new language called *Event Processing SPARQL* (EP-SPARQL). The language extends the SPARQL language with EP and Stream Reasoning capabilities;

- **A logic-based account for Event Processing and Stream Reasoning.** We provide the basic mechanism for EP and Stream Reasoning, grounded in LP. EP-SPARQL is a high-level language based on this mechanism. Our approach is based on *event-driven backward chaining rules* that realize an effective event-driven inferencing. It features both effective EP, and inference capabilities over *temporal* and *static* knowledge. We are aware of no approach that implements both features in one clean, logic framework;

- **Implementation and evaluation.** We provide an open-source prototype implementation of the proposed approach. The prototype is implemented in Prolog (but could be realized in other LP or declarative rule languages, too). We have conducted a set of tests to show the usefulness and effectiveness of our approach with respect to expressivity and run-time performance. However the implementation and tests will be presented later, in Chapter 12.

11.2 The Semantic Web with Event Processing

We argue – and the review of current approaches in the literature clearly witnesses this (see Chapter 4) – that EP and Stream Reasoning in the Semantic Web as two research disciplines may contribute to and complement each other, and hence open new possibilities in direction of the real time Semantic Web. These areas served as design principles we followed when proposing EP-SPARQL.

We see the following dimensions where current research on Stream Reasoning can greatly benefit from EP:

Support for Rapidly Changing Information on the Web. While existing semantic technologies and reasoning engines are constantly being improved in dealing with *time invariant* domain knowledge, they lack in support for processing *real time* streaming data (events). Real time Web data is valuable only if it is captured, processed, and delivered instantly. EP is a set of techniques and tools that help us understand and control real time and event-driven systems [Luck02]. As such, it is a technology that can help in processing real time data on the Web too.

Information Push versus Pull. According to Wikipedia, the Real Time Web is a set of technologies and practices which enable users to receive information as soon as it is published by its authors, rather than requiring periodic updates. Hence, there is no need to *pull* information, it will be delivered to users nearly at the moment it is published. For instance, no more waiting for web services to communicate from one polling instance to another. We notice a paradigm shift from information *pull* to information *push*; or from *request-response* based web services to *event-driven* web services with possibly unforeseen consequences.

On the other hand, Semantic Web technologies clearly surpass current EP approaches in the following aspects:

Structured Events. Various sensors, GPS-enabled devices and the Internet of Things are all sources of events that can easily be structured. Today, event stream systems do not use ontologies to specify common-agreed vocabularies for events and event-driven applications. An important contribution of the Semantic Web to EP is to provide *structured events*. This will enable not only *knowledge-based* EP with Stream Reasoning capabilities, but also easier *communication* between event-driven applications and services, as well as simpler *integration* of heterogeneous data streams and their *interpretation* on the Web.

Stream Reasoning in Knowledge-Based EP. As mentioned above, current EP systems [ADGI08, BGAH07, CCDF$^+$03] do real time pattern matching over unbound event streams. But they cannot combine data streams with *evolving knowledge*, and they cannot perform *reasoning* tasks over streaming data. Semantic technologies can enhance today's EP by providing and evaluating domain knowledge (e.g., in order to *enrich* recorded events, to detect more complex *situations* of interest, to propose certain intelligent *recommendations* on the fly and so forth).

Consequently, the problem addressed in this work combines tasks of EP and Stream Reasoning. That is, we propose an approach to detect *complex events* (specified in an appropriate formal *language*) within a *stream of RDF triples* (atomic events). Detection of complex events may additionally require *reasoning* over background knowledge (expressed as an RDF graph or an RDFS ontology). We assume that the timeliness of this detection is crucial and algorithmically optimize our method towards a *continuous* evaluation of patterns and a fast response behaviour.

11.3 Syntax of EP-SPARQL

In this section, we introduce the syntax of EP-SPARQL, our extension of the SPARQL querying language in order to enable stream-based querying that takes into account temporal situatedness of triple assertions. Thereby, we ensure syntactical and semantic downward-compatibility to plain SPARQL [PrSe08, HiKR09] in the sense detailed below.

Syntactically, we define EP-SPARQL to be SPARQL extended by the binary operators SEQ, EQUALS, OPTIONALSEQ, and EQUALSOPTIONAL used to combine graph patterns in the same way as UNION and OPTIONAL in pure SPARQL. Intuitively, all those operators act like a (left, right or full) join, but they do so in a selective way depending on how the constituents are temporally interrelated, as indicated by their naming: P_1 SEQ P_2 joins P_1 and P_2 only if P_2 occurs[3] strictly after P_1, whereas P_1 EQUALS P_2 performs the

---

[3] in a sense to be defined more precisely in the formal semantics

11.3. Syntax of EP-SPARQL

join if P_1 and P_2 are exactly simultaneous. OPTIONALSEQ and EQUALSOPTIONAL are temporal-sensitive variants of OPTIONAL.

Moreover, we add the function getDURATION() to be used inside filter expressions. This function yields a literal of type xsd:duration giving the length of the time interval associated to the graph pattern the FILTER condition is placed in. Likewise, we add functions getSTARTTIME() and getENDTIME() to retrieve the time stamps (of type xsd:dateTime) of the start and end of the currently described interval.

We provide a few examples to give some intuition on the newly introduced operators. The following EP-SPARQL query is supposed to search for companies whose stock price has decreased by over 30% and then risen by more than 5% (in comparison to its initial value) within a time frame of 30 days.

```
SELECT ?company WHERE
        { ?company hasStockPrice ?price1 }
   SEQ  { ?company hasStockPrice ?price2 }                (11.1)
   SEQ  { ?company hasStockPrice ?price3 }
FILTER ( ?price2 < ?price1*0.7 && ?price3 > ?price2*1.05
         && getDURATION() < "P30D"^^xsd:duration)
```

The next EP-SPARQL query will identify companies with a more than 50% stock price drop and – in case some rating agency previously downrated this company, this rating agency will be indicated as well.

```
SELECT ?company ?ratingagency WHERE
  { ?company downratedby ?ratingagency}
  OPTIONALSEQ                                             (11.2)
  {      { ?company hasStockPrice ?price1 }
    SEQ  { ?company hasStockPrice ?price2 }}
FILTER ( ?price2 < ?price1 * 0.5)
```

It is worth mentioning that – just like for pure SPARQL – negation (i.e., requiring the *absence* of some triple pattern instead of its *presence*) is not an explicit part of the formalism, but can be expressed via OPTIONAL and FILTER. For instance, the following query asks for companies having a larger than 50% stock price increase in less than 15 days without having acquired another company during that period.

```
SELECT ?company WHERE
        { ?company hasStockprice ?price1 }
   SEQ  { { ?company hasAcquired ?othercompany }          (11.3)
          OPTIONALSEQ
          { ?company hasStockPrice ?price2 } }
FILTER ( ?price2 > ?price1 * 1.5 && !BOUND(?othercompany)
         && getDURATION() < "P15D"^^xsd:duration )
```

Moreover, we allow for recursion by employing CONSTRUCT queries, conceiving them as a kind of production rule. Thereby, the result graph of such a query is assumed to be added to the RDF stream. For instance, the following statement gathers "temporally distributed" rating information to create a triple indicating an event of being downrated, which in turn can be used in other CONSTRUCT or SELECT queries.

```
CONSTRUCT  ?company downratedby ?ratingagency
WHERE     { ?rating1 rater ?ratingagency ;
            rated ?company ; score ?score1 }      (11.4)
     SEQ { ?rating2 rater ?ratingagency ;
            rated ?company ; score ?score2 }
FILTER ( ?score2 < ?score1 )
```

Finally, the forthcoming extended SPARQL standard[4] featuring *subqueries* and *expressions* allows for as complex mechanisms as aggregation over sliding windows. As an example we present a query monitoring the average stock price of a company ACME Inc. over the last 10 days. First, we use a construct rule that aggregates counts and sums of stock prices within the given time frame and feeds this information back into the stream. Thereby, the EQUALSOPTIONAL and filter part make sure that no price signal is left out.

```
CONSTRUCT _:aaa   :hasCount ?count . _:aaa   :hasSum   ?sum .
{ SELECT   ?count AS ?prevcount + 1
           ?sum   AS ?prevsum + ?price
   WHERE   {{ ?point :hasCount ?prevcount .
              ?point :hasSum   ?prevsum       . }
         SEQ { :ACME   :hasStockPrice  ?price . }}
         EQUALSOPTIONAL                                    (11.5)
            {{ ?point :hasCount ?prevcount .
               ?point :hasSum   ?prevsum       . }
         SEQ { :ACME   :hasStockPrice  ?inbetween . }
         SEQ { :ACME   :hasStockPrice  ?price . }}
FILTER ( !BOUND(?inbetween) &&
         getDURATION() < "P10D"^^xsd:duration )}
```

Next, we calculate and output the average value as soon as the duration of our time window is exceeded.

```
SELECT ?sum / ?count AS ?average
WHERE {{ :ACME   :hasStockPrice   ?price . }
    SEQ { ?point :hasCount          ?prevcount .
          ?point :hasSum    ?prevsum     . }}
```

---
[4] http://www.w3.org/TR/2009/WD-sparql-features-20090702/

11.4. Semantics of EP-SPARQL

```
EQUALSOPTIONAL
    {{ :ACME    :hasStockPrice    ?price     . }                    (11.6)
    SEQ { :ACME    :hasStockPrice    ?inbetween . }
    SEQ { ?point   :hasCount        ?prevcount .
          ?point   :hasSum          ?prevsum   . }}
FILTER ( !BOUND(?inbetween) &&
         getDURATION() > "P10D"^^xsd:duration )
```

It may take some consideration and checking back with the formal semantics to verify that this realizes the intended behaviour. In practice, additional constructs may be introduced as syntactic sugar to facilitate specification of patterns that are often used.

11.4 Semantics of EP-SPARQL

We define the formal semantics for EP-SPARQL along the same lines as it is done for pure SPARQL [PrSe08], that is, in a relational way. Thereby, the query is first translated into an algebraic expression. Recall that this conversion transforms simple graph patterns[5] (lists of triples) P into expressions of the form $BGP(P)$. Moreover, juxtapositions of graph triples are translated into the function *Join*, UNION into *Union*, OPTIONAL into *LeftJoin*. We reuse but extend this translation to map the new operators as follows: SEQ $\mapsto$ *SeqJoin*, EQUALS $\mapsto$ *EqJoin*, OPTIONALSEQ $\mapsto$ *SeqRightJoin*, and EQUALSOPTIONAL $\mapsto$ *EqLeftJoin*. Each of these functions is meant to return the result of the subquery it describes, which is a formal representation of the corresponding result table – as opposed to plain SPARQL, each row of these intermediary result tables is additionally associated with a time interval.

To make this more formal, note that we pose our query against an *RDF stream* which we define as a set S consisting of *triple occurrences* being pairs $\langle\langle s,p,o\rangle,t,t'\rangle$ where $\langle s,p,o\rangle$ is an RDF triple and t,t' are time stamps denoting the boundaries of the time interval of the occurrence. Now, we say that the tuple $\langle \mu, t_\alpha, t_\omega \rangle$ is a solution for an expression of the form "*BGP(list of triples)*" exactly if the following conditions are satisfied:

1. μ is a partial function the domain of which consists exactly of the variables that occur in the given list of triples.

2. for the triple set $\{\langle s_1,p_1,o_1\rangle,\ldots,\langle s_n,p_n,o_n\rangle\}$ obtained from substituting the variables in the triple list via μ, there exist time stamps $t_1, t'_1, \ldots, t_n, t'_n$ such that

    - $\{\langle\langle s_1,p_1,o_1\rangle,t_1,t'_1\rangle,\ldots\langle\langle s_n,p_n,o_n\rangle,t_n,t'_n\rangle\} \subseteq S$,
    - $t_\alpha = \min(t_1,\ldots,t_n)$, and
    - $t_\omega = \max(t'_1,\ldots,t'_n)$.

---
[5]For the sake of brevity, we assume that the graph patterns do not contain blank nodes, as they can be replaced by (non-distinguished) variables without changing the semantics.

Now define results for the other operators. A pair of solutions $\langle \mu, t_\alpha, t_\omega \rangle$ and $\langle \mu', t'_\alpha, t'_\omega \rangle$ is said to be *compatible* if every variable that is mapped by both μ and μ' is also mapped to the same RDF term by both solutions. If this is the case, their combination $\langle \mu, t_\alpha, t_\omega \rangle \bowtie \langle \mu', t'_\alpha, t'_\omega \rangle$ can be defined as the tuple $\langle \mu'', t''_\alpha, t''_\omega \rangle$ with $t''_\alpha = \min(t_\alpha, t'_\alpha)$, $t''_\omega = \max(t_\omega, t'_\omega)$, and

$$\mu''(x) = \begin{cases} \mu(x) & \text{if } x \text{ occurs in the domain of } \mu \\ \mu'(x) & \text{if } x \text{ occurs in the domain of } \mu' \\ \text{undefined} & \text{in all other cases} \end{cases}$$

Based on this, we define how to evaluate the introduced functions on sets Ψ, Ψ' of solutions. Thereby, we use $\sigma_{t_\alpha t_\omega}$ to denote the operator substituting getDURATION() by $t_\omega - t_\alpha$, getSTARTTIME() by t_α, and getENDTIME() by t_ω in filter expressions.

- *Filter*(F, Ψ) contains those $\langle \mu, t_\alpha, t_\omega \rangle \in \Psi$ for which the expression $\mu(\sigma_{t_\alpha t_\omega}(F))$ evaluates to true.
- *Join*(Ψ, Ψ') contains $\langle \mu, t_\alpha, t_\omega \rangle \bowtie \langle \mu', t'_\alpha, t'_\omega \rangle$ for all compatible $\langle \mu, t_\alpha, t_\omega \rangle \in \Psi$ and $\langle \mu', t'_\alpha, t'_\omega \rangle \in \Psi'$.
- *Union*$(\Psi, \Psi') = \Psi \cup \Psi'$
- *LeftJoin*(Ψ, Ψ', F) contains
  - every $\langle \mu, t_\alpha, t_\omega \rangle \bowtie \langle \mu', t'_\alpha, t'_\omega \rangle$ for every compatible $\langle \mu, t_\alpha, t_\omega \rangle \in \Psi$ and $\langle \mu', t'_\alpha, t'_\omega \rangle \in \Psi'$ with $(\mu \bowtie \mu')(\sigma_{t_\alpha t_\omega}(F)) = $ true and $t'_\omega < t_\omega$.
  - every $\langle \mu, t_\alpha, t_\omega \rangle \in \Psi$ for which there is no compatible $\langle \mu', t'_\alpha, t'_\omega \rangle \in \Psi'$ with $(\mu \bowtie \mu')(\sigma_{t_\alpha t_\omega}(F)) = $ true and $t'_\omega < t_\omega$.
- *SeqJoin*(Ψ, Ψ') contains $\langle \mu, t_\alpha, t_\omega \rangle \bowtie \langle \mu', t'_\alpha, t'_\omega \rangle$ for all compatible $\langle \mu, t_\alpha, t_\omega \rangle \in \Psi$ and $\langle \mu', t'_\alpha, t'_\omega \rangle \in \Psi'$ additionally satisfying $t_\omega < t'_\alpha$
- *SeqRightJoin*(Ψ', Ψ, F) contains
  - all solutions from *Filter*$(F, SeqJoin(\Psi', \Psi))$ as well as
  - all $\langle \mu, t_\alpha, t_\omega \rangle \in \Psi$ for which there is no compatible $\langle \mu', t'_\alpha, t'_\omega \rangle \in \Psi'$ with both $(\mu \bowtie \mu')(\sigma_{t_\alpha t_\omega}(F)) = $ true and $t_\alpha > t'_\omega$.
- *EqJoin*(Ψ, Ψ') contains $\langle \mu, t_\alpha, t_\omega \rangle \bowtie \langle \mu', t'_\alpha, t'_\omega \rangle$ for all compatible $\langle \mu, t_\alpha, t_\omega \rangle \in \Psi$ and $\langle \mu', t'_\alpha, t'_\omega \rangle \in \Psi'$ additionally satisfying $t_\alpha = t'_\alpha$ and $t_\omega = t'_\omega$
- *EqLeftJoin*(Ψ, Ψ', F) contains
  - all solutions from *Filter*$(F, EqJoin(\Psi, \Psi'))$ as well as
  - all $\langle \mu, t_\alpha, t_\omega \rangle \in \Psi$ for which there is no compatible $\langle \mu', t'_\alpha, t'_\omega \rangle \in \Psi'$ with all $(\mu \bowtie \mu')(\sigma_{t_\alpha t_\omega}(F)) = $ true and $t_\alpha = t'_\alpha$ and $t_\omega = t'_\omega$.

We would like to add the following remarks to justify some aspects of our definition of the EP-SPARQL semantics. First, we endorse the principle of *timewise monotonicity*: the querying formalism is intended to work on triple streams (i.e., triples continuously enter the system in the order of their associated time stamps) and query results are supposed to be output as soon as they are detected. This leads to the straightforward requirement that it should not be possible that query results once obtained get invalidated by later triple inputs. More formally, we have to guarantee that for any EP-SPARQL query and any RDF stream S all solutions for the stream $\{\langle \mu, t_\alpha, t_\omega \rangle \mid t_\omega < t_1\}$ are also solutions for the stream $\{\langle \mu, t_\alpha, t_\omega \rangle \mid t_\omega < t_2\}$ given that $t_1 \leq t_2$. Note that a hypothetical constructor SEQOPTIONAL (specifying a mandatory pattern followed by an optional one) defined as the inverse version of OPTIONALSEQ would violate this principle since the solution $\langle \{x \mapsto a\}, 0, 0 \rangle$ would be a solution to the query

SELECT ?x ?y WHERE ?x ?x ?x. SEQOPTIONAL ?y ?y ?y. (11.7)

when posed against the stream $\{\langle \langle a,a,a \rangle, 0, 0 \rangle\}$ but not when posed against the augmented stream $\{\langle \langle a,a,a \rangle, 0, 0 \rangle, \langle \langle b,b,b \rangle, 1, 1 \rangle\}$. As second principle, we obtain *downward compatibility* in the following sense: as a consequence of the syntax definition, every (pure) SPARQL query q is also an EP-SPARQL query. Now, given an RDF graph $\{\langle s_1, p_1, o_1 \rangle, \ldots, \langle s_n, p_n, o_n \rangle\}$, we obtain μ as a result of the SPARQL query q if and only if we obtain $\langle \mu, t, t \rangle$ as a solution to the EP-SPAQL query against the RDF stream $\{\langle \langle s_1, p_1, o_1 \rangle, t, t \rangle, \ldots \langle \langle s_n, p_n, o_n \rangle, t, t \rangle\}$ for any fixed time stamp t.

To finish the semantics definition, we have to consider the CONSTRUCT rules. Given such a statement q with the graph pattern P_q following the CONSTRUCT command and the set Ψ_q^S of solutions to the WHERE part with respect to some given stream S, let $\Psi_q^S(P_q)$ denote the set of tuples $\langle \langle s, p, o \rangle, t, t' \rangle$ for which there is a solution $\langle \mu, t, t' \rangle \in \Psi_q^S$ such that (1) μ has as domain at least all variables occurring in P_q, and (2) $\langle s, p, o \rangle \in \mu(P_q)$. Now, given an RDF stream S and a set Q of CONSTRUCT statements, we define the *Q-closure* of S ($clos_Q(S)$) as the smallest set for which both $S \subseteq clos_Q(S)$ as well as $\Psi_q^{clos_Q(S)}(P_q) \subseteq clos_Q(S)$ for every $q \in Q$. We can see the *Q-closure* of S as the stream S enriched by the triple occurrences following from (possibly iterated) application of the CONSTRUCT rules. Consequently, in the presence of such rules, SELECT-queries get evaluated not against the pure input stream but against its Q-closure. Moreover, in the case of SELECT queries, after calculating the solution set, it is further processed (with respect to variable projection and output formatting) like for normal SPARQL.

11.5 An Example of EP-SPARQL Application

To demonstrate how EP-SPARQL can be used in practise, we provide an example application concerning a sensor-based traffic management system[6]. The system monitors continuously generated traffic events, and diagnoses areas with slow traffic.

The following EP-SPARQL query searches for roads for which two *slow traffic* events have been reported within the the *last hour*. Results from this query could be, for example, used to automatically modify a speed limit on a certain road (or its particular section).

---

[6]The application is similar to the application from Subsection 6.4.1. This time we have implemented background knowledge as an RDF knowledgebase.

```
PREFIX tr:    <http://traffic.example.org/data#>
PREFIX rdfs:  <http://www.w3.org/2000/01/rdf-schema#>
PREFIX xsd:   <http://www.w3.org/2001/XMLSchema#>

SELECT ?road ?speed WHERE
       { ?road    tr:    slowTrafficDue ?observ }
   SEQ { ?road    tr:    slowTrafficDue ?observ }
   AND { ?observ rdfs:  subClassOf tr:SlowTraffCause }
   AND { ?observ tr:    speed ?speed }
FILTER ( getDURATION() < "P1H"^^xsd:duration)
```

Traffic can be slowed down due to various reasons. We provide below a simple RDFS KB to define few of them. The background knowledge will be evaluated when sensor observations (events) get reported. Only events, reporting about `SlowTraffCause` will be selected.

Since (direct or indirect) subclasses of `SlowTraffCause` may also be relevant, ETALIS utilize a *reasoning* procedure to find out *subclass relationships*.

```
tr:Accident       rdfs:subClassOf   tr:SlowTraffCause.
tr:GhostDriver    rdfs:subClassOf   tr:SlowTraffCause.
tr:BadWeather     rdfs:subClassOf   tr:SlowTraffCause.
tr:Rain           rdfs:subClassOf   tr:BadWeather.
tr:Snow           rdfs:subClassOf   tr:BadWeather.
```

We assume that there exist various types of traffic observations. For example, `Observ_1` is a specific type of `tr:Accident`, and in general, there may exist more than one instance of each type (e.g., a traffic accident is classified as a head-on collision, side collision, rollover etc.). Additionally, for each type of an observation there may exist a suggested speed limit, and other relevant details (omitted here for simplicity reasons).

```
Observ_1
  rdf:type   tr:Accident ;
  tr:speed   "70"^^xsd:int .

Observ_2
  rdf:type   tr:GhostDriver ;
  tr:speed   "50"^^xsd:int .

Observ_3
  rdf:type   tr:Snow ;
  tr:speed   "40"^^xsd:int .
```

Finally, to enable detection of *indirect* observations (e.g., of `SlowTraffCause` class), the subclass relation rule (11.8) is utilized.

$$\text{rdf:type}(A,Y) := \text{rdfs:subClassOf}(X,Y), \text{rdf:type}(A,X). \quad (11.8)$$

Note that, by using deductive rules (e.g., rule (11.8)), ETALIS can be used to *infer* implicit knowledge (not only explicitly stated knowledge). This powerful feature is beyond the state of the art EP systems [ADGI08, BGAH07, ArBW06, KrSe09, CCDF$^+$03], and is required in intelligent processing over streaming data.

11.6 Operational Semantics of EP-SPARQL

This section describes how complex events, as defined in Section 11.4 are computed at run-time. We describe an execution mechanism that is based on event-driven backward chaining (EDBC) rules, introduced in [AFRS11a, AFSS09, AFRS$^+$10] and presented in Chapter 7. EP-SPARQL queries are compiled into EDBC rules, which enable timely, event-driven, and incremental detection of complex events (i.e., answers to EP-SPARQL queries). EDBC rules are logic rules, and hence can be mixed with other background knowledge (domain knowledge that is used for Stream Reasoning). Therefore, we provide a unified execution mechanism for EP and Stream Reasoning which was realised for ELE (in Chapter 7) and now extended for EP-SPARQL.

For our encoding, we use a simple correspondence between RDF triples of the form $\langle s,p,o \rangle$ and Prolog predicates of the form $\text{triple}(s',p',o')$ so that s', p', and o' correspond to the RDF symbols s, p, and o, respectively. This means that whenever a triple $\langle s,p,o \rangle$ is satisfied, the corresponding predicate $\text{triple}(s',p',o')$ is satisfied too, and vice versa. Consequently, a time-stamped RDF triple $\langle \langle s,p,o \rangle, t_\alpha, t_\omega \rangle$ corresponds to a predicate $\text{triple}(s',p',o',T'_\alpha,T'_\omega)$ where T'_α and T'_ω denote time stamps. Time stamps are assigned to triples either by a triple source (e.g., a sensor or an application that generates triple updates) or by an EP-SPARQL engine (e.g., our prototype implementation presented in Chapter 12). They facilitate time-related processing, and do not necessarily need to be kept once the stream has been processed (e.g., the pure RDF part could be persisted in a RDF triple store without time stamps).

11.6.1 Sequence

Let us consider a sequence (*SeqJoin* operator) of three timestamped triples (events), represented by Example (11.1) (in Section 11.3) when the FILTER expression is omitted. This EP-SPARQL query can be represented by rule (11.9), where the SEQ operator has the identical meaning, i.e., $\texttt{triple}(\tau, T_1, T_6)$ is detected[7] when $\texttt{triple}(\tau_1, T_1, T_2)$ occurs in a data stream, followed by $\texttt{triple}(\tau_2, T_3, T_4)$, and $\texttt{triple}(\tau_3, T_5, T_6)$. We can always represent this pattern with rule (11.10).

$$\begin{aligned}\texttt{triple}(\tau, T_1, T_6) \leftarrow\ &\texttt{triple}(\tau_1, T_1, T_2)\ \text{SEQ}\\ &\texttt{triple}(\tau_2, T_3, T_4)\ \text{SEQ}\ \texttt{triple}(\tau_3, T_5, T_6).\end{aligned} \quad (11.9)$$

$$\begin{aligned}\texttt{triple}(\tau, T_1, T_6) \leftarrow\ &(\texttt{triple}(\tau_1, T_1, T_2)\ \text{SEQ}\\ &\texttt{triple}(\tau_2, T_3, T_4))\ \text{SEQ}\ \texttt{triple}(\tau_3, T_5, T_6).\end{aligned} \quad (11.10)$$

$$\begin{aligned}\texttt{triple}(\tau', T_1, T_4) &\leftarrow \texttt{triple}(\tau_1, T_1, T_2)\ \text{SEQ}\ \texttt{triple}(\tau_2, T_3, T_4).\\ \texttt{triple}(\tau, T_1, T_6) &\leftarrow \texttt{triple}(\tau', T_1, T_4)\ \text{SEQ}\ \texttt{triple}(\tau_3, T_5, T_6).\end{aligned} \quad (11.11)$$

We recall this rewriting is referred to as *binarization* of patterns (see Chapter 7). Effectively, in binarization we introduce triples that are *binary intermediate goals*. For example, now we can rewrite rule (11.9) as rule (11.10), and further as rules (11.11). Every monitored pattern (capturing either a triple or a derived triple) will be associated with one or more *logic rules*. Rules are fired as soon as certain triples occur, hence they are driven by streaming triples (events). Here we presented a left-associative binarization (events and goals are coupled from left to right). As pointed out in Subsection 7.2.1, the left-associative binarization is a good choice when the rightmost event(s) in a pattern rule have a higher occurrence rate than the others (e.g., event $\texttt{triple}(\tau_3, T_5, T_6)$ occurs more frequently than event $\texttt{triple}(\tau_1, T_1, T_2)$), since in that situation event $\texttt{triple}(\tau_3, T_5, T_6)$ is joined later. Our prototype, described in Chapter 12, currently implements the left-associative binarization, and other types of binarization such as the right-associative coupling, bushy plan and inner plan from [MeMa09] are subject of future work.

In the following, we give more details about rule assignment for each monitored triple, and sketch the execution model for a sequence of triples.

$$\texttt{triple}(\tau, T_1, T_4) \leftarrow \texttt{triple}(\tau_1, T_1, T_2)\ \text{SEQ}\ \texttt{triple}(\tau_2, T_3, T_4). \quad (11.12)$$

Rule (11.12) represents a binary sequence goal, and rules (11.13) and (11.14) represent the pair of EDBC into which (11.12) is translated. The binarization step must therefore precede the rule transformation.

$$\begin{aligned}&\texttt{triple}(\tau_1, T_1, T_2) \leftarrow\\ &\quad \texttt{assert(}\\ &\quad\quad \texttt{goal(triple}(\tau_2,\_,\_), \texttt{triple}(\tau_1, T_1, T_2), \texttt{triple}(\tau,\_,\_))).\end{aligned} \quad (11.13)$$

---

[7]For brevity, we use τ with possible super- and subscripts to denote triplets s, p, o.

11.6. Operational Semantics of EP-SPARQL

```
triple(τ₂,T₃,T₄) ←
    goal(triple(τ₂,_,_),triple(τ₁,T₁,T₂),triple(τ,_,_)),
    T₂ < T₃,
    retract(
        goal(triple(τ₂,_,_),triple(τ₁,T₁,T₂),triple(τ,_,_))),
    triple(τ,T₁,T₄).
```
(11.14)

In general, the EDBC rules created by our translation can be grouped in two different classes of rules. We refer to the first class as *goal-insertion rules*. The second class corresponds to *checking rules*. For example, rule (11.13) belongs to the first class as it asserts a goal. This rule will fire when triple(τ_1,T_1,T_2) occurs, and the meaning of the goal it inserts is as follows: "an event triple(τ_1,T_1,T_2) has occurred at $[T_1,T_2]$, and we are waiting for triple($\tau_2,\_,\_$) to happen in order to detect triple($\tau,\_,\_$)". Obviously, the goal does not carry information about times for triple($\tau_2,\_,\_$) and triple($\tau,\_,\_$), as we do not know when they will occur. In general, the *second* event in a goal always denotes the event (triple) that has just occurred. The role of the *first* event is to specify what we are waiting for to detect an event that is on the *third* position (i.e., a derived triple).

Rule (11.14) belongs to the second class, being a *checking rule*. It checks whether certain prerequisite goals already exist in the knowledgebase, in which case it triggers a more complex event. For example, that rule will fire whenever triple (τ_2,T_3,T_4) (the triple from the rule head) occurs. It checks whether goal(triple($\tau_2,\_,\_$), triple(τ_1, T_1, T_2), triple($\tau, \_, \_$)) already exists (meaning that triple(τ_1,T_1,T_2) has previously happened), in which case it triggers triple(τ,T_1,T_4) by calling that triple. The triple occurrence time span (i.e. $[T_1,T_4]$) is defined based on the occurrence of constituting events (i.e. triple (τ_1,T_1,T_2), and triple (τ_2,T_3,T_4), see Section 11.4). Calling triple(τ,T_1,T_4), this event is effectively either propagated further (if it is an intermediate event) or triggered as a finished complex event.

We see that our *backward* chaining rules compute goals in a *forward* chaining manner. The goals are crucial for computing complex events *incrementally*. Goals can persist over a period of time. It is worth noting that *checking rules* can also delete goals (see retract predicate in rule 11.14). Once a goal is "consumed", it is removed from the knowledgebase[8]. In this respect, goals are kept persistent as long as (but not longer than) they are needed.

So far, we have explained how the SEQ operator is implemented with EDBC rules. OPTIONALSEQ is implemented similarly. The operator allows information to be added to the answer where certain triples are available, but do not reject the answer when some part of the query pattern does not match. Hence the functionality of OPTIONALSEQ operator is the same as for SEQ operator, and OPTIONALSEQ sub-patterns are translated into event-driven rules and computed in the same way as the mandatory part. However, at the end, the pattern is detected when all mandatory conditions are satisfied (regardless

---

[8]Removing "consumed" goals is often needed for space reasons but might be omitted if events are required in a log for further processing or analysing.

whether an optional sub-pattern has been satisfied by that moment or not). The same applies for the EQUALS and EQUALSOPTIONAL operators.

11.6.2 Filter Expression

A FILTER expression in an EP-SPARQL query can be represented as a rule, too.[9] The head of that rule may be part of a goal. When the goal gets evaluated, the corresponding rule will be evaluated, too. For example, let us consider again rule (11.1) from Section 11.3 and its FILTER expression. We said that $\text{triple}(\tau, T_1, T_6)$ can be represented as:

$\text{triple}(\tau, T_1, T_6) \leftarrow \text{triple}(\tau', T_1, T_4)$ SEQ $\text{triple}(\tau_3, T_5, T_6)$

where $\text{triple}(\tau', T_1, T_4)$ is an intermediate triple, specified as:

$\text{triple}(\tau', T_1, T_4) \leftarrow \text{triple}(\tau_1, T_1, T_2)$ SEQ $\text{triple}(\tau_2, T_3, T_4)$.

When the FILTER expression is considered, throughout the binarization process, $\text{triple}(\tau, T_1, T_6)$ is transformed into next two rules:

$\text{triple}(\tau, T_1, T_6) \leftarrow \text{triple}(\tau'', T_1, T_6)$ SEQ
$\qquad\qquad\qquad\qquad\text{condition}(Price1, Price2, Price3)$
$\text{triple}(\tau'', T_1, T_6) \leftarrow \text{triple}(\tau', T_1, T_4)$ SEQ $\text{triple}(\tau_3, T_5, T_6)$

where condition is defined as the following Prolog rule[10]:

$\text{condition}(Price1, Price2, Price3) := $
$\quad P_1$ is $(Price1 * 0.7)$, $P_1 > Price2, P_2$ is $(Price1 * 0.5)$, $Price3 > P_2$.

11.6.3 Background Knowledge

To enable detection of more complex events, our approach combines streams with background knowledge. This knowledge describes the context (domain) in which complex events are detected. As such, it enables detection of real time situations that are identified based on explicit data (e.g., events) as well as on implicit knowledge (derived from the background knowledge).

The background knowledge may be specified either as a Prolog knowledgebase or as an RDFS ontology[11]. This enables our operational semantics to have all relevant parts expressible in a unified (logic rule) formalism, and ultimately to reason over a unified space. For example, while detecting a sequence of two events, we may check whether

---
[9] Here we focus on filters without time constraints. Time constrained filters will be explained later in this section.
[10] Note that $Price1, Price2, Price3$ are contained in τ_1, τ_2, τ_3.
[11] In the latter case, we utilize an existing library www.swi-prolog.org/pldoc/package/semweb.html to transform an RDFS ontology into Prolog rules and facts.

their joined attribute is an instance of a certain class (or any of its subclasses) defined in an ontology (e.g., see a Stream Reasoning test in Subsection 13.1.7.1). To prove this on the fly, an inference procedure needs to be executed. In this respect, our execution model detects time relations among streaming triples (events), and performs reasoning tasks when necessary. Since all components of an EP-SPARQL query – including background knowledge – are represented as (Prolog) rules, we will use a Prolog inference engine (in Chapter 12) to serve as an EP-SPARQL engine.

11.6.4 Equals

Two events are equal if they happen right at the same time (see the definition of *EqJoin* Section 11.4). Hence, in order to implement the EQUALS operator we again use the rules of the type (11.13)-(11.14). Additionally, we use the rule (11.15) to check whether the occurrence intervals of two events are equal, i.e., the rule compares whether the *start* of the first interval (TI_1_S) is equal to the *start* of the second interval (TI_2_S). The same check is done for the *end* of the two intervals.

$$\begin{aligned}
&equals(TI_1, TI_2) \leftarrow \\
&TI_1 = [TI_1\_S, TI_1\_E], validTimeInterval(TI_1), \\
&TI_2 = [TI_2\_S, TI_2\_E], validTimeInterval(TI_2), \\
&TI_1\_S = TI_2\_S, TI_1\_E = TI_2\_E.
\end{aligned} \quad (11.15)$$

$$validTimeInterval(TI) \leftarrow TI = [TI\_S, TI\_E], TI\_S@ < TI\_E. \quad (11.16)$$

Rule (11.16) is an auxiliary rule which makes sure that parameters of rule (11.15) are valid time intervals.

Other operators, such as juxtapositions of graph triples and UNION, are translated into EDBC rules analogously. Hence we omit further discussion here, and refer the interested reader to the conjunction (AND) and disjunction (OR) operations, described in Subsection 7.2.1 and Subsection 7.2.4.

11.7 Memory Management and Time Windows in EP-SPARQL

To *prune* outdated events, we use the three memory management techniques described in Subsection 10.3.1 and Subsection 10.3.2.

The first technique (see Subsection 10.3.1) modifies the binarization step by pushing time window constraints (set by FILTER expressions with time constraints[12], e.g., 30 days in EP-SPARQL query (11.1) from Section 11.3). The technique ensures that time window constraints are checked during the incremental event detection. Therefore, unnecessary

---

[12] Users are encouraged to specify time constraints in queries, as it enables the system to regularly free up its memory.

intermediary sub-complex events will not be generated if time constraints are violated (i.e., time expired).

The second solution (see Subsection 10.3.2) prunes expired events by using system generated events (SGE). Similar to the first technique, rules are defined with time window constraints, and the binarization pushes the constraints to sub-components. This technique, however, does not check its constraints at each step in the event detection incrementally. Instead, events are pruned periodically as SGE are triggered. The third solution (see Subsection 10.3.2) is a variation of the second one. While the second technique makes an assumption that the network delay is the same for all sources, the third technique constructs a garbage collection window for each pattern window individually.

For *time sliding windows*, we also need to prune expired events. This has been realized by using one of the three mentioned memory management techniques. Outdated events are pruned so that an aggregation function can be recomputed on the set of valid events. An output-aggregation event is triggered whenever a new valid event occurs.

Part IV

Practical Considerations

12

Implementation

As a proof of concept, we have provided a prototype implementation of the ETALIS Language for Events (ELE) presented in Chapter 6, as well as an implementation of all of its extensions, introduced in Chapter 9, Chapter 10 and Chapter 11. The system is called the Event-driven Transaction Logic Inference System (ETALIS)[1], and is based on the operational semantics of the language described in Chapter 7, i.e., it is established on goal-directed event-driven backward chaining (EDBC) rules and decomposition of complex event patterns into intermediate events (goals). ETALIS automatically compiles user-defined complex event patterns into EDBC rules. A user may additionally specify deductive rules as background knowledge (see Section 8.4). These rules can be directly written in Prolog, or alternatively, background knowledge can be structured in form of RDF Schema (RDFS) ontologies.

In this chapter we describe the prototype implementation of ETALIS by providing an architecture of the system and characterising its main components [ARFS12b].

12.1 ETALIS Architecture

In the following we give more details about internal processing in ETALIS, i.e., how events specified in ELE can be detected at run time.

ETALIS is a rule-based deductive system that acts as an event-driven engine. Figure 12.1 – as introduced in [ARFS12b] – shows basic operational steps that are undertaken in

---
[1] ETALIS: http://code.google.com/p/etalis/

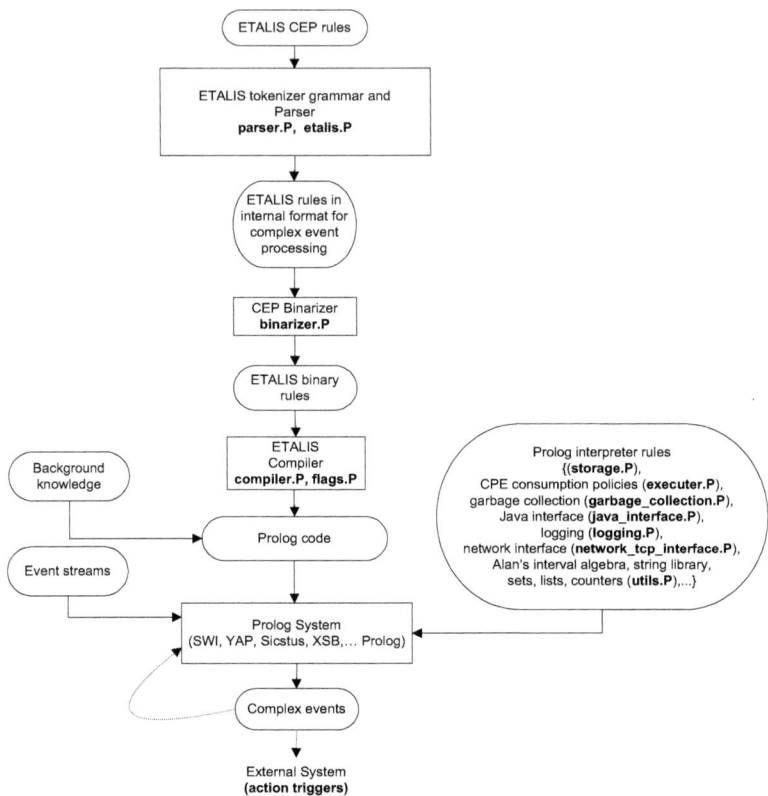

Figure 12.1: System Diagram: ETALIS

ETALIS. Rectangles in the diagram are used to depict certain processes in ETALIS, while ovals represent either (external/internal) inputs to these processes, or (external/internal) outputs from them.

The system diagram starts by user-written *ETALIS CEP rules* provided as input. These rules specify complex event patterns according to ELE (Chapter 6). ETALIS validates these rules with respect to the language grammar, and parses them[2]. As a result, the system produces rules in an *internal format*, ready for the process of *binarization* (see Figure 12.1).

Recall that the binarization eases internal processes in ETALIS for three reasons. First, it is easier to implement an event operator when events are considered on a "two by two" basis. Second, binarization increases the possibility for *sharing* among (complex) events and intermediate events (when the granularity of intermediate patterns is reduced).

---

[2]"parser.P" and "etalis.P" are source files that implement the corresponding functionality (see Figure 12.1) in our open source implementation http://code.google.com/p/etalis/.

12.1. ETALIS Architecture

Third, the binarization facilitates the *management* of rules. Each new use of an event (in a pattern) amounts to appending one or more rules to an existing rule set. What is important is that we never need to *modify* the existing rule set[3].

The *ETALIS Compiler* compiles binary rules into EDBC rules, i.e., executable rules (written in Prolog). EDBC rules are a basic mechanism in ETALIS that "converts" the request-response computation into an *event-driven* processing. It is a mechanism which enables an inference system to derive a complex event at the moment it really occurs (not at the moment when a request is posed). The notable property of these rules is that they are *event-driven*, i.e., a rule will be evaluated when an event, that matches the rule's head, occurs (see Chapter 7).

ETALIS compiler features a number of flags which can be set to tune the compiler[4]. Two important ones are the *revision* and *out-of-order* flag. The former flag enables the compiler to deal with retractions in Event Processing (EP) (see Chapter 9), and the latter one enables out-of-order EP (Chapter 10).

Complex event patterns may be accompanied with background knowledge to describe the domain of interest (as discussed in Section 8.4). Domain knowledge is also expected to be expressed either in Prolog (as shown in Example Application in Subsection 6.4.1), or in a form of an RDFS ontology (as presented in Example Application in Section 11.5).

Compiled rules, together with the domain knowledge, are executed by a standard Prolog system (e.g., SWI, YAP, XSB etc.). EDBC rules are triggered by events from *Event streams* (see Figure 12.1). As a result EDBC rules continuously derive complex events as soon as they happen.

Let us briefly explain the oval on the right hand side of Figure 12.1. Apart from pattern rules, detection of complex events also depends on *consumption policies*. Other important matters in ETALIS are *garbage collection*, and additional *algebra for reasoning* about time intervals, see Figure 12.1.

In EP, consumption policies (or event contexts [CKAK94]) deal with an issue of *selecting* particular events occurrences when there are more than one event instance applicable and *consuming* events after they have been used in patterns. We have implemented three widely used consumption policies: *recent, chronological,* and *unrestricted* policy (see Section 7.4).

ETALIS also features three memory management techniques to *prune* outdated events. The first technique modifies the binarization step by pushing time constraints[5]. The technique ensures that time constraints are checked during the incremental process of events detection. This enables ETALIS to refrain from detecting intermediary (sub-complex) events when time constraints are violated (i.e., time windows have expired). Our second solution for garbage collection is to prune expired events by using periodic events, generated by the system. This technique does not check the constraints at each step during the

---
[3]This property holds, even when patterns with negations are added.
[4]Flags are stored in flags.P file (see Figure 12.1).
[5]users are encouraged to write patterns with certain time window constraints

incremental event detection. Instead, events are pruned periodically as system events are triggered. The third technique is a variation of the second one, but it enables a pruning window to be established for each pattern individually (see Section 10.3).

As an algebra for reasoning about time intervals we have implemented Allen's temporal relationships [Alle83]. Using this algebra, the system can also reason about intervals of detected complex events (e.g., to discover whether one complex event occurred during another complex event, or whether one complex event starts/finishes another event). For more details see Chapter 6.

Finally, it is worth noting that detected complex events are fed back into the system, either to produce more complex events, or to trigger external actions in a timely fashion. Typically, this situation happens when *iterative* event patterns are processed (see Section 7.3). Recursion in the system diagram is denoted by the backward (dashed) edge, see Figure 12.1.

12.2 EP-SPARQL Implementation

Event Processing SPARQL (EP-SPARQL) is implemented as an extension to ELE (see Section 12.1). A system diagram of the EP-SPARQL extension has been introduced in [ARFS12b], and is shown in Figure 12.2.

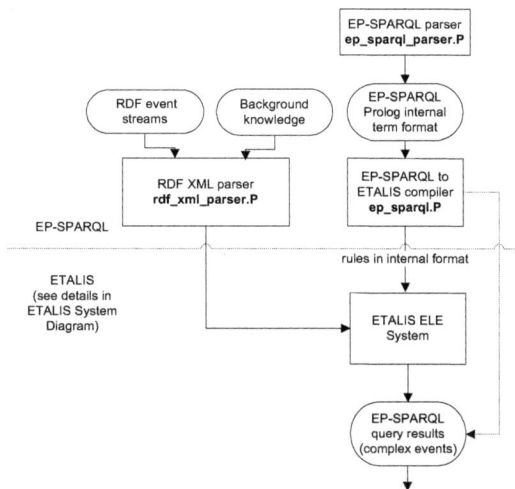

Figure 12.2: System Diagram: EP-SPARQL

A user writes EP-SPARQL queries and deploys them into the engine. These queries act similarly as *continuous* queries in Data Stream Management Systems (DSMS), i.e., once registered, queries are continuously evaluated with respect to streaming data. In our implementation, the engine *incrementally* matches incoming data (events), thereby producing complex events as soon as they occur (see Section 12.1).

Since event streams and a background knowledge are both represented in RDF, we use an RDF/XML parser to convert inputs into an internal ETALIS format (see Figure 12.2). For event streams, the conversion is applied on the fly. It is a straight forward mapping that typically does not cause a significant overhead at run time. As background knowledge (e.g., an RDFS ontology) is static knowledge, it is converted into a Prolog program at design time. Similarly, we have also implemented a parser for the EP-SPARQL syntax and a compiler which produces EDBC rules out of EP-SPARQL expressions. All three inputs (EP-SPARQL queries, event streams and a domain ontology) are then fed into ETALIS, where the processing (as described in Section 12.1) takes place.

12.3 Interacting with ETALIS

An EP system is typically used as a part of an event processing network (EPN). In Section 2.3 we talked about the three main building blocks of an EPN: event producers, event consumers, and event processing (see Figure 2.1). Figure 12.3 is similar in respect that it shows event producers (the left hand part of the figure), event consumers (the right hand part) and ETALIS itself (the middle part), as an an intermediate event processing in between. To enable an easy connection to event producers and consumers, ETALIS features two programming interfaces written in Prolog and Java.

The Prolog interface is the standard one (since ETALIS is written in Prolog). A user may acces ETALIS either through an application programming interface (API), or
through the command line interface. The command line interface is suitable for development, testing, and deployment of an event-driven application.

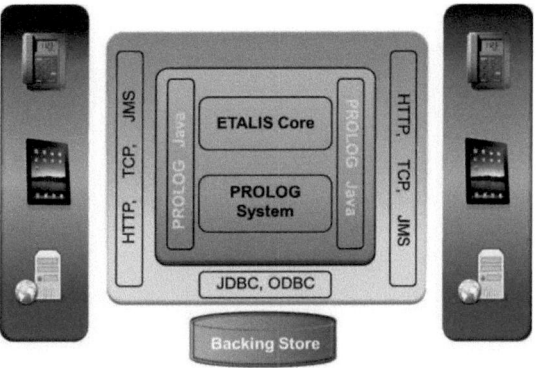

Figure 12.3: ETALIS interfaced with event producers and event consumers

Since EP tools belong to middleware systems (where they serve as a part of other complex systems), ETALIS is designed to be interfaced from other programming languages (e.g.,

Java, C and C#). This also enables ETALIS to be combined with existing programs and libraries. We have built one foreign language interface for Java[6]. The interface enables event producers to pass events to ETALIS, as well as event consumers to get events from the system. It also provides a convenient way for ETALIS to communicate with third part software components via the network, i.e., through Hypertext Transfer Protocol (HTTP), Transmission Control Protocol (TCP), Java Message Service (JMS) and other means for network communication enabled by Java (see Figure 12.3). Finally we provide two interfaces for persisting events in a database, i.e., Java Database Connectivity (JDBC), and Open Database Connectivity (ODBC) (see Figure 12.3).

As a future work we plan to build a graphic user interface, thereby providing another convenient way to interact with ETALIS.

More information about deployment and interactions with ETALIS can be found on ETALIS web site[7].

---

[6]jtalis: http://code.google.com/p/etalis/source/browse/#svn%2Fjtalis
[7]ETALIS: http://code.google.com/p/etalis/

13
Evaluation

In this chapter we present experimental results obtained with ETALIS. We perform evaluation tests for various aspects introduced in this work. Basic event patterns of ELE – introduced in Chapter 6 – are tested in Subsection 13.1.2. Tests where EP is intervened by background knowledge processing are presented in Subsection 13.1.3. From there on, we continue by presenting evaluations of extensions of ETALIS. Subsection 13.1.4 presents evaluation results for retractable EP, Subsection 13.1.5 shows tests related to out-of-order EP, and Subsection 13.1.6 provides evaluation of iterative and aggregative patterns. We conclude the performance evaluation of ETALIS by providing a set of EP-SPARQL tests in Subsection 13.1.7. Where possible, we compare the performance of ETALIS with Esper[1] – a well known open source EP system.

Finally, to show usefulness of ETALIS in practise, we present an implementation of a concrete use case study in Section 13.2.

13.1 Performance Evaluation

Performance evaluation tests discussed in this chapter show *throughput* or *latency* calculated for various aspects introduced in this work. As presented in [EtRS11], there exist different definitions for these two metrics. For instance, throughput can be measured in following ways: *input throughput* (measures the number of input events that the system

---
[1]Esper: http://esper.codehaus.org

can "digest" within a given time interval), *processing throughput* (measures the total processing times divided by the number of event processed within a given time interval), and *output throughput* (measures the number of events that were emitted to event consumers within a given time interval). In our tests we have adopted the input throughput, where the percentage of event instances that are processed in patterns is high.

Regarding the latency, we measure the latency of each event. For events that don't create derived events directly, we measure the time until the system finishes processing them [EtRS11].

The test cases presented here were carried out on a workstation with Intel Core Quad CPU Q9400 2,66GHz, 8GB of RAM running Windows Vista x64[2]. Since our prototype automatically compiles the user-defined complex event descriptions into Prolog rules, we used SWI Prolog version 5.6.64[3] and YAP Prolog version 5.1.3[4]. All tested engines ran in a single dedicated CPU core. The whole output generated from all tests is validated, so we have made sure that all tested systems produce the same, correct, results.

13.1.1 Data Sets

To run tests, we have implemented an event stream generator, which creates time series data with probabilistic values. We have also used a number of real data sets. In particular, event streams with stock data available from Google Finance[5] and Yahoo Finance[6] have been used, as well as live sensor readings from the National Data Buoy Center (NDBC)[7].

To test stream reasoning (SR) characteristics of ETALIS we use various domain ontologies. For instance, to compute subclass relations on the fly we use the Ethan Plants ontology[8], or to explore routes in Milan we use the Milan ontology[9]. Among other information sources, GeoNames ontologies[10] were utilised to identify important geographic locations (e.g., schools, hospitals, motorways, airports, tunnels, railroads etc.) affected by weather observations detected in our use case.

---

[2]Due to unavailability of the workstation, some tests were carried out on a workstation with Pentium dual-core processor 2GHz CPU and 3GB memory running on Ubuntu Linux.
[3]SWI Prolog http://www.swi-prolog.org/.
[4]YAP Prolog: http://www.dcc.fc.up.pt/~vsc/Yap/. Our prototype ran by YAP was using Windows x32, as we could not find YAP version x64 available. Other two systems (Esper and SWI) were running on Windows x64
[5]Google Finance: http://www.google.com/finance
[6]Yahoo Finance: http://finance.yahoo.com/
[7]NDBC: http://www.ndbc.noaa.gov/
[8]http://spire.umbc.edu/ontologies/EthanPlants.owl#Tracheobionta
[9]The Milan ontology was developed in the scope of LarCK project http://www.larkc.eu/, and was generously provided to us by AMAT Milano and CEFRIEL team: http://www.larkc.eu/resources/published-data-sources/
[10]GeoNames Ontolgy: http://www.geonames.org/ontology

13.1. Performance Evaluation

13.1.2 Run-Time Tests for Common Event Patterns

We start the evaluation of ETALIS by presenting experiments related to the sequence operator (SEQ) formally defined in Chapter 6. In particular, Figure 13.1 (a) shows the throughput measurements for a pattern that exhibits a sequence of three events and the join operation on their Id attribute, see rule (13.1). The Y-axis shows the event throughput achieved by the three different EP systems: Esper 3.3.0, and our prototype (P) running on SWI and YAP Prolog, denoted as P-SWI and P-YAP respectively. The X-axis shows different sizes of input event streams, used for detection of complex events as defined by rule (13.1). In this test, our system outperforms Esper 3.3.0. The throughput achieved by the YAP engine is more than twice as big as the one produced by Esper. Also comparing YAP and SWI, our implementation is significantly faster on YAP. This happens because YAP implements several optimizations to improve indexing.

In Figure 13.1 (b) we have evaluated patterns which – apart from the join operation – also contain a selection parameter K (see rule (13.2)). K varies the selectivity of the Y attribute, ranging from 10% till 100%. When 10%-50% of the input events are selected, Esper shows significant advantage over our system. Hence in the future we need to review our implementation so to select events as early as possible. When all events are taken into account (100% selectivity), our system running on YAP is slightly better than Esper. We did this test on a stream of 25000 artificially generated events.

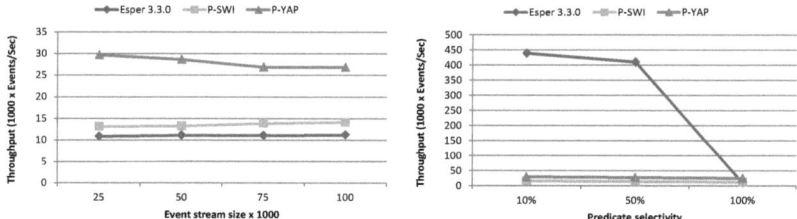

Figure 13.1: Experiments for sequence operator - (a) Throughput (b) Throughput vs. Predicate Selectivity

$$e \leftarrow a \text{ SEQ } b \text{ SEQ } c. \qquad (13.1)$$

$$c(Id, X, Y) \leftarrow a(Id, X) \text{ SEQ } b(Id, Y) \text{ WHERE } (Y < K). \qquad (13.2)$$

In Figure 13.2 (a) we extended the tests (for 100% selectivity) to check out whether the system throughput will remain constant for bigger streams (for example, 50K-100K).

Figure 13.2 (b) presents experimental results for *negation* (NOT). The figure shows results obtained by evaluating a negated pattern from rule (13.3). The pattern is detected when an instance of a is followed by an occurrence of b with no c in between the two events. We have generated input event streams with different percentage of occurrences of events of type c (that is, 10%-100%). We see that our prototype (either run by SWI or

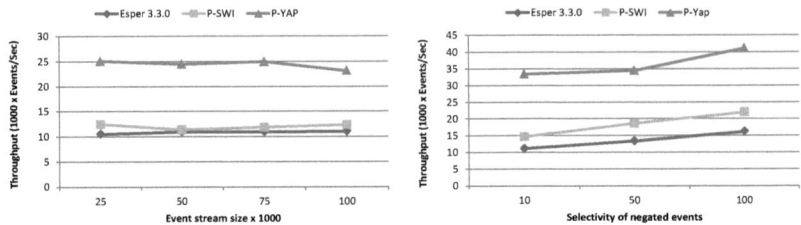

Figure 13.2: (a) Sequence - Throughput vs. Workload Change (b) Negation - Throughput vs. Selectivity

YAP) dominates over Esper. We also notice that the throughput increases as the percentage of c occurrences increases. This is happening as the number of detected complex events decreases by increasing the frequency of occurrences of c. The test is computed on a stream of 25K.

$$d(Id,X,Y) \leftarrow \text{NOT}(c(Id,Z)).[a(Id,X),b(Id,Y)]. \qquad (13.3)$$

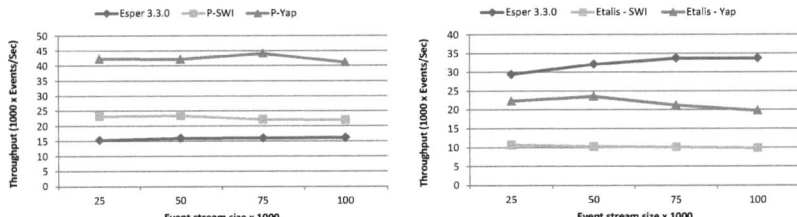

Figure 13.3: (a) Negation - Throughput vs. Workload Change (b) Conjunction - Throughput

Figure 13.3 (a) shows that the throughput does not go down even though we increased the stream size (for example, 50K-100K).

We have tested the conjunction operator (AND) too. The pattern is specified by rule (13.4), and results are presented in Figure 13.3 (b). Esper was faster in this test. Our algorithm for handling conjunction contains twice as many rules as the algorithm for sequence (that is, two events in a conjunct may occur in any order). As a future work, we will try to simplify the conjunction algorithm.

$$d(Id,X,Y) \leftarrow a(Id,X) \text{ AND } b(Id,Y) \text{ AND } c(Id,Z). \qquad (13.4)$$

Figure 13.4 (a) shows results for *disjunction* (OR), and evaluation of rule (13.5). In this test our system running on YAP was the most effective. The throughput for this test

13.1. Performance Evaluation

is similar to results for sequence (Figure 13.1 (a)); this means that the presence of a disjunct does not affect the performance of the sequence.

We have also tested computation of the transitive closure (see rule (13.6)). The throughput change for different sizes of event streams are presented in Figure 13.4 (b). Evaluation results were obtained under chronological consumption policy. Our system on YAP was the fastest, however the difference between evaluations running on YAP and SWI was huge (as discussed earlier, due to better optimizations for indexing in YAP).

Finally, Figure 13.5 compares the tested systems with respect to event plan sharing. We have run an event program containing the same pattern (similar to rule (13.1)) multiplying the pattern one, eight, and sixteen times. The focus was on examining how well the systems can exhibit computation sharing among patterns. In our prototype, we have implemented plan sharing by decoupling events in a complex event pattern. A pattern is represented as a set of binary events, and each couple can be shared among multiply complex event patterns. Despite this feature, our system run by YAP was not resistant to increase of pattern rules. However our prototype executed on SWI was still faster than Esper, see Figure 13.5.

$$d(Id,X,Y) \leftarrow a(Id,X) \text{ SEQ } (b(Id,Y) \text{ OR } c(Id,Y)). \tag{13.5}$$

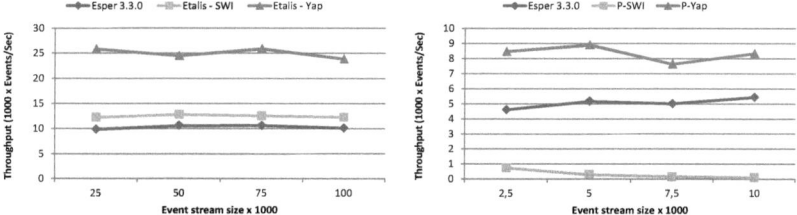

Figure 13.4: (a) Experiments for Disjunction Operator - Throughput (b) Evaluation of Transitive Closure - Workload Change

$$\begin{aligned} \text{tc}(X,Y) &\leftarrow \text{a}(X,Y). \\ \text{tc}(X,Y) &\leftarrow \text{tc}(X,Z) \text{ SEQ } \text{a}(Z,Y). \end{aligned} \tag{13.6}$$

It is worth mentioning that the cost of compilation of an *ELE* event program into Prolog rules is minor. Typically a program is compiled in few micro seconds. Hence the compilation phase does not cause a significant overhead. This observation holds for other tests in this chapter, as well as for use of ELE and ETALIS in genaral.

In this subsection, we have provided measurement results for few common event operators. Even though there is a lot of room for improvements, preliminary results show

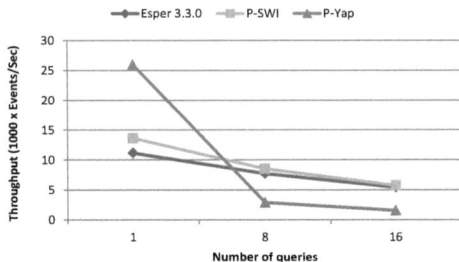

Figure 13.5: Experiment for Testing Computation Sharing for Sequence Operator

that logic-based event processing has the capability to achieve significant performance. Taking inference capability into account, logic-based EP goes beyond the state of the art in providing a powerful combination of *deductive* capabilities and *temporal* features[11], while at the same time exhibiting competitive run-time characteristics. We will present inference capability of ETALIS in the following subsection, as well as in other parts of this chapter.

13.1.3 Performance Evaluation for Knowledge-Based Event Processing

As a concrete example, we show the evaluation of the *trendIncrease* complex pattern from Subsection 9.2.1. We varied the pool of companies in the transitive closure, ranging from 100 to 100,000 *linked* companies. Figure 13.6 shows the throughput in thousands of events/second, obtained after detection of *stockIcr* events. To prove the supply-chain connectivity between two companies, the system needs to evaluate transitive closure rules, i.e., it needs to perform SR (see *inSupChain* rules from Subsection 9.2.1). It can be seen that the computation of the recursive relation *inSupChain* has a relatively small effect, ~10% (the throughput dropped from 24148 to 21739 Events/Sec), on the overall complex processing execution time (even when the system needs to traverse 100,000 *links* in between two *stockIcr* events). Our system detects more 20000 complex events per second, where for each complex event, the system additionally needed to process background knowledge consisting of 100000 facts.

In the remaining parts of this chapter we will show few additional tests related to knowledge-based Event Processing.

---

[11] We have skipped comparative tests requiring interval-based operators (for example, PAR, DURING and so forth), as Esper language semantics is based on time points and does not support these operators.

13.1. Performance Evaluation

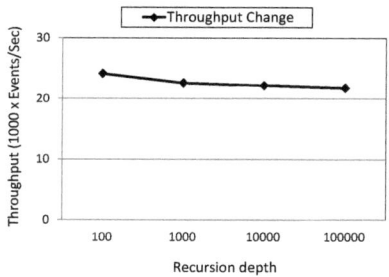

Figure 13.6: EP combined with Stream Reasoning

13.1.4 Performance Evaluation for Event Processing with Retractions

Figure 13.7 (a) shows experimental results we obtained for an event pattern represented by rule (13.7). In particular, Figure 13.7 (a) shows the throughput comparison with and without handling event revision. We did the measurement for a pattern that exhibits different event operators (i.e., BIN instantiated by SEQ, AND, OR) of two events and the join operation on their ID attribute. The Y-axis shows the event throughput achieved by our prototype when events are retractable and are not retractable (denoted by Revision Flag on/off, respectively). The X-axis shows different event operators in rule (13.7). The performance loss when revision is handled is moderate, and it happens mainly due to the fact that more events (goals) are kept in memory; hence more data needs to be indexed and processed.

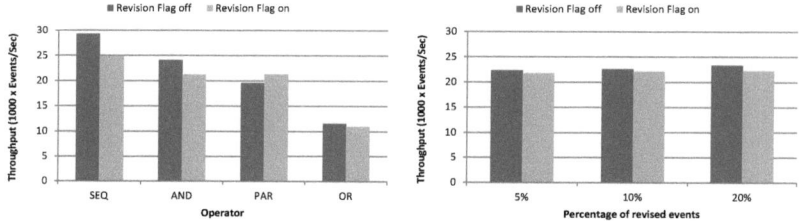

Figure 13.7: (a) Throughput comparison (b) Negation and revision

$$e(ID) \leftarrow a(ID) \text{ BIN } b(ID). \tag{13.7}$$

We also present an in-comparison throughput for negation. The tested pattern with negation is depicted by rule (13.8). The pattern detects an event a followed by an event b, with no occurrence of an event c in between (provided that all event instances must have the same ID). Figure 13.7 (b) shows evaluation results for this pattern. We compare two throughputs, one obtained by processing streams without retracted events; and another with retracted events. The percentage of negated events (i.e., those of type c) in both streams varies from 5% to 20%. Additionally, streams with retracted events contain negated events with the same percentage (i.e., from 5% to 20%). The achieved results are similar to those from other operators.

$$e(ID) \leftarrow \text{NOT}(c(ID)).[a(ID) \text{ SEQ } b(ID)]. \tag{13.8}$$

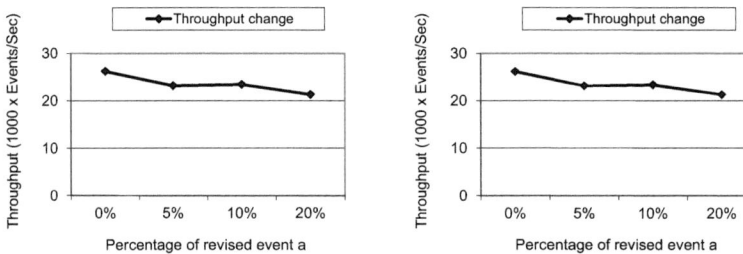

Figure 13.8: (a) Sequence - 1st event retracted (b) 2nd event retracted

Further, we tested how retraction of certain events and percentage of retracted events influence the overall performance. Figure 13.8 (a) and Figure 13.8 (b) show how retraction of each of the two constituting events in the sequence (rule (13.7)) influences the performance[12]. In Figure 13.8 (a), only event a is retractable while in Figure 13.8 (b), event b is retracted. We again compare the throughput with and without revision (retraction), although this time by varying the percentage of retracted events (from 0%, i.e., no revision till 20%).

To test the parallel operator, events in the pattern must have intervals with a non-zero overlap (i.e., synchronous events). One such pattern is presented with rule (13.9). Evaluation results for this pattern are shown in Figure 13.9 (a).

$$e(ID) \leftarrow (a(ID) \text{ SEQ } b(ID)) \text{ PAR } c(ID). \tag{13.9}$$

For sake of completeness, we made equivalent tests for conjunction and disjunction (based on rule (13.7)). Results are presented in Figure 13.9 (b) and Figure 13.10 (a), respectively. Overall we see that the throughput for all operators does not decline rapidly even for some rather big percentages of retracted events (e.g., 20%).

---

[12]Recall that each pattern – written in the proposed formalism – is broken into binarized patterns (see Section 13.1), the components of which are treated differently upon execution (goal assertion vs. goal retraction). Hence we could speculate whether there could exist a systematic difference depending on what component of a binary pattern is retracted.

13.1. Performance Evaluation

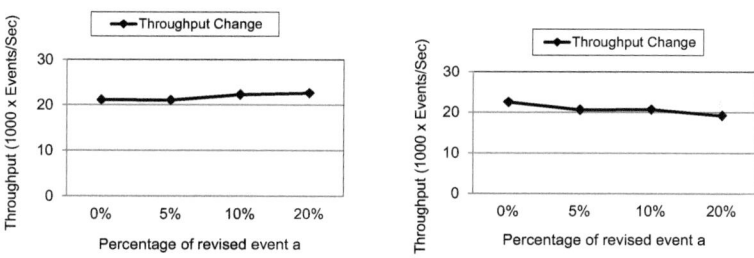

Figure 13.9: (a) Parallel - 1st event retracted (b) Conjunction - 1st event retracted

We have also tested the *latency* caused by retraction of a hierarchy of complex events (i.e., not only complex events detected directly from an input stream). Complex events in this test are chained events, as represented by rule (13.10). That is, when event e_1 occurs, it will trigger other n events in a chain. Also if event e_1 is retracted, all n chained events will be retracted. We have created event chains of different sizes, ranging from 1000 events to 50000 events. Once the chains are created, we retract the first event in the chain and measure the time required to retract all other triggered events. Figure 13.10 (b) shows the experiment results. Retraction of 1000 event is done in 31 ms; and until 10000 events, the delay seems fairly negligible (less than a second). However to retract 20000 and more (e.g., 50000 events), the time increases exponentially (i.e., approx. 3 s and 16 s). Note that this test is rather hard as we assumed that all 50000 events have the same *ID*, so no goal could have been removed while computing and retracting all of them. Obviously, this fact has its consequences on the performance.

$$e_2(ID) \leftarrow e_1(ID).$$
$$e_3(ID) \leftarrow e_2(ID).$$
$$\ldots$$
$$e_{n+1}(ID) \leftarrow e_n(ID).$$
(13.10)

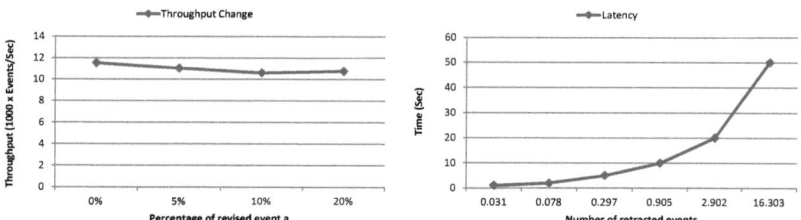

Figure 13.10: (a) Disjunction - 1st event retracted (b) Event latency

We have implemented time-based windows for all operators with revision. In general, windows in EP are used to discard outdated events and hence to free up the system memory. A *revision time-based* window specifies a period of time in which retraction of an event, as well as, retraction of its consequences (on other complex events) is still possible. We have tested how the length of the revision time-based *windows* influence the performance of our implementation. The length X from rule (13.11) was varied between 0.1 s and ∞ (i.e., revision possible anywhere in the stream). It is obvious that for $X = \infty$ and an infinite input stream, the system will get out of memory at some point. Therefore we constrained the input stream to 50000 events. The percentage of revision tuples was kept constant (1%). Figure 13.11 (a) shows results of this test. We see that the time required to process the input stream goes up (linearly) as the revision window increases. This happens simply as for larger windows more revisions need to be computed.

$$\text{rule}_1([\text{property}(window, X)]) : e(ID) \leftarrow a(ID) \text{ SEQ } b(ID). \tag{13.11}$$

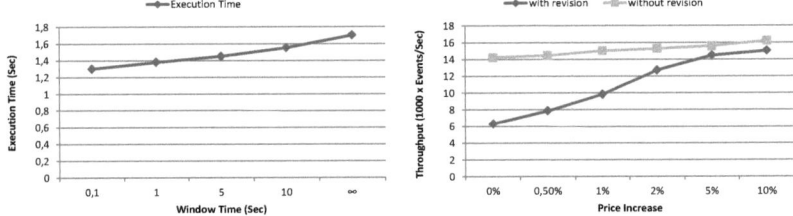

Figure 13.11: (a) Revision time-based windows (b) Stock price change on a real data set

All presented tests so far were carried out with probabilistic synthetic data streams. We could not find available real data sets with revision tuples (as they are usually kept proprietarily). Still to present a more realistic scenario, we took a stream of IBM stocks from 1962. year up to now, provided by Yahoo Finance[13]. We inserted 5% of revision tuples to this stream artificially. The format of events provided by Yahoo Finance is stock(*ID, Date, Opn, High, Low, Cls, Vol, Adj*) where *ID* is a company ID; *Date* is a current date; *Opn, High, Low, Cls* denote the opening, the highest, the lowest, and closing price, respectively; *Adj* is the closing price adjusted for dividends and splits. The event pattern is represented by rule (13.12). We monitored the price increase of two successive stock updates with respect to *Adj* data. Additionally a filter for the price increase was specified by X, where X varied between 0% and 10%. Figure 13.11 (b) compares results obtained for the original stream and the one modified with revision tuples.

---

[13] Yahoo Finance: http://finance.yahoo.com/

13.1. Performance Evaluation

$$\begin{aligned}
&\texttt{stockIncr}(ID, Adj_1, Adj_2) \leftarrow \\
&\quad \texttt{stock}(ID, Date_1, Opn_1, High_1, Low_1, Cls_1, Vol_1, Adj_1) \\
&\quad \text{SEQ} \\
&\quad \texttt{stock}(ID, Date_2, Opn_2, High_2, Low_2, Cls_2, Vol_2, Adj_2) \\
&\quad \text{WHERE } (Adj_1 * X < Adj_2).
\end{aligned} \qquad (13.12)$$

First, we see that the throughput without revision is lower than the one obtained from a similar test (see Figure 13.7 (a)). Our closer investigation has shown that this difference was not caused by the use of real data set. Instead it has to do with more efficient indexing in the former test (Figure 13.7 (a)). Note that in the real stream, all events are of the same type (i.e., *stock*) whereas in the synthetic data set we have two types (i.e., a and b). Our engine is more effective when events are discriminated upon their types (rather than on data attributes, e.g., an *ID*). Second, we can observe that the throughput without revision slightly increases as the filter condition gets tighter. This result is understandable, since in this case, less complex events, are computed and the throughput (based on the input stream) raises up.

Finally, we notice that the difference between the throughput with revision and without it at the beginning is significant, and then it gets smaller as the filter condition gets tighter. This happens again as a consequence of the number of computed complex events and their revisions. For 0%, the current price needs to be higher than the price of the previous stock update, no matter for how much this is ($X = 1$). Since more complex events and their revisions need to be processed, the difference is significant. For 10%, the current price needs to be for more that 10% higher than the price of the previous stock update ($X = 1.1$). In this case less revisions are computed, and consequentially the difference is smaller.

13.1.5 Performance Evaluation of Out-of-Order Event Processing

We have implemented techniques for dealing with out-of-order events in ETALIS (see Chapter 10). To test out-of-order event processing in our system, we have developed an automatic event stream generator. We have created different sets of event streams where probability of occurrences of out-of-order events varies between $p=0$ and $p=0,33$, i.e., between 0% and 33% of events are out-of-order. We also discuss a test, conducted with real data set.

In the remaining part of this section we report results obtained from the experiments. Unfortunately, since related approaches for dealing with out-of-order events [LLDR[+]07, BGAH07, BFSF08] are not open source systems we could not compare performance of ETALIS with them.

As a test program in this experiment, we consider rules (10.1)-(10.2). The test program is executed in two modes: first with the in-order events, and second with streams that contain out-of-order events.

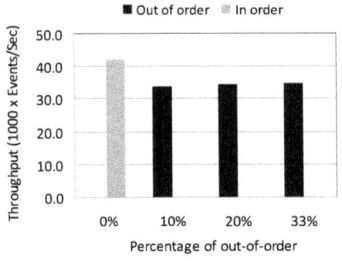
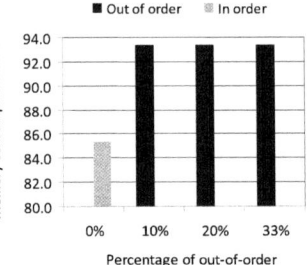

Figure 13.12: (a) Throughput comparison (b) Memory consumption

Figure 13.12 (a) shows experimental results we obtained for the *sequence* operator (i.e., rules (10.1)-(10.2)). In particular, Figure 13.12 (a) shows the throughput comparison with in-order and out-of-order event streams achieved by ETALIS (the Y-axis). The X-axis shows different percentages of out-of-order events, ranging between 0% (in-order events) until 33% (in average, every third event in the stream is an out-of-order event). We see that the performance loss when out-of-order events are handled is moderate even for high percentage of out-of-order events. It happens mainly due to the fact that more events (goals) are kept in memory; hence more data needs to be indexed and processed. This is evident in Figure 13.12 (b) which shows considerable bigger memory consumption with out-of-order events. However ETALIS was capable to keep memory consumption constant, even for frequent out-of order events.

For example, an approach presented in [LLDR+07] completes a similar test with a 60,000 stream in 200 seconds, a 80,000 stream in 400 seconds, i.e., approximatively between 200 and 300 events/second (see Figure 9 in [LLDR+07]). It is also evident that the presented throughput depends exponentially on the number of events. The results were obtained on two Pentium 4 3,0 GHz machines, each with 512M RAM. Our tests on ETALIS were performed on an 100000 event streams, and we have achieved a linearly-dependent throughput ranging between 30000 and 40000 events per second (for different percentages of out-of-order events). Moreover our approach to processing out-of-order events does not introduces *delay* through buffering and reordering as it occurs in related work in [LLDR+07, BGAH07, BFSF08].

13.1.5.1 Knowledge-Based Event Processing with Out-of-Order events

We continue tests related to EP and *background knowledge* processing. Additionally, we assume that events may come out-of-order. To demonstrate this scenario, let us consider the following example. Suppose we want to detect the stock price increase in a supply chain system of companies. The following pattern monitors two *stock price increases* in two companies (occurred within certain time window), and checks whether the compa-

13.1. Performance Evaluation

nies are parts of the *supply chain system*.

```
trendIncrease() ←
  (stockIcr(CompanyA) SEQ stockIcr(CompanyB)).10
  WHERE inSupChain(CompanyA,CompanyB).
```

The supply chain system is represented as a set of explicit links between companies, e.g., with linked(*CompanyA,CompanyB*) we represent two interconnected businesses involved in the ultimate provision of a product. We assume that such explicit relationships are continuously being updated via according *information events* (e.g., a data mining tool processes different information sources and generates these events). The following transitive closure pattern can then be used to span over semantic relationships between companies scenario where direct supply relationships are represented *explicitly*, and hence discover *implicit* relationships.

```
inSupChain(X,Y) ← linked(X,Y).
inSupChain(X,Z) ← linked(X,Y) AND inSupChain(Y,Z).
```

We tested this application scenario with presence of *out-of-order* events, and results are shown in Figure 13.13 and Figure 13.14. In particular, Figure 13.13 shows throughput obtained for trendIncrease complex events. To detect a trendIncrease event, ETALIS needs to detect stock price increases of two companies and check the *supply-chain* connectivity (inSupChain relations) among them. To prove inSupChain relations the system needs to traverse up to 1000 links between companies' relations in real time (on the fly) when respective events occur. Percentage of out-of-order events was 20%. For this, rather hard test, we see that throughput declines as ETALIS needs to evaluate more background knowledge (and out-of-order events occur), though memory consumption is kept constant.

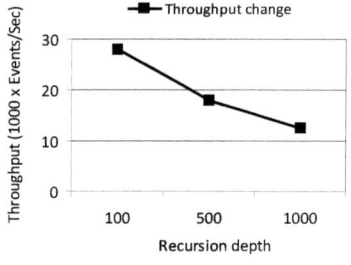
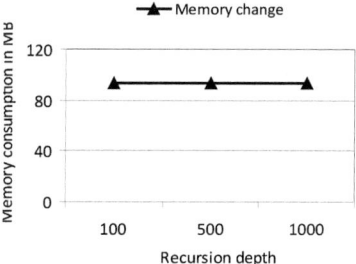

Figure 13.13: Throughput change as the size of companies' relations varies from 100 to 1000

Figure 13.14: Memory consumption in the knowledge-based EP test

13.1.5.2 Test with Real Dataset and Out-of-Order Events

So far, the presented tests with out-of-order events were carried out with probabilistic synthetic data streams.

Similarly as for retracted events, we could not find real out-of-order data sets available (as they are usually kept proprietarily). Still to present a more realistic scenario, we have reconstructed the test with a history stream of IBM stocks (see Subsection 13.1.4). We have modified timestamps of 10% of events so to appear as out-of-order. Recall that format of events, provided by Yahoo Finance, is stock($ID, Date, Opn, High, Low, Cls, Vol, Adj$) where ID is a company ID; $Date$ is a current date; Opn, $High$, Low, Cls denote the opening, the highest, the lowest, and closing price, respectively; Adj is the closing price adjusted for dividends and splits. The event pattern is represented by rule (13.12) from Subsection 13.1.4. We monitored the price increase of two successive stock updates with respect to Adj data. Additionally, a filter for the price increase was specified by X, where X varied between 0% and 10%. Figure 13.15 (a) compares results obtained for the original stream (in-order) and the one modified with out-of-order timestamps. The second graph in Figure 13.15 (b) shows the memory consumption for these two cases.

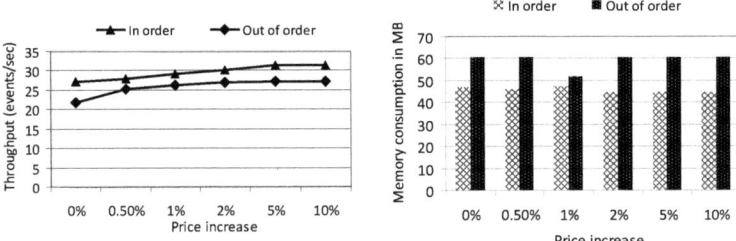

Figure 13.15: Stock price change on a real data set: (a) throughput (b) memory consumption

We see that the throughput with in-order and out-of-order events is different due to the price we pay for computation of delayed events. We can also observe that the throughput with and without out-of-order events slightly increases as the filter condition gets tighter. This result is understandable since in this case less complex events are computed and the throughput (based on the input stream) raises up.

13.1.6 Performance Evaluation for Iterative Patterns

We have conducted few performance tests related to iterative and aggregative patterns [ARFS11a]. For an introduction to iterative and aggregative rules, the interested reader is referred to Section 7.3 and [ARFS11a].

13.1. Performance Evaluation

13.1.6.1 Test 1: Sum with Sequance

We have evaluated the *sum* aggregation function, defined by iterative pattern (13.13). The moving sum is computed over the stream of complex events. Complex events are defined as a *sequence* of two events, joined on their *ID* (see pattern rule (13.14)). The sum is aggregated on the attribute X of complex events a(ID,X,Y). Figure 13.16 shows the performance results. In particular, the figure shows how the throughput depends on different sizes of the sliding window. Our system ETALIS was run in two modes: using the window implementation based on the stack and the difference lists, denoted as P-Stack and P-Dlists, respectively. In both modes our implementation has outperformed Esper 3.3.0., see Figure 13.16.

$$\begin{aligned}
&\text{sum}(StartCntr = 0, StartVal) \leftarrow \texttt{start\_event}(StartVal).\\
&\text{sum}(OldCntr + 1, NewSum) \leftarrow \\
&\quad \text{sum}(OldCntr + 1, OldSum) \text{ SEQ a}(AggArg)\\
&\quad \text{WHERE } \{\texttt{assert}(AggArg),\\
&\quad\quad \texttt{window}(WndwSize, OldCntr,\\
&\quad\quad\quad OldSum + AggArg, AggArg, NewSum)\}.
\end{aligned} \quad (13.13)$$

$$\begin{aligned}
&\texttt{window}(WndwSize, OldCntr, CurrSum, NewSum): -\\
&\quad OldCntr + 1 >= WindowSize - >\\
&\quad \texttt{retract}(LastItem),\\
&\quad NewSum = CurrSum - LastItem;\\
&\quad NewSum = CurrSum - LastItem.
\end{aligned}$$

$$\text{a}(ID, X, Y) \leftarrow \text{b}(ID, X) \text{ AND } \text{c}(ID, Y). \quad (13.14)$$

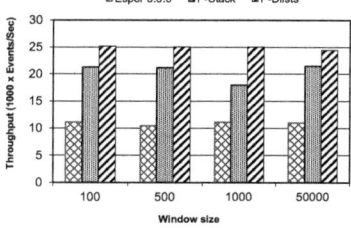

Figure 13.16: SUM-SEQ: throughput vs. window size

13.1.6.2 Test 2: Average with Sequence

In the next test we computed the moving *average* (avg) over the stream of complex events. Complex events were defined by rule (13.14) where operator AND was replaced with the *sequence* operator (SEQ). Again, ETALIS was run with windows implemented with the stack and different lists. Results are presented in Figure 13.17, showing the dominance of our system.

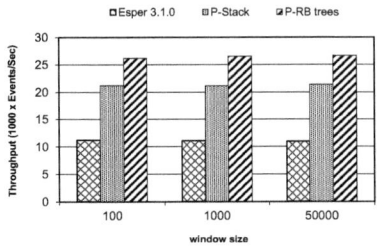

Figure 13.17: AVG-SEQ: throughput vs. window size

13.1.6.3 Test 3: Maximum with Disjunction

When calculating aggregates, that require search over sliding windows (e.g., min, max, etc.), it is convenient to use balanced binary search trees. For this purpose ETALIS utilizes the red-black trees[14]. The following test shows computation of the *maximum* over the stream of complex events using the iterative pattern (13.15). Complex events are defined as a *sequence* that involves *disjunction* of events (see rule (13.16)). We searched for the maximum on the attribute Y of complex events a(ID,X,Y). Figure 13.18 shows again the dominance of ETALIS over Esper. However, while Esper throughput is rather constant, the performance of our implementation has been dropping for larger windows (and then was kept constant). Hence we will continue experimenting with other data structures to achieve a more stable throughput.

Results for the minimum aggregation function has shown to be similar as for the maximum, hence we omit the presentation of this test here.

$$\begin{aligned}
&\max(StartCntr = 0, StartVal) \leftarrow \text{start\_event}(StartVal).\\
&\max(OldCntr+1, NewMax) \leftarrow \\
&\quad \max(OldCntr+1, OldMax) \text{ SEQ } a(AggArg)\\
&\quad \text{WHERE } \{\text{assert}(AggArg),\\
&\quad\quad \text{window}(WndwSize, OldCntr, NewMax)\}.
\end{aligned} \quad (13.15)$$

$$\begin{aligned}
&\text{window}(WndwSize, OldCntr, NewMax) : -\\
&\quad OldCntr + 1 >= WindowSize - >\\
&\quad \text{retract}(LastItem), get(NewMax);\\
&\quad get(NewMax).
\end{aligned}$$

---
[14]Red-black tree: http://en.wikipedia.org/wiki/Red%E2%80%93black_tree

13.1. Performance Evaluation

$$a(ID, X, Y) \leftarrow b(ID, X) \text{ SEQ } (c(ID, Y) \text{ OR } d(ID, Y)). \tag{13.16}$$

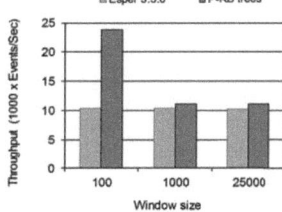

Figure 13.18: MAX-OR: throughput vs. window size

13.1.6.4 Test 4: Count with Negation

Finally, we present test results for the *count* pattern (13.17) over complex events with *negation*, see rule (13.18). We computed the count aggregation for different event streams. Probability of occurrence of the negated events was changed so to obtain selectivity of 10%, 50%, and 100% (i.e., 10%, 50%, and 100% of complex events contributed in iterative patterns). Results are shown in Figure 13.19 where we see that ETALIS is around three times faster than Esper 3.3.0.

$$\begin{aligned}
&\texttt{iteration}(StartCntr = 0, StartVal) \leftarrow \texttt{start\_event}(StartVal).\\
&\texttt{iteration}(NewCntr) \leftarrow \\
&\quad \texttt{iteration}(OldCntr) \text{ SEQ } \texttt{a}(AggArg)\\
&\quad \text{WHERE } \{NewCntr = \texttt{getCount}([T_2, T_1]), \texttt{window}(3min)\}.
\end{aligned} \tag{13.17}$$

$$a(ID, X, Y) \leftarrow \text{NOT}(d(ID, Z)).[b(ID, X), c(ID, Y)] \tag{13.18}$$

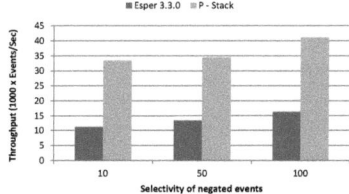

Figure 13.19: COUNT-NOT: throughput vs. window size

In the remaining part of this section we present two application scenarios that involve – apart from EP capabilities – on line *knowledge processing* and *stream reasoning*. Since these features are beyond of Esper capabilities we show the evaluation for ETALIS only.

13.1.6.5 Application 1: Supply Chain

EP can be combined with evaluation of *background knowledge* to detect real time situations of interest. To demonstrate this functionality, let us consider the following example. Suppose we monitor a shipment delivery process in a supply chain system. The following rules represent a complex pattern (delivery event), triggered by every shipment event. This iterative pattern may be used to *aggregate* certain values carried by shipment events; or for example, one can conclude whether the shipment has been delivered within the *expected* time by observing timestamps of the first and last delivery event.

$$\begin{aligned} &\text{delivery}(Start, Start) \leftarrow \text{shipment}(Start). \\ &\text{delivery}(From, To) \leftarrow \text{delivery}(From, PrevTo) \\ &\qquad \text{SEQ shipment}(To) \\ &\qquad \text{WHERE inSupChain}(From, To). \end{aligned} \qquad (13.19)$$

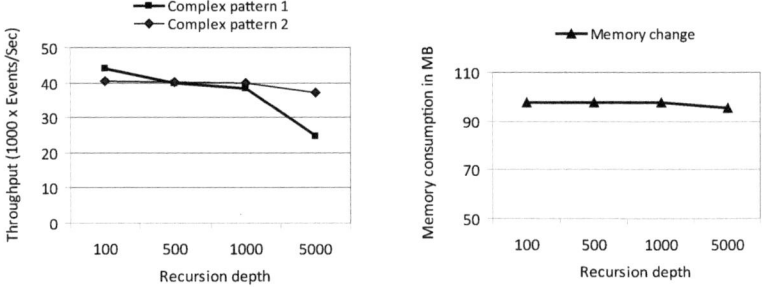

Figure 13.20: (a) Throughput comparison (b) Memory consumption

In our example application there is an additional constraint, i.e., every shipment on its way passes a number of sites where the *delivery path* is strictly defined. For example, a shipment is sent from site number 3, it needs to pass the site number 4, and to reach its final destination, the site number 5. Every shipment contains the next address (*To*) it needs to reach on its way (see shipment(*To*)). To be accepted as a valid delivery, this address is challenged with respect to the predefined path. Valid paths are represented as sets of explicit links between sites, e.g., with linked($site_3, site_4$) we represent two connected sites. If for that shipment there exists also another connection linked($site_4, site_5$), the system can *infer* that the path $site_3, site_4, site_5$ is a valid path (performing the *reasoning* over the following transitive closure and available background knowledge):

inSupChain(*X*,*Y*) : − linked(*X*,*Y*).
inSupChain(*X*,*Z*) : − linked(*X*,*Y*) AND inSupChain(*Y*,*Z*).

13.1. Performance Evaluation

The knowledge about connected (valid) paths represents our background knowledge. This knowledge is continuously updated as some links may be temporary unavailable; and other new links may be added in the system. Therefore the transitive closure `inSupChain` is evaluated on the fly whenever a new `shipment` event occurs.

We have evaluated the iterative `delivery` pattern for different sizes of supply chain paths (between 100 and 5000 links), see Figure 13.20 (a). We have achieved a high throughput despite the fact that for each detected complex event, ETALIS additionally needed to evaluate the background knowledge. In "Complex pattern 1" we enforce that for each new `shipment` event, the valid path must be proved from its beginning (see `inSupChain(From,To)` in rule (13.19)). For longer paths (e.g., 5000 links) this is a significant overhead, and we see that the throughput declines. If we however relax the check so that for every new event the path must be checked with respect only to the last `delivery` event, i.e., we replace `inSupChain(From,To)` with `inSupChain(PrevTo, To)` in rule (13.19)) we obtain the throughput which is almost constant (see "Complex pattern 2" in Figure 13.20 (a)).

Figure 13.21 (b) shows the total memory consumption for the presented test. There is no difference in memory consumption for complex patterns 1 and 2, hence we present only one curve.

13.1.6.6 Application 2: Stock Trade

There is an increasing need to process events from Web 2.0 sources (e.g., microblogs, social networks etc.) in near real time. For example, tweets[15] can be converted into events and used for detection of some more complex situations. These situations represent *topics of interest* which need to be detected nearly in *real time* (e.g., developing news stories such as buyout speculations).

We combined events from Twitter with stock events from Google Finance[16] to detect interesting situations. In particular, at the beginning of August 2010 we detected a hot discussion on Twitter about a company 3PAR, and a buyout race for that company between Hewlett-Packard and Dell Inc. This news event triggered ETALIS to monitor real 3PAR stocks from Google Finance[17]. We have created two patterns, one to monitor the *average* price (using a modified version of the pattern (13.13)) and the other one to compute the *maximum* price (using the pattern (13.15)) on a 10-day sliding window.

Figure 13.21 shows results from these two patterns. When the news event occurred on Twitter (at the beginning of August 2010) there was no big difference between the average and maximum values. Later, when it was certain that the buyout will happen (around August 13th) 3PAR stocks rapidly increased.

---

[15]from Twitter: http://twitter.com/
[16]Google Finance: http://google.com/finance
[17]We have manually triggered ETALIS to start monitoring stocks of 3PAR. Proper detection of an interesting situation should involve natural language processing and machine learning techniques, which are out of scope of this work.

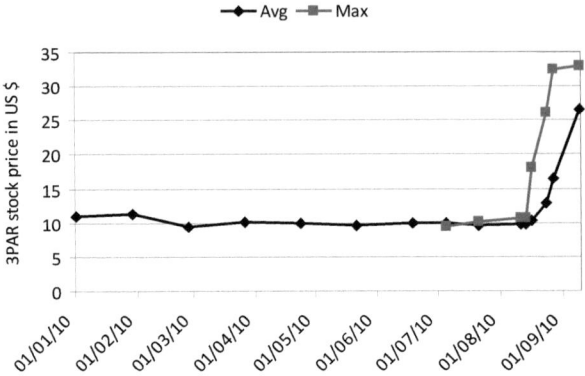

Figure 13.21: Average and maximum stock prices

In the test, our intention was to realize the *machine processable* detection of a period of time in which trade of 3PAR shares could have been considered as indeed beneficial (between the news event and August 13th). This is a viable approach to monitor stock fluctuations, and to cope with the amount of information sources currently available on line.

Moreover we extended this application to include also certain domain knowledge. Typically, companies *related* to 3PAR benefit as merger and acquisition rumours abound. Therefore we created small domain knowledge containing companies related to 3PAR[18]. When ETALIS started to monitor 3PAR stocks, it automatically applied the same event patterns on related companies too. The monitoring showed that few other related companies (e.g., Micron Technology, NetApp Inc., Dot Hill Systems Corp., Xyratex Ltd., ADPT Corporation, Compellent Technologies, Inc.) benefited from the bidding war between Dell Inc and Hewlett-Packard. In particular, ETALIS registered that shares of these companies, during the monitored period, increased between 10% and 50%.

In this subsection we arguably demonstrated the performance and versatility of the introduced approach for *iterative* and *aggregative* patterns, combined in a declarative framework for *on line knowledge* processing. First, we showed that such an approach is efficient on a set of common aggregation functions. Second, it enables new powerful applications that are beyond the state of the art. Third, we showed that with our approach it is possible to realise not only a set of event patterns, but rather *event-driven applications* which include expressive event patterns, as well as domain knowledge, and enable inference procedures under time constraints.

---

[18]Google Finance offers this knowledge for every company listed in the stock market, see for example 3PAR related companies: http://google.com/finance/related?q=NYSE:PAR

13.1.7 Experimental Results for EP-SPARQL

To evaluate EP-SPARQL, introduced in Chapter 11 and [AFRS11a], we have created few performance tests. This section includes a test which demonstrates SR features of ETALIS (Subsubsection 13.1.7.1), as well as two example applications that use both EP and SR capabilities of ETALIS (Subsubsection 13.1.7.2).

13.1.7.1 Test 1: Stream Reasoning

To provide a performance evaluation for the SR functionality, we have reconstructed an experiment from [WJFY08]. The goal of the test is to listen to streaming triples, and to infer whether the subject of a triple is an instance of the class of concern (or any of its subclasses). Suppose we process streaming triples about plants as part of a scientific experiment. Our system needs to check whether each triple in the stream carries an instance of a certain plant. The class of concern is defined in an ontology[19]. The ontology has 40,080 subclasses with a maximum class-hierarchy depth of eight.

This test has been reconstructed from [WJFY08] to check performance of ETALIS. Hence, similarly as in [WJFY08], we measured delay caused by the automated reasoning process needed to determine whether an entry in a streaming triple is an instance of the class of concern. The work in [WJFY08] provides three implementations: the first based on Jena[20], the second based on pre-computed inference results stored in a hash table, and the third based on a streaming database engine TelegraphCQ [CCDF+03] (none of which was available for download and testing). According to [WJFY08], the fastest implementation is the third one (which also pre-computes all inferences and stores them in a PostgreSQL database).

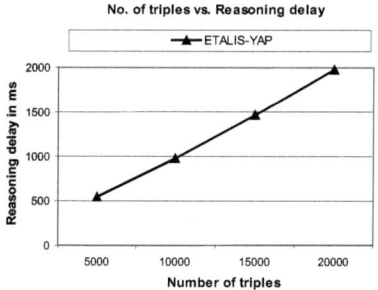

Figure 13.22: Delay caused by stream reasoning

Figure 13.22 shows results of the same test with ETALIS. Our system is more than 20 times faster. On one hand, we did the test on a machine that is faster than the one from

---
[19]http://spire.umbc.edu/ontologies/EthanPlants.owl#Tracheobionta
[20]Jena: http://jena.sourceforge.net/

[WJFY08]. On the other hand, ETALIS was doing SR on the fly (with no persisted inferences), and still performed significantly faster.

In the future, we also plan to provide persistence of inferences (as in [WJFY08]) in order to speed up query processing. FILTER sub-patterns which demand access and reasoning over *static* knowledge (ontologies) can be pre-computed. These results can then be reused every time a query needs to be executed. This approach may be beneficial when large ontologies are used, and events are streamed with a high frequency (e.g., hundred thousands events per second).

13.1.7.2 Test 2: Example Applications

We developed an application using both event streams and static RDF knowledgebases. The application implements the Goods Delivery System in the city of Milan. The system comprises of a set of delivery agents that need to deliver the manufactured products to the consumers. Each of them has a list of locations that it needs to deliver goods to. While an agent is visiting a particular location, the system "knows" her next location and "*listens*" to traffic-update events on that route(s). If the agent requests the next route at the moment when the route is currently inaccessible (e.g., due to traffic jam), the system will find another route (calculating a transitive closure on the fly over the background ontology). We use a Milan ontology[21] to explore routes in Milan. The application has been implemented on top of EP-SPARQL and ETALIS. Due to space limitations we cannot show patterns from the whole application here. Instead, we show in Figure 13.23 results obtained for 1 and 10 delivery agents (visitors) when each visiting 20 locations (the time spent at a location is irrelevant for the test, hence it is ignored). We simulated situations where more than 50% of the connections between the visiting locations were inaccessible, so that the system needed to recalculate the traffic routes frequently (as response to traffic-update events).

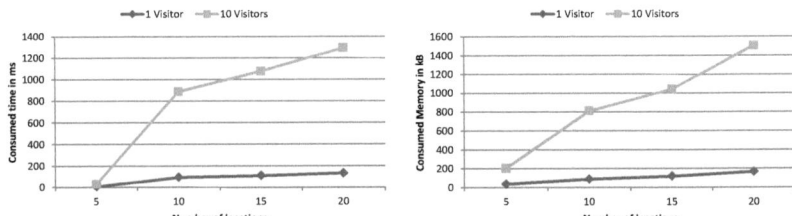

Figure 13.23: Goods Delivery System: (a) Delay caused by processing (b) Memory consumption

The goal of the test was to show the usefulness of our formalism in a real-use scenario, as well as to show that the application scales well with the increase of number of agents

---

[21]Milan ontology was developed in the scope of LarCK project http://www.larkc.eu/, and was generously provided to us by AMAT Milano and CEFRIEL team: http://www.larkc.eu/resources/published-data-sources/

13.1. Performance Evaluation

(throughput for one agent is about 10 times higher than the throughput for 10 agents (visitors), indicating a *linear* relationship in the investigated range, see Figure 13.23 (a)). Similarly, Figure 13.23 (b) shows memory consumption for the same test (likewise indicating a linear space dependency with respect to the number of agents).

Next, we have developed a real time service for detection of tsunamis. A tsunamis gauge is designed to detect and report tsunamis based on buoy sensor data. Data is provided by the National Data Buoy Center (NDBC)[22]. We have implemented a tsunami detection algorithm[23] which works by predicting the amplitudes of the pressure fluctuations within the tsunami frequency band, and then it tests these amplitudes against a threshold value. The prediction is calculated by the following formula:

$$H_p(t') = \sum_{i=0}^{3} w(i) H^*(t - i \cdot \Delta t)$$

where $w(i)$ are coefficients that come from Newton's formula for forward extrapolation. The NDBC uses the following values for these coefficients:

$$w(0) = 1.16818457031250$$
$$w(1) = -0.28197558593750$$
$$w(2) = 0.14689746093750$$
$$w(3) = -0.03310644531250$$

Buoy sensor data is updated every 15 seconds, providing the sea level pressure, air temperature, wind speed, wave hight etc. The asterisk H^* denotes average pressure. Four values are continuously produced over a 3 hour sliding window ($i = 0,..,3$ where a new value is outputted every hour, i.e., $\Delta t = 1$ hour), and t' is the prediction time which is set to 5,25 minutes. A tsunami is detected if the difference between the observed pressure (current sensor value) and the prediction H_p exceeds a threshold (30 mm for the North Pacific as prescribed by the NDBC). The difference magnitude was continuously calculated over historic NDBC data from May 2005 until September 2010. In this period, 44310 sensor readings were reported to ETALIS. The system detected pressure differences higher than 30 mm only 3 times (all 3 times during 3 hours, on 23.03.2010). Results are shown as a histogram in Figure 13.24. The chosen sensor station[24] is located in the Bering Sea, close to Alaska ($55°0'40''N 171°58'50''W$).

Further on, we have utilized GeoNames[25] as a worldwide geographical knowledgebase. If a sensor detects a tsunami, GeoNames can provide all geographical places within a certain radius from the sensor location. These places can then automatically be warned of

---

[22]NDBC : http://www.ndbc.noaa.gov/
[23]http://www.ndbc.noaa.gov/dart/algorithm.shtml
[24]http://www.ndbc.noaa.gov/station_page.php?station=46073
[25]GeoNames: http://www.geonames.org/

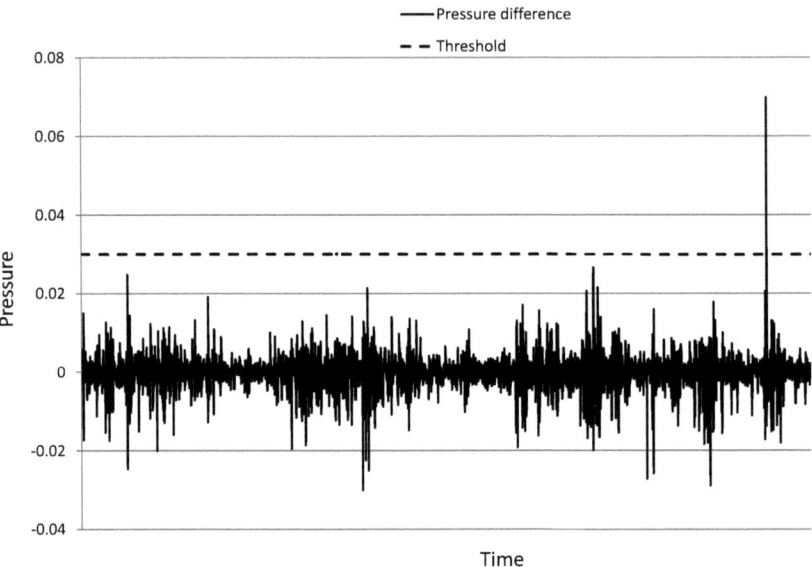

Figure 13.24: Tsunami detection histogram

a detected tsunami. We have set up an on line demo for this application[26] to continuously monitor live data provided by NDBC and detect tsunami warnings in real time.

13.2 Use Case: On The Live Measurements of Environmental Phenomena

To demonstrate the usefulness of our framework in practice, we have developed a use case using real sensor data. The use case is connected to a sensor network called MesoWest[27], which provides measurements of environmental phenomena (e.g., weather observations such as wind, temperature, humidity, precipitation, visibility and so forth). The goal of our use case application is to demonstrate how simple sensor readings can be analysed on the fly, and hence used to detect more complex weather observations (e.g., blizzards, hurricanes etc.). Further on, we demonstrate how sensor data can be integrated over *time* and geographical *space*. For instance, observations of a blizzard, detected by few nearby sensors within a certain time frame, identify an affected blizzard area. A blizzard warning may be issued as soon as the application detects such a situation. Moreover, the application utilizes GeoNames semantic information[28] to identify all important geographic

---
[26]See http://etalis.fzi.de
[27]MesoWest: http://mesowest.utah.edu/
[28]GeoNames Ontolgy: http://www.geonames.org/ontology

locations (e.g., schools, hospitals, motorways, airports, tunnels, railroads etc.) affected by that weather observation, so that further (security) actions can be taken in case of an emergency.

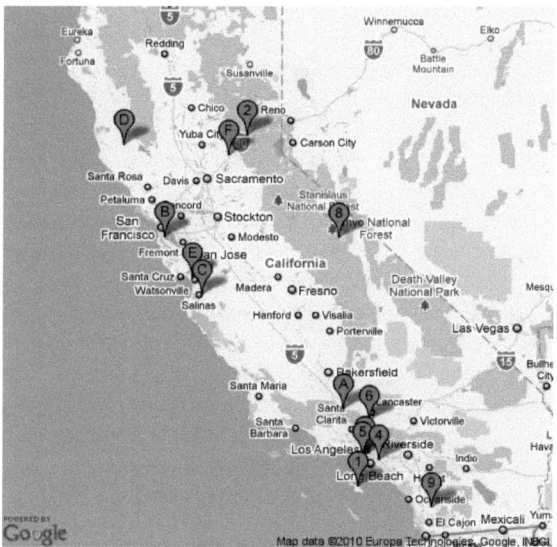

Figure 13.25: Sensor Location Map

MesoWest is a cooperative project between researchers at the University of Utah, forecasters at the Salt Lake City National Weather Service Office, the NWS Western Region Headquarters, and many other participating agencies, universities, and commercial firms. The network includes around 20,000 weather stations in the United States. For this experiment we have selected 15 sensors from California (we have chosen California since density of available sensors in that US state is high). Locations of the selected sensors are indicated by red markers in Figure 13.25 (enumerated with hexadecimal numbers: 1,2,3,...,F). Experiments are conducted on sensor data starting from 2007-12-31 until 2010-20-11. In our running example, the goal was to detect a blizzard from MesoWest streaming data. According to National Oceanic and Atmospheric Administration[29] (NOAA), a blizzard occurs when the following conditions prevail over a period of 3 hours or longer: high wind speed (35 miles an hour or greater); considerable falling snow; and low visibility (less than 1/4 mile). The following event pattern (13.20) is used to detect a blizzard settling situation:

---

[29]NOAA: http://www.noaa.gov/

$$\texttt{blizzardSettling}(T_1, T_1, ID, 1) \leftarrow$$
$$\texttt{sensor}(T_1, ID, Temp, Wind, WtherCond, Visib)$$
$$\text{WHERE } (Wind > 35, WtherCond ==' snow', Visib < 0.25).$$

$$\texttt{blizzardSettling}(T_1, T_3, ID, C+1) \leftarrow \qquad (13.20)$$
$$\texttt{blizzardSettling}(T_1, T_2, ID, C) \text{ SEQ}$$
$$\texttt{sensor}(T_3, ID, Temp, Wind, WtherCond, Visib)$$
$$\text{WHERE } (Wind > 35, WtherCond ==' snow', Visib < 0.25).$$

The first rule operates on sensor reading events that carry a timestamp T[30], as well as, a number of other parameters: a weather station *ID*, the current temperature *Temp*, wind speed *Wind*, weather condition *WtherCond*, and visibility measure *Visib*. The rule detects a sensor reading which satisfies the blizzard condition, and triggers a blizzard Settling event. This event will start the second, iterative rule in (13.20). Every new sensor reading (matching the same *ID*, and passing the filter condition) will trigger a new blizzardSettling event and increase a counter C. The counter is used to implement the situation in which the blizzard conditions *prevail* over a period of time. This means that, in order to detect a blizzard, not every sensor reading needs to satisfy the conditions. Instead, it is enough to detect sufficiently many of satisfying readings. Since in average MesoWest sensor updates its readings every 30 minutes, 4 events would be sufficient to satisfy this condition (as 6 events in total happen within 3 hours). Note that with each next iteration blizzardSettling event will have a longer time interval (T_1, T_3) which the event is defined on. Finally, if the interval gets at least three hours long (with at least 4 iterations passed), rule (13.21) will detect a blizzardWarning event. To ensure the upper interval limit in settling a blizzardWarning, we can set a garbage collection (e.g., between 3 and 6 hours, see Section 10.3).

$$\texttt{blizzardWarning}(T_1, T_2, ID) \leftarrow$$
$$\texttt{blizzardSettling}(T_1, T_2, ID, C) \qquad (13.21)$$
$$\text{WHERE } (C \geq 4, T_2 - T_1 \geq 3hours).$$

Table 13.1 presents evaluation results that we have obtained from MesWest sensor data. The first two columns show the sensor ID and the number of events produced by the corresponding sensor (in the period from 2007-12-31 until 2010-20-11). The third and fourth columns show the number of complex events, produced by evaluating pattern (13.21) and pattern (13.23), respectively. To increase the number of complex detections we have weakened the blizzard definition. In particular, we have removed the requirement for the considerable falling snow, and have decreased the wind speed condition to 15 mph or greater (instead of 35 mph).

A blizzardWarning event is detected from data provided by a single sensor. Very often to monitor development of a blizzard (or other phenomena) in an area, it is neces-

---

[30]Since sensor is an atomic event, it is defined on the time point (not an interval $[T_1, T_2]$)

13.2. Use Case: On The Live Measurements of Environmental Phenomena

Table 13.1: Complex Events from Live Sensor Data.

Sensor ID	No. of Events	Pattern (13.20)	Pattern (13.21)
KAVX	38156	2995	161
KBLU	1998	2327	157
KCQT	1164	0	0
KFUL	29341	28	0
KHHR	30118	31	0
KMER	28999	281	16
KMHS	1364	0	0
KMMH	36783	161	2
KRNM	1307	148	8
KSDB	1464	1167	89
KSFO	1277	241	12
KSNS	31958	794	32
KUKI	1267	52	2
KWVI	34132	420	28

sary to *integrate* different observations from multiple sensors in that area. To analyze the observations over a certain geographical space, the system will require awareness of sensor locations in that space. Real time integration of sensor observations from different geographic locations is not the only challenge. The heterogeneity of data provided by various sensors pose a big challenge too. For example, not all sensors provide the same measurements (e.g., some weather stations measure the wind speed, and other do not); measurements from various sensors are not provided in the same format, metric unit, or precision.

To overcome these and similar challenges, we utilize a domain specific *ontology* as a single view over the whole sensors network. Such an ontology for the MesoWest sensor network is available from [PSHS10]. This sensor ontology, for example, defines concepts such as *Observation* (specified as an act of observing a property or phenomenon, with the goal of producing an estimate of the value of the property), and *Feature* (defined as an abstraction of real world phenomenon). Further on, it defines major properties of an observation such as a feature of interest (*featureOfInterest*), observed property (*observedProperty*), sampling time (*samplingTime*) and so forth.

The work in [PSHS10] also provides an RDF dataset containing expressive descriptions of about 20000 weather stations across the United States. On average, there are five sensors per weather station measuring phenomena such as temperature, visibility, precipitation, pressure, wind speed, humidity, see Section A.1 (Appendix) for description of one such a weather station. The description also contains the sensor location (altitude, latitude, and longitude). In our application we utilize this information in order to eventually detect a blizzard area (once a station detects a blizzard).

The first rule in the complex event pattern (13.22) is triggered whenever a `blizzard Warning` event occurs. To evaluate the WHERE clause of the rule, ETALIS will access the background knowledge (i.e., the weather station RDF descriptions) and retrieve the

Table 13.2: Computation for pattern (13.23) from live sensor data.

Area	Start [date/time]	End [date/time]	Iterations
KSDB, KRNM	2008-01-14 02:00	2008-01-15 12:30	1
KAUN, KBLU	2008-02-01 10:35	2008-02-01 13:30	1
KBLU, KWVI	2008-02-23 09:53	2008-02-24 03:00	5
KWVI, KBLU	2008-02-24 07:47	2008-02-24 13:07	1
KBLU, KWVI	2008-02-24 07:54	2008-02-25 02:22	5
KSDB, KAVX	2010-01-03 02:52	2010-01-03 07:02	7
KAVX, KSDB	2010-01-03 09:52	2010-01-04 07:02	1
KSDB, KAVX	2010-01-05 03:22	2010-01-05 09:02	3
KAVX, KSDB	2010-01-05 11:42	2010-01-06 08:02	1
KBLU, KSFO	2010-02-02 04:21	2010-02-02 12:58	1
KWVI, KSFO	2010-11-07 08:06	2010-11-07 08:22	1

sensor location. The first rule will also start an iteration, which is then continued by the second rule. This rule will fire an `areaSettling` event every time there is a new `blizzardWarning` in an area close to the initial `blizzardWarning`. The distance is calculated by the `getDistance` predicated, and its implementation is provided as a background rule see Section A.2 (Appendix). In our example pattern we want to make sure that the distance is less than 300 km (or 186 miles).

$$\begin{aligned}
&\texttt{areaSettling}(ID, ID, Lat, Lng) \leftarrow \\
&\quad \texttt{blizzardWarning}(T_1, T_2, ID) \\
&\quad \text{WHERE } \texttt{getLatLong}(ID, Lat, Lng).
\end{aligned}$$

$$\begin{aligned}
&\texttt{areaSettling}(ID_1, ID_2, Lat_1, Lng_1) \leftarrow \\
&\quad \texttt{areaSettling}(ID_1, Lat_1, Lng_1) \text{ SEQ} \\
&\quad \texttt{blizzardWarning}(T_1, T_2, ID_2) \\
&\quad \text{WHERE } \big(\texttt{getLatLong}(ID_2, Lat_2, Lng_2) \\
&\quad\quad \texttt{getDistance}(Lat_1, Lng_1, Lat_2, Lng_2, Dist), \\
&\quad\quad 0 < Dist < 300\big).
\end{aligned} \quad (13.22)$$

Finally, a `blizzardArea` event is detected when an `areaSettling` event occurs within the next 9 hours.

$$\begin{aligned}
&\texttt{blizzardArea}(T_1, T_2, ID) \leftarrow \\
&\quad \big(\texttt{areaSettling}(ID_1, ID_2, Lat_1, Lng_1)\big).9hours.
\end{aligned} \quad (13.23)$$

Table 13.2 shows results for the complex event pattern (13.23). ETALIS has detected different areas (with weather conditions as defined above) eleven times. The table presents which weather stations contributed to a particular area; a starting and ending date/time of an observation; and how many iterations were involved in creating that observation.

Figure 13.26 shows marked wind areas as calculated from patterns (13.20)-(13.23). Weather stations that have detected one or more blizzards (during the observed period)

13.2. Use Case: On The Live Measurements of Environmental Phenomena 189

are marked yellow, and those that have not are small and blue. Finally, the wind areas are marked red.

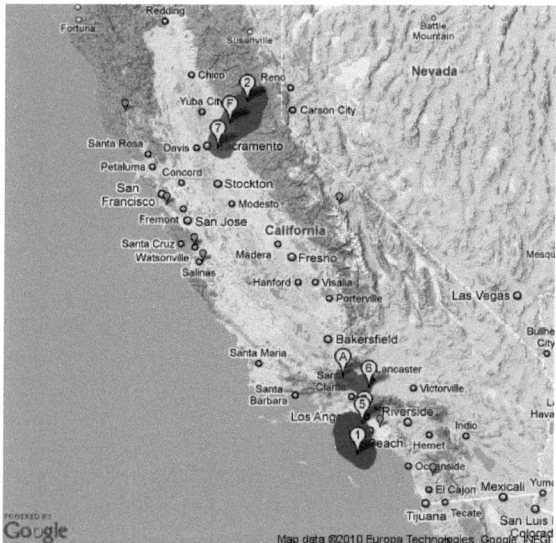

Figure 13.26: Sensor location map with marked wind areas

In addition to location attributes (latitude, longitude, and elevation), the RDF dataset contains also links to locations in GeoNames[31] near a weather station, see Section A.1 in Appendix. The distance from a GeoNames location to a weather station is also provided. As said, GeoNames provides all important geographic locations (e.g., schools, hospitals, motorways, airports etc.) within a certain radius from the sensor location, so that our application can issue an early warnings. Table 13.3, for example, shows GeoNames locations[32] triggered by the blizzard event for the KSFO weather station (i.e., the San Francisco International Airport).

Performance results for patterns (13.20)-(13.23) are presented in Figure 13.27. The throughput is obtained so that time between sensor readings is ignored. Different sensors produce data with different frequency. The goal of our performance test was to take into account ETALIS processing time, and to show the throughput accordingly. When only event processing time is considered (network latencies are ignored), the throughput for patterns (13.20)-(13.23) are 24696, 37437, and 3900 events per second, respectively (see Figure 13.27 (a)).

We also see that the throughput for patterns (13.20) and (13.21) is significantly higher than for pattern (13.23). This pattern is however the most complex one, as for every

---
[31]GeoNames: http://www.geonames.org/
[32]For space reasons we have listed only 7 locations. The complete list for this weather station contains 51 items.

Table 13.3: GeoNames locations nearby KSFO weather station (SFO Airport).

GeoName ID	Location name	Latitude	Longitude
5394116	Seaplane Harbor	37.63216	-122.38164
7229706	San Mateo School	37.61196	-122.42842
7256223	Exit 5B	37.62861	-122.43167
7256211	Exit 41	37.59639	-122.41917
7256225	Exit 6A	37.63361	-122.40528
7256243	Exit 421	37.6025	-122.38028
7256245	Exit 423A	37.63111	-122.40278
...	...	...	...

`blizzardWarning` event the system needs to on the fly find the location from the RDF dataset; to compute the distance; and further to find out whether two sensors are close to each other. Taking into account that in average MesoWest sensors update information every half an hour, the throughput of 3900 events per second (or 7020000 events per 30 minutes) arguably demonstrates the use of our framework for real time event recognition and reasoning, as this means that the same number of sensors can be handled by a single instance of our running system. Note that the complexity of the overall processing is high, i.e., additional knowledgebases are accessed and evaluated in the real time during the detection of complex events, hence the achieved throughput is indeed promising.

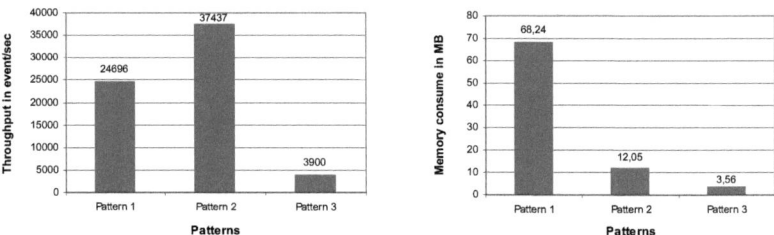

Figure 13.27: (a) Complex event throughput (b) Memory consumption

Figure 13.27 (b) shows the memory consumption for patterns (13.20)-(13.23). We have calculated the overall memory consumption (i.e., not only memory picks). Pattern (13.23) has the lowest consumption (despite its complexity) and pattern (13.20) has the highest one. This comes as a consequence of the number of produced complex events. For example, from the KAVAX sensor stream, pattern (13.20) has been detected 2995 times and pattern (13.21) only 161 times, see Table 13.1. This stream has contributed to pattern (13.23) only four times. Hence although ETALIS needed to keep certain ontology data in memory (i.e., not only events), it still had a low memory consumption.

13.2.1 Additional Use Cases

We have implemented two additional use cases with ETALIS. The first use case was developed in the scope of the SYNERGY project[33], and it deals with the collaborative drug design in the pharmaceutical industry. The goal of the drug design was to potentially provide a new medicine against malaria. The project was carried out through the scientific work related to predictions of toxicological properties of certain proteins and other substances. The scientific work was distributed among different parties which were collaborating as a virtual organisation.

The SYNERGY project aimed to develop a real time collaboration platform for virtual organisations. The framework was developed as a service-oriented architecture (SOA) where different parties can collaborate via services. Since the collaboration is performed in real time, the SYNERGY platform was developed as an event-driven architecture (EDA) too. ETALIS has been used as a main event processing component of this architecture which enables real time collaborations in a virtual organisation.

In particular, a virtual organisation in SYNERGY has dealt with a drug discovery process. Members of the virtual organisation have gathered themselves to work on discovery of a new drug against malaria. Since this work involves a lot of expensive experiments handled on different sites, early warnings in this process may save the overall project costs. Based on event pattern rules, ETALIS was used to discover real time situations which indicated unsuccessful experiments, and trigger early warnings. More details about the project and ETALIS implementation can be obtained from the mentioned web site of SYNERGY.

The second use case is *Fast Flowers Delivery* scenario developed in [EtNi10]. This use case is about a flower stores association which operates in a large city in order to provide a flower delivery service. The service is implemented through a network of local independent van drivers. The communication between flower stores and drivers is handled via events[34]. The authors of [EtNi10] have offered the use case to be implemented with existing EP systems. We have participated in this project by providing an ETALIS implementation of Fast Flowers Delivery use case. The implementation demonstrates capabilities of ETALIS to support various event processing agents (EPAs) from an EPN. The implementation is publicly available[35].

---

[33] SYNERGY project: http://www.synergy-ist.eu/
[34] The use case is accessible from: http://www.ep-ts.com/content/view/80/111/
[35] Our running implementation of the use case is available at: http://code.google.com/p/etalis/wiki/Fast_Flower_Delivery_Use_Case

Part V

Conclusions and Outlook

14
Summary and Conclusion

The objective of this work was to establish synergies between Event Processing (EP) and deductive reasoning in logic programming (LP), thereby shifting EP towards a more *intelligent* EP and reasoning towards *stream* reasoning. We conclude by summing up the results that have been accomplished toward that goal (Section 14.1). Finally, we give an extended overview of future research topics that, in our view, represent prospective directions of our work (Section 14.2).

14.1 Summary of the Results

To summarise and discuss the results of this work, we refer to the research questions specified in Section 1.4.

- **Knowledge representation formalism to express both, complex event patterns and contextual knowledge.** In this work we have investigated practical and theoretical issues related to EP. While in existing EP approaches, complex events consist merely of simple (temporally situated) events, we argued that in *knowledge-rich* applications such complex events are not expressive enough to assess complex situations in real time. We proposed a *logic-based* event processing, advocating a richer formalism for EP. The formalism is capable not only to match patterns based on *temporal* relations among events, but also to evaluate *contextual knowledge*. We call this formalism the ETALIS Language for Events (ELE). It comes with a *rule-based* syntax and a clear *declarative* formal semantics. Notable property of this knowledge representation formalism is that it can express both, events and contextual knowledge, in a unified and compact way.

- **Logic inferencing to derive complex events in a timely fashion.** In our view an event is equivalent to a *declaration* that something has occurred or there is a change in the current state of affairs. Formally, we represented an event with a special kind of a logic *fact*. A complex event may be derived as a *logic consequence* of this fact (and possibly other available knowledge). We have proposed a powerful inferencing mechanism that allows finding, not only *temporal* relations between events, but to *reason* about their non-temporal *semantic* relations in a timely fashion, too.

- **Synergism between EP and LP to enable detection of situations (otherwise undetectable).** One question – that arises from motivation of our work – is whether LP-based EP can be used to detect real time situations that are otherwise undetectable with sole EP. From what we have learnt so far, it is difficult to justify this statement in general. Different non LP approaches in EP can be used to detect various complex events that were presented in this work, too. However some complex events can be more *effectively* represented by our approach. For instance, by using an ontology as background knowledge we are able to write *fewer* pattern rules to capture *more* situations. We have seen such an example in Subsection 8.4.3 where different entities in an ontology were structured through class/subclass relationships. Thanks to the multiple inheritance provided by an ontology, conditions expressed as instances, properties or classes in a pattern do not necessarily need to be explicitly stated. Instead, they can be *inferred* as certain events occur. This was demonstrated in an example from Subsubsection 13.1.7.1. There, to check whether an event carries an instance of a class of interest (or any of its 40,080 subclasses), we did not write 40,080 event patterns. In fact, we wrote only one pattern and used an ontology which defines all relationships. Moreover, since LP inferencing enables us to derive new, *implicit* knowledge, an LP-based EP can be used in detecting situation that are otherwise undetectable (with approaches that do not have a mechanism for discovery of implicit knowledge).

  It can be argued that all relationships defined in an ontology can always be precomputed and persisted in a database (i.e., to be made explicit). However, in some scenarios this knowledge is dynamic (i.e., acquired on the fly), or there is already structured knowledge available. In these, and other similar cases it is more appropriate to use already proven knowledge representation (KR) techniques to process this knowledge. Our approach is built on some of these techniques – in particular, it adheres to well-established concepts from LP.

- **Efficient implementation of an event-driven, and LP-based computation model.** The execution model of ELE is established on *goal-directed* event-driven backward chaining (EDBC) rules and decomposition of complex event patterns into *two-input intermediate events* (goals). Goals are automatically asserted by rules as relevant events occur. They can persist over a period of time, waiting to

14.1. Summary of the Results

support detection of a more complex goal. This process of asserting more and more complex goals shows the progress towards detection of a complex event. Important characteristics of these goals are that they are asserted only if they are used later on (to support a more complex goal or an event pattern), goals are unique, and persistent as long as they are relevant. Goals are asserted by rules which are executed in the backward chaining mode. The notable property of these rules is that they are event-driven. Hence, although the rules are executed backwards, overall they exhibit a forward chaining behaviour.

EDBC rules integrate logic programming with event-based programming. They serve as an execution mechanism for an expressive formalism for EP (presented in Chapter 6). They enable a seamless integration of EP with query processing, as well as with processing of background (domain) knowledge. Further on, EDBC rules provide an event-driven incremental reasoning capability. Finally, they facilitate event at a time processing in Event-driven Transaction Logic Inference System (ETALIS) (see Chapter 5), and are general enough to accommodate various other extensions as mentioned in the following.

- **Extensibility of an LP approach for EP.** ELE is a general, expressive formalism for EP. Orthogonal to expressivity of a language, our goal was to address few extensions that are usually found as specific features in EP formalisms. In particular, we have discarded an assumption of many EP approaches that events are immutable and therefore always correct. This has led us to the problem of *revision* in EP, where an EP system is required to behave similar to a transaction processing system. Secondly, we have addressed the problem of *out-of-order* events. In this case we have ignored yet another assumption that events are *totally ordered*, i.e., the order in which events are received by the system is the same as their timestamp order. In such a setting an EP system needs to deal with more historical data and late events.

    In both extensions we have demonstrated that our approach can meet additional requirements while retaining existing expressivity of the language, and with no significant overhead in run time performance.

    Finally, we developed a formalism for EP and stream reasoning (SR) called Event Processing SPARQL (EP-SPARQL). EP-SPARQL can be considered as a new language (rather as an extension of ELE). However since the underlying ground concepts, as well as the execution model are the same as for ELE, we treat it as an extension of the ELE formalism. EP-SPARQL is specially tailored for event-driven applications in the realm of the Semantic Web.

- **Trade-off between performance and expressibility in an LP approach for EP.** We have implemented *ETALIS Language for Events* with its extensions in a Prolog-based prototype. The implementation is open source[1]. We have conducted a number of performance tests to present run time characteristics of our implementation.

---

[1] ETALIS source code: http://code.google.com/p/etalis/

In some cases we have also compared performance of our implementation with an existing open source system. It has been shown that our LP-based approach for EP does not necessarily need to compromise performance due to its expressivity and an execution mechanism that is rooted in logic. In particular, this observation is true for more complex event patterns, e.g., when iterative and aggregative patterns are processed on a stream of *complex* events, or when *nested hierarchies* of events are built where each level contains atomic or complex events. We have also proved that SR can be conjunctively used with EP. We have constructed different knowledgebases, and presented performance tests that demonstrate feasibility for on the fly knowledge processing.

14.2 Future Work

As the next steps, we will continue to investigate and exploit the advantages of our framework over non-logic-based EP. In particular, we plan to investigate how a rule representation of complex events (in large pattern bases) may help in *verification* of event patterns (e.g., discovering patterns that can never be detected according to inconsistency problems). We also plan to utilize *machine learning* techniques to automatically generate both event patterns and the domain knowledge required for knowledge-based EP (see [APPS10], and XHAIL system [Ray09]).

Dynamic event pattern management (i.e., patterns are created or discarded on the fly when certain situations are detected) is another interesting topic where the logic approach may help to control event-driven computation.

One promising line of research, in our view, will go toward a tight integration of an *action logic* with our "logic" for EP. While we have been investigating thoroughly detection of *events*, it is worth to pay more attention to possible automated *actions* triggered by detected events. This research filed is not particularly new. It has been investigated in the scope of event-condition-action (ECA) rules and production rules (PR). We have also provided work in this area [ApSA09, AnSt08a, AnSt08b]. Nevertheless we still see potential for benefiting from our *logic-based* view on this research subject. In particular we believe that dynamic and adaptive actions will increasingly appear in many domains. These actions will not only be triggered automatically, but will need to *adapt* (change) automatically too. Changes will be initiated by occurring events, and the adaptivity will be initiated and proved by a certain *logic*.

In the following we identify an area where this idea could be applied, and give more insights into the idea itself.

14.2.1 Event-Driven Business Processes

An increasing dynamics in today's business requires flexible infrastructures that can *sense* a problem or opportunity and *react* accordingly. There is a tendency today in providing

14.2. Future Work

support for business processes with *flexibility*. It is especially true for the business processes which are underpinning both complex work and unexpected situations, e.g., emergency (disaster) management scenarios. In such scenarios there can be many parameters changed every second, so that any *a priory* coded adaptivity, or an exception handling approach, will fail. If one tried to define adaptivity at design-time, there would be too many situations that cannot be calculated in advance. For example, if during fighting against fire a very strong wind starts, the correct action can be calculated only in the moment of the execution, since there are so many parameters that can influence the decision and which will be known in the real time, e.g., the intensity of the fire, the number of available firemen, the environment characteristics etc. It means that the system must detect these events in real time in order to respond adequately upon them. Such responses are known as *ad-hoc* process changes, and we call corresponding processes *event-driven ad-hoc processes*. On one hand, any pre-coding of the possible changes (alternative paths in the process execution) decreases the flexibility of the process, i.e. the efficiency of the running process instance. On the other hand, approaches that would fully automate event-driven ad-hoc processes are indeed challenging. The main requirement is to enable the process flexibility so that it is not completely defined in advance. Instead, it is calculated in real time based on certain constraints. Constraints may be defined either at the design or run-time.

To fulfil this requirement, our approach will be based on EP. That is, to structure the course of affairs and describe more complex *dynamic* situations, we compose simple (atomic) events into complex events. Complex events, detected in real time, may signify situations that require *modification* in a running process (workflow). Further on, our approach will be *declarative*. In comparison to an imperative approach, declarative workflows enable more flexible management with respect to *ad-hoc changes* [PSSVDA07, vdAPS09]. Flexibility of declarative workflows come from the fact that they do not prespecify a single possible execution path. This feature may be of great value in the presence of ad-hoc changes. Our approach will explore this value, and unlike [PSSVDA07, vdAPS09], it will combine declarative workflows with EP. We have published the outline of this idea in [AnSt08a]. Our goal is to propose a framework that includes both sufficiently *expressive* techniques for workflow modelling, as well as *inference* capabilities to reason over those specifications. The framework enables detection of real time situations that demand workflow modifications. Modifications are expressed as declarative *constraints* (logic rules), and their on line *verification* is ensured.

14.2.1.1 A Unifying Framework for Event-Driven Ad-Hoc Processes

Figure 14.1 depicts, in our view, the main aspects of *event-driven ad-hoc* processes. In particular, the figure shows the conceptual relationships between executing *tasks*, the workflow *scheduler*, and the *dynamic change manager*. Tasks that need to be executed are scheduled by the scheduler. The scheduler orders executing tasks according to the model specified by a concrete workflow. The dynamic change manager (DCM) may alter

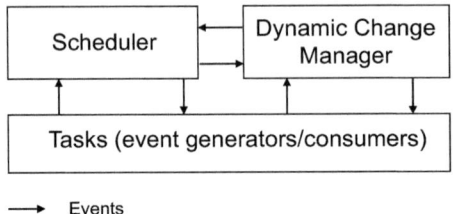

Figure 14.1: Conceptual architecture of event-driven ad-hoc processes.

the scheduling plan, i.e., the order in which tasks are scheduled for execution. This may happen due to detection of certain events that represent unexpected situations.

In the presented conceptual architecture, tasks are seen as external event sources. The scheduler receives a stream of events from these sources, and schedules them in real time. The incoming event stream is denoted by the arc pointing from tasks to the scheduler (see Figure 14.1). As events may represent the state of executing tasks (e.g., start, end and so forth), scheduling of an event amounts to scheduling of a task (process). The process of scheduling must ensure that it satisfies all *constraints*, specified by a workflow (possibly after reordering some events in the incoming stream). Reordering is realised by sending events from the scheduler back to tasks (depicted by the arc in the reverse direction). For example, such an event may carry information that a corresponding task is either allowed (for execution), rejected, or delayed.

Task events are also gathered by the dynamic change manager, which additionally receives external events (e.g., events from various information sources or sensors etc.). The manager correlates these events into complex events (relevant with respect to a particular business domain). Hence the manager utilises EP to detect real time situations that require certain decisions. Decisions may deviate an ongoing workflow instance. They are made by humans, however DCM with its EP capabilities helps in discovering situations (that might require deviations). The deviation (adaptation) is typically driven by the need to take into account new emerging issues (e.g., something accidentally happen) or to optimise the execution with respect to certain events (that just happened). Finally, complex events may further be used externally for e.g., activity monitoring, various analytics and so forth.

14.3 Conclusions

There has been a significant paradigm shift toward real time information processing due to emerging mobile applications and services, Internet of Things, real-time Web, and various other technology fields. Event Processing (EP) brings a new concept to this paradigm shift in the form of event-driven architecture (EDA) and underlying principles of event-driven computation.

14.3. Conclusions

In this work we have investigated a logic programming (LP) approach for EP. Our approach was motivated by the need to enable detection of real time situations based on processing of events and domain knowledge. In *knowledge-rich* applications detection of real time situations demand, not merely temporally situated events, but also evaluation of *contextual knowledge*, and *reasoning* about their non-temporal *semantic* relations.

Our contribution includes a seamless integration of EP concepts with logic rules. We have proposed an expressive declarative language called the ETALIS Language for Events (ELE), and an execution model which detects complex events in a data-driven fashion (based on *goal-directed event-driven rules*). The approach goes beyond existing event-driven systems by providing declarative semantics and an efficient logic-programming-based execution model that enables event-driven deductive *reasoning*. We have also provided an open-source implementation of our formalism, which allows for specification of complex events and their detection at occurrence time.

The results of this work can be extended in few directions. Hitherto, approaches to ad-hoc and dynamic process-aware information systems acted on the assumption that decision on process changes are not strictly time sensitive. The emphasis was rather on full support to process modifications. In many practical cases (e.g., emergency management) the time to react on certain situations is limited. Further on, decisions on ad-hoc process modifications need to be carefully assessed taking into account many changing parameters. To address these requirements, we will work on a framework for *event-driven ad-hoc processes* and *actions*. The framework features both EP capabilities as well as capabilities to accept on line process changes. The framework will be based on declarative rules, and as such it will feature a greater flexibility with respect to ad-hoc changes. We also plan to provide an integrated implementation of the proposed formalism with the Event-driven Transaction Logic Inference System (ETALIS).

Another application area where we have started to apply EP with ETALIS is the Smart Grid. The Smart Grid aims at making the current energy grid more efficient and eco-friendly. We propose EP to be used as a key technology for intelligent monitoring, control, communication and optimised consumption of energy. Since smart grids are electricity networks that integrate behaviour and actions of all users connected to it (generators and consumers), we need a way to publish and discover resource in the networks. Linked Data principles may be used for enabling decentralised publishing and resource discovery, ultimately fostering data integration. In [WASS+10] we have investigated (and we will continue to investigate) how ETALIS can be applied efficiently in processing events and Linked Data from the smart grids.

A similar, energy efficiency scenario can be realised with sensor networks. We are considering the use of cheap sensors in commercial buildings to enable more efficient energy consumption, and applying EP to provide real time situational awareness, describe sensor locations, and other sensor parameters as background knowledge [XSSA+11, SMXS+11].

Further questions of course may be raised, but the above are most related to the research that we have already started.

In summary, this work covers research topics related to EP and stream reasoning (SR). The work provides the foundational background, as well as the application aspects of the topics. Finally, it also opens up a wide range of possible future research directions.

Appendix

A.1 Linked Sensor Data for Weather Stations

An RDF dataset that describes sensors of KFSO weather station is shown below (see [PSHS10]). In particular, the station measures phenomena such as temperature, dew point, humidity, visibility, wind direction, wind gust, and wind speed. The description also contains geo-location of the station, as well as a GeoNames link with all known nearby locations.

```
<rdf:RDF xmlns="http://knoesis.wright.edu/ssw/ont/sensor-observation.owl#"
    xmlns:log="http://www.w3.org/2000/10/swap/log#"
    xmlns:om-owl="http://knoesis.wright.edu/ssw/ont/sensor-observation.owl#"
    xmlns:owl="http://www.w3.org/2002/07/owl#"
    xmlns:rdf="http://www.w3.org/1999/02/22-rdf-syntax-ns#"
    xmlns:rdfs="http://www.w3.org/2000/01/rdf-schema#"
    xmlns:sens-obs="http://knoesis.wright.edu/ssw/"
    xmlns:weather="http://knoesis.wright.edu/ssw/ont/weather.owl#"
    xmlns:wgs84="http://www.w3.org/2003/01/geo/wgs84_pos#"
    xmlns:xsd="http://www.w3.org/2001/XMLSchema#">

    <LocatedNearRel rdf:about="http://knoesis.wright.edu/ssw/LocatedNearRelKSFO">
        <distance rdf:datatype="http://www.w3.org/2001/XMLSchema#float">0.9813</distance>
        <hasLocation rdf:resource="http://sws.geonames.org/5391989/"/>
        <uom rdf:resource="http://knoesis.wright.edu/ssw/ont/weather.owl#miles"/>
    </LocatedNearRel>

    <System rdf:about="http://knoesis.wright.edu/ssw/System_KSFO">
        <ID>KSFO</ID>
        <hasLocatedNearRel rdf:resource="http://knoesis.wright.edu/ssw/LocatedNearRelKSFO"/>
        <hasSourceURI rdf:resource="http://mesowest.utah.edu/cgi-bin/droman/meso_base.cgi?stn=KSFO"/>
        <parameter rdf:resource="http://knoesis.wright.edu/ssw/ont/weather.owl#_AirTemperature"/>
        <parameter rdf:resource="http://knoesis.wright.edu/ssw/ont/weather.owl#_DewPoint"/>
        <parameter rdf:resource="http://knoesis.wright.edu/ssw/ont/weather.owl#_RelativeHumidity"/>
        <parameter rdf:resource="http://knoesis.wright.edu/ssw/ont/weather.owl#_Visibility"/>
        <parameter rdf:resource="http://knoesis.wright.edu/ssw/ont/weather.owl#_WindDirection"/>
        <parameter rdf:resource="http://knoesis.wright.edu/ssw/ont/weather.owl#_WindGust"/>
        <parameter rdf:resource="http://knoesis.wright.edu/ssw/ont/weather.owl#_WindSpeed"/>
        <processLocation rdf:resource="http://knoesis.wright.edu/ssw/point_KSFO"/>
```

```
    </System>

  <wgs84:Point rdf:about="http://knoesis.wright.edu/ssw/point_KSFO">
      <wgs84:alt rdf:datatype="http://www.w3.org/2001/XMLSchema#float">10</wgs84:alt>
      <wgs84:lat rdf:datatype="http://www.w3.org/2001/XMLSchema#float">37.61972</wgs84:lat>
      <wgs84:long rdf:datatype="http://www.w3.org/2001/XMLSchema#float">-122.36472</wgs84:long>
  </wgs84:Point>
</rdf:RDF>
```

A.2 Distance Calculation

Distance between two points, defined by their latitude and longitude (Lat_1, $Long_1$, Lat_2, $Long_2$, respectively) is calculated with the following formula where the Earth Radius (ER) is equal to 6378,137.

$$\texttt{getDistance} = \left(2 \cdot \arcsin\left(\left(\left[\sin\frac{rad(Lat_1) - rad(Lat_2)}{2}\right]^2 + \cos[rad(Lat_1)] \cdot \cos[rad(Lat_2)] \cdot \left[\sin\frac{rad(Long_1) - rad(Long_2)}{2}\right]^2\right)^{1/2} \right)\right) \cdot ER$$

The following rule (written in Prolog syntax) implements the above formula. The rule was evaluated in the WHERE clause of the second rule in complex event pattern (13.22), every time when BlizzardWarning event occurred (see experiments from Section 13.2).

```
getDistance(Lat1,Long1,Lat2,Long2,Distance) :-
    ER is 6378.137,
    getRad(Lat1,RadLat1),
    getRad(Long1,RadLong1),
    getRad(Lat2,RadLat2),
    getRad(Long2,RadLong2),
    A is RadLat1 - RadLat2,
    B is RadLong1 - RadLong2,
    TempA1 is A / 2,
    TempB1 is B / 2,
    SinA is sin(TempA1),
    SinB is sin(TempB1),
    TempA2 is SinA ** 2,
    TempB2 is SinB ** 2,
    CosA is cos(RadLat1),
    CosB is cos(RadLat2),
    Temp1 is CosA * CosB,
    Temp2 is Temp1 * TempB2,
    Temp3 is TempA2 + Temp2,
    Sqrt is sqrt(Temp3),
    Asin is asin(Sqrt),
    S is Asin * 2,
    Distance is S * ER.

getRad(Deg,Rad) :-
    Temp1 is Deg * pi,
    Rad is Temp1 / 180.
```

Bibliography

[AbHV95] Serge Abiteboul, Richard Hull, and Victor Vianu. *Foundations of Databases*. Addison-Wesley, 1995.

[ACCE+09] P. Alvaro, T. Condie, N. Conway, K. Elmeleegy, J. M. Hellerstein, and R. C. Sears. BOOM: Data-Centric Programming in the Datacenter. Technical Report UCB/EECS-2009-113, EECS Department, University of California, Berkeley, 2009.

[AdBE00] Asaf Adi, David Botzer, and Opher Etzion. Semantic Event Model and its Implication on Situation Detection. In Hans Robert Hansen, Martin Bichler, and Harald Mahrer, editors, *Proceedings of the 8th European Conference on Information Systems, Trends in Information and Communication Systems for the 21st Century*, ECIS '00, pages 320–325, Vienna, Austria, 2000.

[AdCh06] Raman Adaikkalavan and Sharma Chakravarthy. SnoopIB: Interval-based event specification and detection for active databases. *Data Knowledge Engineering*, 59(1):139–165, 2006.

[AdEt04] Asaf Adi and Opher Etzion. Amit - the situation manager. *The VLDB Journal*, 13:177–203, May 2004.

[ADGI08] Jagrati Agrawal, Yanlei Diao, Daniel Gyllstrom, and Neil Immerman. Efficient pattern matching over event streams. In Jason Tsong-Li Wang, editor, *Proceedings of the 28th ACM SIGMOD Conference*, SIGMOD'08, pages 147–160. New York, USA, 2008.

[AFRS+10] Darko Anicic, Paul Fodor, Sebastian Rudolph, Roland Stühmer, Nenad Stojanovic, and Rudi Studer. A Rule-Based Language for Complex Event Processing and Reasoning. In Pascal Hitzler and Thomas Lukasiewicz, editors, *Proceedings of the 4th International Conference on Web Reasoning and Rule Systems*, RR'10, pages 42–57, Berlin,Heidelberg, 2010. Springer-Verlag.

[AFRS11a] Darko Anicic, Paul Fodor, Sebastian Rudolph, and Nenad Stojanovic. EP-SPARQL: a unified language for event processing and stream reasoning. In Sadagopan Srinivasan, Krithi Ramamritham, Arun Kumar, M. P. Ravindra, Elisa Bertino, and Ravi Kumar, editors, *Proceedings of the 20th International Conference on World Wide Web*, WWW'11, pages 635–644, New York, NY, USA, 2011. ACM.

[AFRS+11b] Darko Anicic, Paul Fodor, Sebastian Rudolph, Roland Stühmer, Nenad Stojanovic, and Rudi Studer. ETALIS: Rule-Based Reasoning in Event Processing. In Sven Helmer, Alexandra Poulovassilis, and Fatos Xhafa, editors, *Reasoning in Event-Based Distributed Systems*, volume 347 of *Studies in Computational Intelligence*, pages 99–124. Springer Berlin / Heidelberg, Berlin, Heidelberg, 2011.

[AFSS09] Darko Anicic, Paul Fodor, Roland Stühmer, and Nenad Stojanovic. Event-Driven Approach for Logic-Based Complex Event Processing. In *Proceedings of the 12th IEEE International Conferences on Computational Science and Engineering (CSE'09)*, CSE'09, pages 56–63, Washington, DC, USA, 2009. IEEE Computer Society.

[AlBB06] José Júlio Alferes, Federico Banti, and Antonio Brogi. An Event-Condition-Action Logic Programming Language. In Michael Fisher, Wiebe van der Hoek, Boris Konev, and Alexei Lisitsa, editors, *Proceedings of the 10th European Conference on Logics in Artificial Intelligence*, JELIA'06, pages 29–42, Berlin,Heidelberg, 2006. Springer-Verlag.

[Alle83] James F. Allen. Maintaining knowledge about temporal intervals. *Communications of the ACM*, 26:832–843, 1983.

[Alve09] Alexandre Alves. Extensions to logic programming inference engines to support CEP (a short paper). In *Proceedings of the 2009 International Symposium on Rule Interchange and Applications*, RuleML '09, Berlin, Heidelberg, 2009. Springer-Verlag.

[AnSt08a] Darko Anicic and Nenad Stojanovic. Future Internet Collaboration Workflow. In John Domingue, Dieter Fensel, and Paolo Traverso, editors, *First Future Internet Symposium*, Lecture Notes in Computer Science, pages 141–151, Berlin,Heidelberg, 2008. Springer-Verlag.

[AnSt08b] Darko Anicic and Nenad Stojanovic. Towards Creation of Logical Framework for Event-Driven Information Systems. In José Cordeiro and Joaquim Filipe, editors, *Proceedings of the Tenth International Conference on Enterprise Information Systems, Volume ISAS-2*, ICEIS'08, pages 394–401, Berlin,Heidelberg, 2008. Springer-Verlag.

[AnSt09] Darko Anicic and Nenad Stojanovic. Expressive Logical Framework for Reasoning about Complex Events and Situations. In Nenad Stojanovic,

Andreas Abecker, Opher Etzion, and Adrian Paschke, editors, *Intelligent Event Processing, Papers from the 2009 AAAI Spring Symposium*, number SS-09-05 in Technical Report, pages 14–20, Menlo Park, CA, 2009. AAAI Press.

[ApBW88] K. R. Apt, H. A. Blair, and A. Walker. Towards a theory of declarative knowledge. In Jack Minker, editor, *Foundations of Deductive Databases and Logic Programming*, pages 89–148. Morgan Kaufmann Publishers Inc., San Francisco, CA, USA, 1988.

[APPS10] Alexander Artikis, Georgios Paliouras, François Portet, and Anastasios Skarlatidis. Logic-based representation, reasoning and machine learning for event recognition. In Jean Bacon, Peter R. Pietzuch, Joe Sventek, and Ugur Çetintemel, editors, *Proceedings of the 4th ACM International Conference on Distributed Event-Based Systems*, DEBS'10, pages 282–293, New York, NY, USA, 2010. ACM.

[ApSA09] Dimitris Apostolou, Nenad Stojanovic, and Darko Anicic. Responsive Knowledge Management for Public Administration: An Event-Driven Approach. *IEEE Intelligent Systems*, 24:20–30, 2009.

[Apt90] Krzysztof R. Apt. Logic Programming. In Jan V. Leeuwen, editor, *Handbook of Theoretical Computer Science: Formal Models and Semantics*, volume B, chapter 10, pages 493–574. Elsevier, 1990.

[ApvE82] Krzysztof R. Apt and Maarten H. van Emden. Contributions to the Theory of Logic Programming. *Journal of the ACM (JACM)*, 29:841–862, July 1982.

[ArBW06] Arvind Arasu, Shivnath Babu, and Jennifer Widom. The CQL Continuous Query Language: Semantic Foundations and Query Execution. *VLDB Journal*, 15(2):121–142, 2006.

[ARDRSP+07] Michael P. Ashley-Rollman, Michael De Rosa, Siddhartha S. Srinivasa, Padmanabhan Pillai, Seth Copen Goldstein, and Jason D. Campbell. Declarative Programming for Modular Robots. In *Workshop on Self-Reconfigurable Robots/Systems and Applications, collocated with International Conference on Intelligent RObots and Systems*, IROS '07, October 2007.

[ARFS11a] Darko Anicic, Sebastian Rudolph, Paul Fodor, and Nenad Stojanovic. A declarative framework for matching iterative and aggregative patterns against event streams. In Nick Bassiliades, Guido Governatori, and Adrian Paschke, editors, *Proceedings of the 5th international conference on Rule-based reasoning, programming, and applications*, RuleML'11, pages 138–153, Berlin, Heidelberg, 2011. Springer-Verlag.

[ARFS11b] Darko Anicic, Sebastian Rudolph, Paul Fodor, and Nenad Stojanovic. Retractable Complex Event Processing and Stream Reasoning. In Nick Bassiliades, Guido Governatori, and Adrian Paschke, editors, *Proceedings of the 5th International Symposium on Rules*, RuleML'11, pages 122–137, Berlin,Heidelberg, 2011. Springer-Verlag.

[ARFS12a] Darko Anicic, Sebastian Rudolph, Paul Fodor, and Nenad Stojanovic. Real-Time Complex Event Recognition and Reasoning – A Logic Programming Approach. *The Applied Artificial Intelligence journal*, 26:6–57, 2012.

[ARFS12b] Darko Anicic, Sebastian Rudolph, Paul Fodor, and Nenad Stojanovic. Stream Reasoning and Complex Event Processing in ETALIS. *Semantic Web Journal - Interoperability, Usability, Applicability*, pages 1–11, 2012.

[BBCG10] Davide Francesco Barbieri, Daniele Braga, Stefano Ceri, and Michael Grossniklaus. An execution environment for C-SPARQL queries. In Ioana Manolescu, Stefano Spaccapietra, Jens Teubner, Masaru Kitsuregawa, Alain Leger, Felix Naumann, Anastasia Ailamaki, and Fatma Ozcan, editors, *Proceedings of the 13th International Conference on Extending Database Technology*, EDBT'10, pages 441–452. ACM, 2010.

[BBCV+10] Davide Francesco Barbieri, Daniele Braga, Stefano Ceri, Emanuele Della Valle, and Michael Grossniklaus. Incremental Reasoning on Streams and Rich Background Knowledge. In Lora Aroyo, Grigoris Antoniou, Eero Hyvönen, Annette ten Teije, Heiner Stuckenschmidt, Liliana Cabral, and Tania Tudorache, editors, *Proceedings of the 7th Extended Semantic Web Conference*, ESWC'10, pages 1–15, Berlin,Heidelberg, 2010. Springer-Verlag.

[BFSF08] Andrey Brito, Christof Fetzer, Heiko Sturzrehm, and Pascal Felber. Speculative out-of-order event processing with software transaction memory. In Roberto Baldoni, editor, *Proceedings of the 2nd international conference on Distributed event-based systems*, DEBS '08, pages 265–275, New York, NY, USA, 2008. ACM.

[BGAH07] Roger S. Barga, Jonathan Goldstein, Mohamed H. Ali, and Mingsheng Hong. Consistent Streaming Through Time: A Vision for Event Stream Processing. In Gerhard Weikum, Joe Hellerstein, and Mike Stonebraker, editors, *Proceedings of the 3rd Biennial Conference on Innovative Data Systems Research*, CIDR'07, pages 363–374, 2007.

[BMSU86] Francois Bancilhon, David Maier, Yehoshua Sagiv, and Jeffrey D Ullman. Magic sets and other strange ways to implement logic programs (extended abstract). In *Proceedings of the fifth ACM SIGACT-SIGMOD symposium on Principles of database systems*, PODS '86, pages 1–15, New York, NY, USA, 1986. ACM.

[BoGJ08] Andre Bolles, Marco Grawunder, and Jonas Jacobi. Streaming SPARQL - Extending SPARQL to Process Data Streams. In Sean Bechhofer, Manfred Hauswirth, Jörg Hoffmann, and Manolis Koubarakis, editors, *Proceedings of the 5th European Semantic Web Conference*, ESWC'08, pages 448–462, Berlin,Heidelberg, 2008. Springer-Verlag.

[BrEc07a] François Bry and Michael Eckert. Rule-Based Composite Event Queries: The Language XChange^{EQ} and Its Semantics. In Massimo Marchiori, Jeff Z. Pan, and Christian de Sainte Marie, editors, *Proceedings of the 1st International Conference on Web Reasoning and Rule Systems*, RR'07, pages 16–30, Berlin, Heidelberg, 2007. Springer-Verlag.

[BrEc07b] François Bry and Michael Eckert. Towards Formal Foundations of Event Queries and Rules. In *Proceedings of the 2nd International Workshop on Event-Driven Architecture, Processing and Systems EDA-PS, collocated with the 33rd International Conference on Very Large Data Bases*, Vienna, Austria, 2007.

[BrEc07c] François Bry and Michael Eckert. Twelve Theses on Reactive Rules for the Web. In K. Mani Chandy, Opher Etzion, and Rainer von Ammon, editors, *Event Processing*, Dagstuhl Seminar Proceedings. Internationales Begegnungs- und Forschungszentrum fuer Informatik (IBFI), Schloss Dagstuhl, Germany, 2007.

[BrGM04] Dan Brickley, R.V. Guha, and Brian McBride, editors. *RDF Vocabulary Description Language 1.0: RDF Schema*. W3C Recommendation, 10 February 2004. http://www.w3.org/TR/rdf-schema/.

[CBBC$^+$03] Mitch Cherniack, Hari Balakrishnan, Magdalena Balazinska, Donald Carney, Ugur Çetintemel, Ying Xing, and Stanley B. Zdonik. Scalable Distributed Stream Processing. In Gerhard Weikum, Joseph Hellerstein, and Michael Stonebraker, editors, *Proceedings of the 1st Biennial Conference on Innovative Data Systems Research*, CIDR'03. www.crdrdb.org, 2003.

[CcCC$^+$02] Don Carney, Uğur Çetintemel, Mitch Cherniack, Christian Convey, Sangdon Lee, Greg Seidman, Michael Stonebraker, Nesime Tatbul, and Stan Zdonik. Monitoring streams: a new class of data management applications. In Raghu Ramakrishnan Philip A. Bernstein, Yannis E. Ioannidis and Dimitris Papadias, editors, *Proceedings of the 28th International Conference on Very Large Data Bases*, VLDB '02, pages 215–226. VLDB Endowment, 2002.

[CCDF+03] Sirish Chandrasekaran, Owen Cooper, Amol Deshpande, Michael J. Franklin, Joseph M. Hellerstein, Wei Hong, Sailesh Krishnamurthy, Samuel Madden, Vijayshankar Raman, Frederick Reiss, and Mehul A. Shah. TelegraphCQ: Continuous Dataflow Processing for an Uncertain World. In Gerhard Weikum, Joseph Hellerstein, and Michael Stonebraker, editors, *Proceedings of the 1st Biennial Conference on Innovative Data Systems Research*, CIDR'03. www.crdrdb.org, 2003.

[CCHM08] Tyson Condie, David Chu, Joseph M. Hellerstein, and Petros Maniatis. Evita Raced: Metacompilation for Declarative Networks. *Proceedings of the VLDB Endowment*, 1:1153–1165, August 2008.

[CGSP+09] Antonio Cunei, Rachid Guerraoui, Jesper Honig Spring, Jean Privat, and Jan Vitek. High-Performance Transactional Event Processing. In John Field and Vasco T. Vasconcelos, editors, *Proceedings of the 11th International Conference on Coordination Models and Languages*, COORDINATION '09, pages 27–46, Berlin, Heidelberg, 2009. Springer-Verlag.

[Chak97] Sharma Chakravarthy. SENTINEL: An Object-Oriented DBMS With Event-Based Rules. In Joan Peckham, editor, *Proceedings of the 1997 ACM SIGMOD International Conference on Management of Data*, SIGMOD '97, pages 572–575. ACM Press, 1997.

[ChEA11] Mani K. Chandy, Opher Etzion, and Rainer von Ammon. Executive Summary and Manifesto – Event Processing. In K. Mani Chandy, Opher Etzion, and Rainer von Ammon, editors, *Event Processing*, number 10201 in Dagstuhl Seminar Proceedings, Dagstuhl, Germany, 2011. Schloss Dagstuhl - Leibniz-Zentrum fuer Informatik, Germany.

[Chen97] Yangjun Chen. Magic Sets and Stratified Databases. *International Journal of Intelligent Systems*, 12(3):203–231, 1997.

[ChMi94] Sharma Chakravarthy and D. Mishra. SNOOP: An Expressive Event Specification Language for Active Databases. *Data & Knowledge Engineering*, 14(1):1–26, 1994.

[ChSc10] K. Mani Chandy and W. Roy Schulte. *Event Processing: Designing IT Systems for Agile Companies*. McGraw-Hill, Inc., New York, NY, USA, 2010.

[ChWa96] Weidong Chen and David S. Warren. Tabled Evaluation with Delaying for General Logic Programs. In *Journal of the ACM*. ACM, 1996.

[CKAK94] Sharma Chakravarthy, V. Krishnaprasad, Eman Anwar, and S.-K. Kim. Composite Events for Active Databases: Semantics, Contexts and Detection. In Jorge B. Bocca, Matthias Jarke, and Carlo Zaniolo, editors, *Proceedings of 20th International Conference on Very Large Data Bases*, VLDB'94, pages 606–617. Morgan Kaufmann Publishers Inc., 1994.

[Clar79] Keith L. Clark. Predicate logic as a computational formalism. In *Research Report DOC 79/59*. Imperial College, Department of Computing, London, 1979.

[CuMa11] Gianpaolo Cugola and Alessandro Margara. Processing Flows of Information: From Data Stream to Complex Event Processing. *ACM Computing Surveys*, 2011.

[DEGV01] Evgeny Dantsin, Thomas Eiter, Georg Gottlob, and Andrei Voronkov. Complexity and expressive power of logic programming. *ACM Computing Surveys*, 33(3):374–425, 2001.

[DeJG07] Alan J. Demers and et al. Johannes Gehrke. Cayuga: A General Purpose Event Monitoring System. In *Proceedings of the 3rd Biennial Conference on Innovative Data Systems Research (CIDR'07)*. Stanford University, USA, 2007.

[DGLO+09] Nihal Dindar, Baris Güç, Patrick Lau, Asli Ozal, Merve Soner, and Nesime Tatbul. DejaVu: Declarative pattern matching over live and archived streams of events. In Carsten Binnig and Benoit Dageville, editors, *Proceedings of the 35th SIGMOD International Conference on Management of Data*, SIGMOD '09, pages 1023–1026, New York, NY, USA, 2009. ACM.

[DMRH04] Luping Ding, Nishant Mehta, Elke A. Rundensteiner, and George T. Heineman. Joining Punctuated Streams. In Elisa Bertino, Stavros Christodoulakis, Dimitris Plexousakis, Vassilis Christophides, Manolis Koubarakis, Klemens Böhm, and Elena Ferrari, editors, *9th International Conference on Extending Database Technology*, pages 587–604, Berlin, Heidelberg, EDBT'04. Springer-Verlag.

[DoFl06] Kevin Donnelly and Matthew Fluet. Transactional events. In *Proceedings of the eleventh ACM SIGPLAN International Conference on Functional Programming*, ICFP '06, pages 124–135, New York, NY, USA, 2006. ACM.

[Doyl78] Jon Doyle. Truth maintenance systems for problem solving. Technical Report AI-TR-419, Massachusetts Institute of Technology, Cambridge, MA, USA, 1978.

[Doyl87] Jon Doyle. *A truth maintenance system*, pages 259–279. Morgan Kaufmann Publishers Inc., San Francisco, CA, USA, 1987.

[Ecke08] Michael Eckert. *Complex Event Processing with XChangeEQ: Language Design, Formal Semantics and Incremental Evaluation for Querying Events*. Dissertation/Ph.D. thesis, Institute of Computer Science, LMU, Munich, 2008. Institute for Informatics, University of Munich, 2008.

[EiGS05] Jason Eisner, Eric Goldlust, and Noah A. Smith. Compiling Comp Ling: Practical Weighted Dynamic Programming and the Dyna Language. In *Proceedings of the conference on Human Language Technology and Empirical Methods in Natural Language Processing*, HLT '05, pages 281–290, Stroudsburg, PA, USA, 2005. Association for Computational Linguistics.

[EtNi10] Opher Etzion and Peter Niblett. *Event Processing in Action*. Manning Publications Co., Greenwich, CT, USA, 2010.

[EtRS11] Opher Etzion, Ella Rabinovich, and Inna Skarbovsky. Non functional properties of event porcessing. In David M. Eyers, Opher Etzion, Avigdor Gal, Stanley B. Zdonik, and Paul Vincent, editors, *Proceedings of the 5th ACM International Conference on Distributed Event-Based System*, DEBS '11, pages 365–366, New York, NY, USA, 2011. ACM.

[FoAR11] Paul Fodor, Darko Anicic, and Sebastian Rudolph. Results on out-of-order event processing. In Ricardo Rocha and John Launchbury, editors, *Proceedings of the 13th International Conference on Practical Aspects of Declarative Languages*, PADL'11, pages 220–234, Berlin, Heidelberg, 2011. Springer-Verlag.

[Forg82] Charles L. Forgy. Rete: A Fast Algorithm for the Many Pattern/ Many Object Pattern Match Problem. *Artificial Intelligences*, 19(1):17–37, 1982.

[FSSB05] Andrew D. H. Farrell, Marek J. Sergot, Mathias Sallé, and Claudio Bartolini. Using the event calculus for tracking the normative state of contracts. *International Journal of Cooperative Information Systems*, 14(2-3):99–129, 2005.

[GaAu02] Antony Galton and Juan Carlos Augusto. Two Approaches to Event Definition. In Abdelkader Hameurlain, Rosine Cicchetti, and Roland Traunmüller, editors, *Proceedings of the 13th International Conference on Database and Expert Systems Applications*, DEXA '02, Berlin, Heidelberg, 2002. Springer-Verlag.

[GaDi92] Stella Gatziu and Klaus R. Dittrich. SAMOS: an Active Object-Oriented Database System. In *IEEE Bulletin of the TC on Data Engineering*, 1992.

[GaDi94] Stella Gatziu and Klaus R. Dittrich. Detecting composite events in active database systems using Petrinets. In *Proc. Fourth International Workshop on Active Database Systems Research Issues in Data Engineering*, pages 2–9, 1994.

[GADI08] Daniel Gyllstrom, Jagrati Agrawal, Yanlei Diao, and Neil Immerman. On Supporting Kleene Closure over Event Streams. In *Proceedings of the 24th International Conference on Data Engineering*, ICDE '08, pages 1391–1393. IEEE, 2008.

[GeJS92a] N. H. Gehani, H. V. Jagadish, and O. Shmueli. Event specification in an active object-oriented database. *SIGMOD Record*, 21(2):81–90, 1992.

[GeJS92b] Narain H. Gehani, H. V. Jagadish, and Oded Shmueli. Composite Event Specification in Active Databases: Model & Implementation. In Li-Yan Yuan, editor, *Proceedings of the 18th International Conference on Very Large Data Bases*, VLDB'92, pages 327–338, San Francisco, CA, USA, 1992. Morgan Kaufmann Publishers Inc.

[GHMA+05] T. Ghanem, M. Hammad, M. Mokbel, W. G. Aref, and A. Elmagarmid. Query Processing Using Negative Tuples in Stream Query Engines. Technical Report CSD 04-040, Pudue University, 2005.

[GMSa87] Hector Garcia-Molina and Kenneth Salem. Sagas. In Umeshwar Dayal, editor, *Proceedings of the 1987 ACM SIGMOD International Conference on Management of Data*, SIGMOD '87, pages 249–259, New York, NY, USA, 1987. ACM.

[GoÖ5] Lukasz Golab and M. Tamer Özsu. Update-Pattern-Aware Modeling and Processing of Continuous Queries. In Fatma Özcan, editor, *Proceedings of the 2005 ACM SIGMOD International Conference on Management of Data*, SIGMOD '05, pages 658–669, New York, NY, USA, 2005. ACM.

[Gran10] Fabio Grandi. T-SPARQL: a TSQL2-like Temporal Query Language for RDF. In *International Workshop on on Querying Graph Structured Data*, ADBIS'10, pages 21–30. CEUR (online), 2010.

[GuHV07] Claudio Gutierrez, Carlos A. Hurtado, and Alejandro A. Vaisman. Introducing Time into RDF. *The IEEE Transactions on Knowledge and Data Engineering*, 19(2):207–218, 2007.

[GuMu99] Ashish Gupta and Inderpal Singh Mumick. Materialized views. chapter Maintenance of materialized views: problems, techniques, and applications, pages 145–157. MIT Press, Cambridge, MA, USA, 1999.

[Hale87] Paul Haley. Data-Driven Backward Chaining. In *International Joint Conferences on Artificial Intelligence*. Milan, Italy, 1987.

[HiKR09] Pascal Hitzler, Markus Krötzsch, and Sebastian Rudolph. *Foundations of Semantic Web Technologies*. Chapman & Hall/CRC, August 2009.

[KlCa04] Graham Klyne and Jeremy J. Carroll, editors. *Resource Description Framework (RDF): Concepts and Abstract Syntax*. W3C Recommendation, 10 February 2004. http://www.w3.org/TR/rdf-concepts/.

[KoKy10] Manolis Koubarakis and Kostis Kyzirakos. Modeling and Querying Metadata in the Semantic Sensor Web: The Model stRDF and the Query Language stSPARQL. In Lora Aroyo, Grigoris Antoniou, Eero Hyvönen, Annette ten Teije, Heiner Stuckenschmidt, Liliana Cabral, and Tania Tudorache, editors, *Proceedings of the 7th Extended Semantic Web Conference (ESWC'10)*, Lecture Notes in Computer Science, pages 425–439, Berlin,Heidelberg, 2010. Springer-Verlag.

[KoSe86] R Kowalski and M Sergot. A logic-based calculus of events. *New Generation Computing*, 4:67–95, January 1986.

[Kowa74] Robert A. Kowalski. Predicate Logic as a Programming Language. *Information Processing Letters*, 74:569–574, 1974.

[Kowa79a] Robert A. Kowalski. Algorithm = logic + control. *Communications of the ACM*, 22:424–436, July 1979.

[Kowa79b] Robert A. Kowalski. *Logic for problem solving*. North-Holland Publishing Co., Amsterdam, The Netherlands, The Netherlands, 1979.

[KPNR+06] Alex Kozlenkov, Rafael Penaloza, Vivek Nigam, Loic Royer, Gihan Dawelbait, and Michael Schroeder. Prova: Rule-based Java Scripting for Distributed Web Applications: A Case Study in Bioinformatics. In *EDBT Workshops*, 2006.

[KrSe09] Jürgen Krämer and Bernhard Seeger. Semantics and implementation of continuous sliding window queries over data streams. *ACM Transactions on Database Systems*, 34(1):1–49, 2009.

[LaLM98] Georg Lausen, Bertram Ludäscher, and Wolfgang May. On Active Deductive Databases: The Statelog Approach. In Burkhard Freitag, Hendrik Decker, Michael Kifer, and Andrei Voronkov, editors, *Transactions and Change in Logic Databases*, Lecture Notes in Computer Science, pages 69–106, Berlin,Heidelberg, 1998. Springer-Verlag.

[LFWK09] Senlin Liang, Paul Fodor, Hui Wan, and Michael Kifer. OpenRuleBench: an analysis of the performance of rule engines. In Juan Quemada, Gonzalo León, Yoëlle S. Maarek, and Wolfgang Nejdl, editors, *Proceedings of the 18th International Conference on World Wide Web*, WWW '09, pages 601–610, New York, NY, USA, 2009. ACM.

[LLDR+07] Ming Li, Mo Liu, Luping Ding, Elke A. Rundensteiner, and Murali Mani. Event Stream Processing with Out-of-Order Data Arrival. In *Proceedings of the 27th International Conference on Distributed Computing Systems Workshops*, ICDCSW'07, pages 67–77, Washington, DC, USA, 2007. IEEE Computer Society.

[LLGR+09] Mo Liu, Ming Li, Denis Golovnya, Elke A. Rundensteiner, and Kajal Claypool. Sequence Pattern Query Processing over Out-of-Order Event Streams. In *Proceedings of the 25th International Conference on Data Engineering*, pages 784–795, Washington, DC, USA, 2009. IEEE Computer Society.

[Lloy87] John Wylie Lloyd. *Foundations of Logic Programming*. Springer-Verlag New York, Inc., Secaucus, NJ, USA, 2nd edition, 1987.

[Luck02] David Luckham. *The Power of Events: An Introduction to Complex Event Processing in Distributed Enterprise Systems*. Addison-Wesley, Reading, MA, USA, 2002.

[LuSc11] David Luckham and W. Roy Schulte. *Event Processing Glossary - Version 2.0*. Event Processing Technical Society, 2nd edition, July 2011.

[MaCh08] Anurag S. Maskey and Mitch Cherniack. Replay-based approaches to revision processing in stream query engines. In *Proceedings of the 2nd International Workshop on Scalable Stream Processing System*, SSPS '08, pages 3–12, New York, NY, USA, 2008. ACM.

[McDa89] Dennis McCarthy and Umeshwar Dayal. The architecture of an active database management system. In *Proceedings of the 1989 ACM SIGMOD International Conference on Management of Data*, SIGMOD '89, pages 215–224, New York, NY, USA, 1989. ACM.

[MeMa09] Yuan Mei and Samuel Madden. ZStream: a cost-based query processor for adaptively detecting composite events. In *Proceedings of the 29th ACM SIGMOD Conference*, pages 193–206, 2009.

[MiSh99] Rob Miller and Murray Shanahan. The Event Calculus in Classical Logic - Alternative Axiomatisations. *Electronic Transactions on Artificial Intelligence*, 3(A):77–105, 1999.

[MoZa95] Iakovos Motakis and Carlo Zaniolo. Composite Temporal Events in Active Database Rules: A Logic-Oriented Approach. In Tok Wang Ling, Alberto O. Mendelzon, and Laurent Vieille, editors, *Proceedings of the 4th International Conference on Deductive and Object-Oriented Databases*, DOOD '95, pages 19–37, London, UK, 1995. Springer-Verlag.

[MWAB+02] Rajeev Motwani, Jennifer Widom, Arvind Arasu, Brian Babcock, Shivnath Babu, Mayur Datar, Gurmeet Manku, Chris Olston, Justin Rosenstein, and Rohit Varma. Query Processing, Resource Management, and Approximation in a Data Stream Management System. Technical Report 2002-41, Stanford InfoLab, 2002.

[NiMa95] Ulf Nilsson and Jan Maluszynski. *Logic, Programming, and PROLOG*. John Wiley & Sons, Inc., 2nd edition, 1995.

[PaDi99] Norman W. Paton and Oscar Diaz. Active database systems. In *ACM Computing Surveys*. ACM, 1999.

[PaKB10] Adrian Paschke, Alexander Kozlenkov, and Harold Boley. A Homogeneous Reaction Rule Language for Complex Event Processing. *CoRR*, abs/1008.0823, 2010.

[PeSJ11] Matthew Perry, Amit P. Sheth, and Prateek Jain. SPARQL-ST: Extending SPARQL to Support Spatiotemporal Queries. In Naveen Ashish and Amit P. Sheth, editors, *Geospatial Semantics and the Semantic Web*, volume 12 of *Semantic Web And Beyond Computing for Human Experience*, pages 61–86, Berlin,Heidelberg, 2011. Springer-Verlag.

[PrSe08] Eric Prud'hommeaux and Andy Seaborne. SPARQL Query Language for RDF. In *http://www.w3.org/TR/rdf-sparql-query/*, 2008.

[PSHS10] Harshal Patni, Satya S. Sahoo, Cory Henson, and Amit Sheth. Provenance Aware Linked Sensor Data. In *2nd Workshop on Trust and Privacy on the Social and Semantic Web, Greece*. CEUR Workshop Proceedings, 2010.

[PSSVDA07] M. Pesic, M. H. Schonenberg, N. Sidorova, and W. M. P. Van Der Aalst. Constraint-based workflow models: change made easy. In Robert Meersman and Zahir Tari, editors, *Proceedings of the 2007 OTM Confederated International Conference on On the move to meaningful internet systems: CoopIS, DOA, ODBASE, GADA, and IS - Volume Part I*, OTM'07, pages 77–94, Berlin, Heidelberg, 2007. Springer-Verlag.

[Ray09] Oliver Ray. Nonmonotonic Abductive Inductive Learning. *Journal of Applied Logic*, 7(3):329–340, 2009.

[RMCZ06] Esther Ryvkina, Anurag S. Maskey, Mitch Cherniack, and Stan Zdonik. Revision Processing in a Stream Processing Engine: A High-Level Design. In *Proceedings of the 22nd International Conference on Data Engineering*, ICDE '06, page 141, Washington, DC, USA, 2006. IEEE Computer Society.

[Robi65] John Alan Robinson. A Machine-Oriented Logic Based on the Resolution Principle. *Journal of the ACM (JACM)*, 12:23–41, January 1965.

[RoMM09] A. Rodriguez, R. E. McGrath, and J. Myers. Semantic Management of Streaming Data. In David De Roure Kerry Taylor, Arun Ayyagari, editor, *Proceedings of the 2nd International Workshop on Semantic Sensor Networks, collocated with the 8th International Semantic Web Conference (ISWC '09)*, SSN09. CEUR (online), 2009.

[SASM+09] Roland Stühmer, Darko Anicic, Sinan Sen, Jun Ma, Kay-Uwe Schmidt, and Nenad Stojanovic. Lifting Events in RDF from Interactions with Annotated Web Pages. In Abraham Bernstein, David R. Karger, Tom Heath, Lee Feigenbaum, Diana Maynard, Enrico Motta, and Krishnaprasad Thirunarayan, editors, *Proceedings of the 8th International Semantic Web Conference*, ISWC '09, pages 893–908, Berlin, Heidelberg, 2009. Springer-Verlag.

[SeSt10] Sinan Sen and Nenad Stojanovic. GRUVe: a methodology for complex event pattern life cycle management. In Barbara Pernici, editor, *Proceedings of the 22nd International Conference on Advanced Information Systems Engineering*, CAiSE'10, pages 209–223, Berlin, Heidelberg, 2010. Springer-Verlag.

[SMXS+11] Nenad Stojanovic, Dejan Milenovic, Yongchun Xu, Ljiljana Stojanovic, Darko Anicic, and Rudi Studer. An intelligent event-driven approach for efficient energy consumption in commercial buildings: smart office use case. In David M. Eyers, Opher Etzion, Avigdor Gal, Stanley B. Zdonik, and Paul Vincent, editors, *Proceedings of the 5th ACM international conference on Distributed event-based system*, DEBS '11, pages 303–312, New York, NY, USA, 2011. ACM.

[StKa02] Thomas Strandenæs and Randi Karlsen. Transaction Compensation in Web Services. In *The Norwegian Computer Science Conference*. Buskerud College, Norway, 2002.

[TaBe09] Jonas Tappolet and Abraham Bernstein. Applied Temporal RDF: Efficient Temporal Querying of RDF Data with SPARQL. In *Proceedings of the 6th European Semantic Web Conference*, ESWC'09, pages 308–322, Berlin, Heidelberg, 2009. Springer-Verlag.

[Ullm88] Jeffrey D. Ullman. *Principles of Database and Knowledge-Base Systems, Volume I*. Computer Science Press, 1988.

[Ullm89] Jeffrey D. Ullman. *Principles of Database and Knowledge-Base Systems, Volume II*. Computer Science Press, 1989.

[Ullm90] J. D. Ullman. *Principles of Database and Knowledge-Base Systems, Volume I and II*. W. H. Freeman & Co., New York, NY, USA, 2nd edition, 1990.

[vdAPS09] Wil M. P. van der Aalst, Maja Pesic, and Helen Schonenberg. Declarative workflows: Balancing between flexibility and support. *Computer Science - R&D*, 23(2):99–113, 2009.

[vEKo76] Maarten H. van Emden and Robert A. Kowalski. The Semantics of Predicate Logic as a Programming Language. *Journal of the ACM*, 23:733–742, October 1976.

[Warr92] David S. Warren. Memoing for logic programs. *Communications of the ACM*, 35:93–111, March 1992.

[WASS+10] Andreas Wagner, Darko Anicic, Roland Stühmer, Nenad Stojanovic, Andreas Harth, and Rudi Studer. Linked Data and Complex Event Processing for the Smart Energy Grid. In Manfred Hauswirth Sören Auer, Stefan Decker, editor, *Proceedings of Linked Data in the Future Internet at the Future Internet Assembly*, volume 700, Ghent Belgium, 2010.

[WJFY08] Onkar Walavalkar, Anupam Joshi, Tim Finin, and Yelena Yesha. Streaming Knowledge Bases. In *International Workshop on Scalable Semantic Web Knowledge Base Systems, collocated with the 7th International Semantic Web Conference (ISWC '08)*, Karlsruhe, Germany, 2008.

[WuDR06] Eugene Wu, Yanlei Diao, and Shariq Rizvi. High-performance complex event processing over streams. In Surajit Chaudhuri, Vagelis Hristidis, and Neoklis Polyzotis, editors, *Proceedings of the 2006 ACM SIGMOD International Conference on Management of Data*, SIGMOD '06, pages 407–418, New York, NY, USA, 2006. ACM.

[XSSA+11] Yongchun Xu, Nenad Stojanovic, Ljiljana Stojanovic, Darko Anicic, and Rudi Studer. An Approach for More Efficient Energy Consumption Based on Real-Time Situational Awareness. In Grigoris Antoniou, Marko Grobelnik, Elena Paslaru Bontas Simperl, Bijan Parsia, Dimitris Plexousakis, Pieter De Leenheer, and Jeff Z. Pan, editors, *Proceedings of the 8th Extended Semantic Web Conference - Volume Part II*, ESWC'11, pages 270–284, Berlin, Heidelberg, 2011. Springer-Verlag.

[YoBa05] Eiko Yoneki and Jean Bacon. Unified Semantics for Event Correlation over Time and Space in Hybrid Network Environments. In Robert Meersman, Zahir Tari, Mohand-Said Hacid, John Mylopoulos, Barbara Pernici, Özalp Babaoglu, Hans-Arno Jacobsen, Joseph P. Loyall, Michael Kifer, and Stefano Spaccapietra, editors, *OTM Conferences*, Lecture Notes in Computer Science, pages 366–384, Berlin,Heidelberg, 2005. Springer-Verlag.

[ZhDI10] Haopeng Zhang, Yanlei Diao, and Neil Immerman. Recognizing patterns in streams with imprecise timestamps. *Proceedings of the VLDB Endowment*, 3:244–255, September 2010.

Index

active databases, 39
agent
   aggregate, 22
   compose, 22
   enrich, 22
   filter, 22
   pattern detectio, 22
   project, 22
   split, 22
   transformation, 22
   translate, 22
aggregation, 20, 104
Allen's interval algebra, 11
Amit, 42
artificial intelligence, 7
atom, *see* atomic formula
atomic event, 5, 59
atomic formulas, 26

background knowledge, 5, 7
backward chaining, 80
backward-chaining evaluation, *see* top-down evaluation
binary event goals, 83
body (of the rule), 26
bottom-up evaluation, 34
built-in predicates, 26
business processes, 196
   ad-hoc, 196
   event-driven, 196

C-SPARQL, 53
CEDR, 42
checking rules, 79
chronological policy, 95, 98
classification, 106

clause, 26
complex event, 59, *see* derived event
Complex Event Processing, 17
composition of events, 20, 104
concurrent event patterns, 85
consumption policies, 57, 94
   intervals, 96
   time points, 95
consumption policy, 58, 70
context, 5, 7
Continuous Computation Language, 42
Coral8, 42

declarative
   language, 65
   programming, 57
declarative programming, 25
declarative semantics, 30
deductive reasoning, 7, 11
deductive rule, 7, 11
deductive rules, 105
definite clause, 26
definite goal, 26
definite program, 26
definite programs, 25, 30
derived event, 3, 5, 12
domain knowledge, 11
dynamic filtering, 100

ELE, 11
enrichment, 20, 102
EP-SPARQL, 11, 14, 135
   operational semantics, 145
   semantics, 141
   syntax, 138
Esper, 42

ETALIS, 14, 153
    architecture, 153
ETALIS Language for Events, 11, 14, 52, 65, 70
    implementation, 153
    syntax, 67
evaluation, 159
    basic patterns, 161
    EP-SPARQL, 178
    iterative patterns, 172
    knowledge-based Event Processing, 164
    out-of-order Event Processing, 169
    retraction in Event Processing, 164
    use case, 182
event, 3, 17
    channel, 23
    consumer, 21
    producer, 21
event at a time, 62
event binarization, 78
event classification, 5
event clustering, 5
event conjunction, 83
event disjunction, 85
event enrichment, 5
event filtering, 5
event pattern, 3
Event Processing, 17
event processing, 3, 11, 14, 20
    agent, 22
    architecture, 20
    language, 23
event processing architecture, 20
Event Processing Language, 42
event processing language, 3
event producer, 21
event revision, 3, 11, 14
event rules, 67
event-driven, 7, 11, 19
event-driven backward chaining rules, 78
event-driven computation model, 7

fact, 11, 26
filtering, 20, 100
    event content, 100
    event type, 100
fixpoint theory, 34
forward chaining, 80
forward-chaining evaluation, *see* bottom-up evaluation
function symbols, 26

garbage collection of events, 131
    general garbage collection, 133
    pattern-based garbage collection, 133
    pushed constraints, 132
goal inserting rules, 79
ground atom, 26

head (of the rule), 26
Herbrand Base, 30
Herbrand Model, 30
Herbrand Universe, 30
HiPAC, 39
Horn clause, 26, *see* definite clause
Horn program, *see* definite program
Horn rule, 26

implicit knowledge, 5, 7
incremental reasoning, 61
inductive reasoning, 7
inferencing, 7
information pull, 19
information push, 19
intelligent event processing, 7
interpretation
    definite programs, 30
    ETALIS Language for Events programs, 71
interval-based temporal semantics, 59

knowledge representation, 11, 25
knowledge-based EP, 5
knowledge-rich EP, 5

late event, 14, *see* out-of-order event
late events, *see* out-of-order events

Index

literal, 26
logic programming, 7, 11, 25
logic rule, 7
logic-based EP, 49

memory management, 131
model, *see* model-theory
    ETALIS Language for Events programs, 71
model-theory, 30
multiplying, *see* splitting

naive evaluation, 34

Ode, 39
operational semantics, 33, 77
out-of-order event, 3, 11
out-of-order event processing, 11, 14, 125
out-of-order events, 48

pattern detection, 20, 101
pattern matching, *see* pattern detection
point-based temporal semantics, 59
program
    definite, 26
projection of events, 20, 101
Prova, 49

RDF, 52
RDF Schema, 7
reasoning, 7, 105
reasoning over events, 7
recent policy, 95, 97
request-response, 19
request-response interaction, 11
request-response interaction model, 7
retraction in EP, 46, 113
revised event, 14, *see* event revision
revision in EP, *see* retraction in EP
revoked event, *see* event revision
rule
    Horn, 27, 68

SASE, 42
semantic condition, 3

Semantic Web, 11
semantics, 26
semi-naive evaluation, 34
set at a time, 62
signature
    Horn logic, 27, 68
SLD Resolution, 35
SPARQL, 52
splitting, 20, 103
static knowledge, 7
static rules, 67
stream reasoning, 7, 14
StreamBase, 42
Streaming SPARQL, 53
StreamInsight, 42
StreamSQL, 42
subclass relationships, 108
syntax, 26

TelegraphCQ, 42
temporal condition, 3
terms, 26
The Fast Flower Delivery, 11
The Real Time Web, 19
top-down evaluation, 35
total order assumption, 11
transaction processing, 46
transactions, 114
transformation of events, 20, 101
transitive closure, 105
translation of events, 20, 102
truth maintenance system, 46

unrestricted policy, 70, 96

variable assignment, 30

XChange^{EQ}, 49

ZStream, 42

i want morebooks!

Buy your books fast and straightforward online - at one of world's fastest growing online book stores! Environmentally sound due to Print-on-Demand technologies.

Buy your books online at
www.get-morebooks.com

Kaufen Sie Ihre Bücher schnell und unkompliziert online – auf einer der am schnellsten wachsenden Buchhandelsplattformen weltweit! Dank Print-On-Demand umwelt- und ressourcenschonend produziert.

Bücher schneller online kaufen
www.morebooks.de

VDM Verlagsservicegesellschaft mbH
Heinrich-Böcking-Str. 6-8   Telefon: +49 681 3720 174   info@vdm-vsg.de
D - 66121 Saarbrücken   Telefax: +49 681 3720 1749 www.vdm-vsg.de

Printed by Books on Demand GmbH, Norderstedt / Germany